Desktop Scanners

Image Quality Evaluation

ISBN 0-13-080904-7

9 780130 809049

90000

Hewlett-Packard Professional Books

Atchison	Object-Oriented Test & Management Software Development in C++
Blinn	Portable Shell Programming: An Extensive Collection of Bourne Shell Examples
Blommers	Practical Planning for Network Growth
Caruso	Power Programming in HP OpenView: Developing CMIS Applications
Chew	The Java/C++ Cross-Reference Handbook
Cook	Building Enterprise Information Architectures
Costa	Planning and Designing High Speed Networks Using 100VG-AnyLAN, Second Edition
Crane	A Simplified Approach to Image Processing: Classical and Modern Techniques
Day	The Color Scanning Handbook: Your Guide to Hewlett-Packard ScanJet Color Scanners
Derickson	Fiber Optic Test and Measurement
Eisenmann and Eisenmann	Machinery Malfunction Diagnosis and Correction: Vibration Analysis and Troubleshooting for the Process Industries
Fernandez	Configuring the Common Desktop Environment
Fristrup	USENET: Netnews for Everyone
Fristrup	The Essential Web Surfer Survival Guide
Gann	Desktop Scanners: Image Quality Evaluation
Grady	Practical Software Metrics for Project Management and Process Improvement
Greenberg	A Methodology for Developing and Deploying Internet and Intranet Solutions
Grosvenor, Ichiro, O'Brien	Mainframe Downsizing to Upsize Your Business: IT-Preneuring
Gunn	A Guide to NetWare® for UNIX®
Helsel	Graphical Programming: A Tutorial for HP VEE
Helsel	Visual Programming with HP VEE, Second Edition
Holman, Lund	Instant JavaScript
Kane	PA-RISC 2.0 Architecture
Knouse	Practical DCE Programming
Lee	The ISDN Consultant: A Stress-Free Guide to High-Speed Communications
Lewis	The Art & Science of Smalltalk
Lichtenbelt, Crane, Naqvi	Introduction to Volume Rendering
Loomis	Object Databases in Practice
Lund	Integrating UNIX® and PC Network Operating Systems
Madell	Disk and File Management Tasks on HP-UX
Mahoney	High-Mix Low-Volume Manufacturing
Malan, Letsinger, Coleman	Object-Oriented Development at Work: Fusion In the Real World
McFarland	X Windows on the World: Developing Internationalized Software with X, Motif®, and CDE
McMinds/Whitty	Writing Your Own OSF/Motif Widgets
Norton, DiPasquale	Thread Time: The Multithreaded Programming Guide
Orzessek, Sommer	ATM: & MPEG-2: A Practical Guide to Computer Security
Phaal	LAN Traffic Management
Pipkin	Halting the Hacker: A Practical Guide to Computer Security
Poniatowski	The HP-UX System Administrator's "How To" Book
Poniatowski	HP-UX 10.x System Administration "How To" Book
Poniatowski	Learning the HP-UX Operating System
Poniatowski	The Windows NT and HP-UX System Administrator's How-To Book
Poniatowski	The HP-UX System Administration Handbook and Toolkit
Poniatowski	HP NetServer Guide for Windows NT™
Ryan	Distributed Object Technology: Concepts and Applications
Simmons	Software Measurement: A Visualization Toolkit
Thomas	Cable Television Proof-of-Performance: A Practical Guide to Cable TV Compliance Measurements Using a Spectrum Analyzer
Weygant	Clusters for High Availability: A Primer of HP-UX Solutions
Witte	Electronic Test Instruments
Yawn, Stachnick, Sellars	The Legacy Continues: Using the HP 3000 with HP-UX and Windows NT

Desktop Scanners
Image Quality Evaluation

Robert Gann, PH.D.

http://www.hp.com/go/retailbooks

Prentice Hall PTR
Upper Saddle River, New Jersey 07458
http://www.phptr.com

Library of Congress Cataloging-in-Publication Data

Gann, Robert, Ph.D.
  Desktop scanners: image quality evaluation / Robert Gann.
    p.   cm. -- (Hewlett-Packard Professional books)
  Includes bibliographical references and index.
  ISBN 0-13-080904-7
  1. Scanning systems. 2. Image systems--Image quality.
  I. Title. II. Series.
  TK7882.S3G36   1999
  006.6'2--dc21   98-28791
                                                               CIP

Editorial/production supervision: *Nicholas Radhuber*
Manufacturing manager: *Alexis Heydt*
Acquisitions editor: *John Anderson*
Marketing manager: *Miles Williams*
Cover design: *Talar Agasyon*
Cover design director: *Jerry Votta*
Manager, Hewlett-Packard Press: *Patricia Pekary*

Prentice Hall books are widely used by corporations and government agencies for training, marketing, and resale. The publisher offers discounts on this book when ordered in bulk quantities. For more information, contact:
        Phone: 800-382-3419, Fax: 201-236-7141
        E-mail: corpsales@prenhall.com
        or write:
        Corporate Sales Department
        Prentice Hall PTR
        1 Lake Street
        Upper Saddle River, NJ 07458

Printed in the United States of America
10 9 8 7 6 5 4 3 2 1

ISBN 0-13-080904-7

Prentice-Hall International (UK) Limited, *London*
Prentice-Hall of Australia Pty. Limited, *Sydney*
Prentice-Hall Canada Inc., *Toronto*
Prentice-Hall Hispanoamericana, S.A., *Mexico*
Prentice-Hall of India Private Limited, *New Delhi*
Prentice-Hall of Japan, Inc., *Tokyo*
Simon & Schuster Asia Pte. Ltd., *Singapore*
Editora Prentice-Hall do Brasil, Ltda., *Rio de Janeiro*

Colophon

This document was designed and written by Robert Gann, Ph.D. of Hewlett-Packard Company. Illustrations were created by Rich Kurz of Marketing By Design, Fort Collins, Colorado. Some photos are by Western Sky Photography, Fort Collins, Colorado. The document was published using Adobe FrameMaker 5.5, Photoshop 4.0, and Illustrator and Corel Draw. Images were scanned using a variety of scanners, including the HP ScanJet IIcx, 4c, 4p and 5p.

Acknowledgments

Many people helped with this book, both directly and indirectly – my thanks to them all. Special thanks, first and foremost, to my wife, Charlie, and son Justin, for supporting me through long nights and weekends while I struggled along. Thanks to the Scanner Image Quality team and Nancy Mundelius at HP GHC for review efforts and lots of ideas. Thanks to Rod Wilson for sponsoring my efforts and to HP Press for giving me the opportunity.

Table of Contents

List of Figures

List of Tables

Desktop Scanners

Image Quality Evaluation

Chapter 1

What's *Desktop Scanners: Image Quality Evaluation* All About?

Desktop Scanners: Image Quality Evaluation is based upon a previous series of books titled *Reviewing and Testing Desktop Scanners.* That series was written to help technical writers evaluate desktop scanners and write accurate articles about them. Along the way we found that many other people, from design engineers to marketing experts, from technical writers to novice scanner users, found the book useful. Since the previous editions were never "published" in the sense that you could buy them in the store, we kept running out of copies. In this book we've built upon those previous books and tried to address scanners and scanner technology from a wide range of viewpoints. While technical, the book is also written for the somebody who doesn't need to understand the details, but just the concepts. The book ranges from simple descriptions to detailed step-by-step analysis procedures.

■ Answers to Your Questions

Can one book really answer all the questions about scanners? Well, no. But many of them are addressed here. Plus, you will find the information you need to be able to ask the right questions. You will also find in-depth technical discussions and testing procedures. Finally, we've tried to organize the book so you won't even have to dig too hard to find what you need.

For the first-time scanner buyer and user:

- I want to buy a scanners, what do I need to know?
- What kind of scanner is best for me?
- What do specifications like dpi and bit depth mean? Do I care?
- Is there a difference in scanners, or should I just get the lowest price I can?
- What interface is best for me (SCSI, parallel, USB, Firewire)?
- What software do I need? Do all scanners come with what I need?
- How much computer power do I need?
- Do I need an automatic document feeder or a transparency adapter?
- How do scanners work, and what difference does it make?
- What's more important, the software or the hardware?
- Should I buy a digital camera or a scanner, or both?
- Do I really need to know how a scanner works, just to use one?

For the web user:

- What kind of scanner do I need for web publishing?
- What about color accuracy on the web?
- How much resolution do I need?
- What file formats work best?

For the experienced user:

- Do these new low-cost scanners meet my needs?
- What about scanning transparencies?
- What kind of technology is used in my scanner and how can I get the best out of it?
- What is limiting my output quality?
- What do "gamma correction" and those other strange terms really mean?
- How much resolution and bit depth do I need, or do those specifications really mean anything? (*Hint: not really!*)

For technical reviewers or those responsible for recommending scanners:

- What technologies are used in scanners?
- How are they different than digital cameras?
- How can I test a scanner, in detail and analytically, to prove or disprove the claimed performance?
- How are scanners changing, and what technologies are important?
- What information do I need to present to my reader?

For engineers and scientists

- What are the technological trade-offs and trends I need to worry about?
- Are scanners "designed" or "assembled" today?
- What determines color accuracy of a scanner or its resolution, and so on?
- What color space should I use to evaluate scanners?
- What do users need?

■ How to Use the Book

The book is written to allow you to pick and choose what you need, so you don't need to read it cover to cover (but you can). The first few chapters provide information for all users. In the following chapters you will find more detailed information and, in many cases, a step-by-step procedure on how to measure some aspect of a scanner analytically. This last part is designed for the technical reviewer or engineer, and to perform the tasks you will need a special test target discussed in the appendix. Of particular interest is Chapter 2 • "A Guide to the Book" on page 7; it will help you decide which parts of the book are more important to you.

Finally, on the included CDROM you will find example images, further explanations, tools and some on-line presentations to review. Please respect the copyrighted material on the CDROM – it cannot be reproduced or used without the express permission of Hewlett-Packard and the author.

A word about figures in the book. Throughout the book you will find black and white versions of figures. For figures in which color would help, there is a color version in the color section.

■ What's New in *Desktop Scanners: Image Quality Evaluation*

Desktop Scanners: Image Quality Evaluation is a significant enhancement over the *Reviewing and Testing Desktop Scanners* series. New information includes:

- ■ New technologies.
- ■ New sections devoted to buying and using scanners.
- ■ Digital cameras.
- ■ Trends in users and use models.
- ■ Scanner cost trends.
- ■ A CDROM with extra "stuff" like a spreadsheet for color calculations.
- ■ Expanded information on spectral matching, metamerism and color errors.

■ A Word from the Author

With the help of some friends and colleagues, I originally wrote the book *Reviewing and Testing Desktop Scanners* for the technical press reviewers trying to learn how to objectively test and write about desktop scanners. Since this is my field and since it was a fairly new field, I thought I could help. In fact, the first edition was so well received that we needed a second, then a third. The information in those books has been the basis for many seminars, classes and presentations. This book, *Desktop Scanners: Image Quality Evaluation,* builds upon the previous books and, I hope, answers many of the questions people have about scanners. On the associated CDROM you will find some presentations based upon the book. Note, please respect the copyright of information on the CDROM. The presentations are intended for the reader of the book and may not be reproduced or presented to audiences without the express permission of the author.

■ About the Author

Desktop Scanners: Image Quality Evaluation was written (with a lot of help from others) by a design engineer working at Hewlett-Packard in Greeley, Colorado. Hewlett-Packard is the home of the HP ScanJet scanner, the first desktop scanner, and is really responsible for bringing the scanner to the desktop. The primary author, Dr. Robert (Bob) Gann, has been responsible for image quality specification and testing on desktop scanners at Hewlett-Packard for over 8 years and has taught many seminars on testing scanners and scanner image quality around the world. Bob received his Ph.D. in Electrical Engineering from Colorado State University in 1986. He is a native Coloradoan, is a volunteer fireman and lives with his lovely wife Charlene and his son Justin in the mountains of Colorado, along with various cats, dogs and horses.

Chapter **2**

A Guide to the Book

In this chapter you will find suggested reading for various people. You will also find a chapter-by-chapter description of the book. Some redundancy exists in the book, descriptions of the same thing may appear in multiple places. The reason for that is to make it easy to find things and to help each section stand on its own.

■ For the Scanner Buyer

There is information scattered about the book for you, but you might start with these chapters.

■ For the Reviewer

This is where the heart of the book is. Start with Chapter 4 • "For the Technical Reviewer" on page 43. Nearly all the chapters will have value to you. Look at the descriptions of each chapter given in "A Guide to Each Chapter" on page 8.

■ For the User

Look at the items under "For the Scanner Buyer" on page 7 and add the following chapters:

- ■ Chapter 6 • "Scanner Trends" on page 79.
- ■ Chapter 10 • "More on Image Quality" on page 121.
- ■ Chapter 11 • "Some Scanner Technologies" on page 139.

■ For the Engineer or Scientist

You can approach the book as a tutorial and read it all, or look in detail at the analytical test descriptions starting at Chapter 11 • "Some Scanner Technologies" on page 139 and work on through the book. Be sure to look carefully at Chapter 10 • "More on Image Quality" on page 121 and Chapter 6 • "Scanner Trends" on page 79. Finally, much of the forward progress in scanning is in software, so look at Chapter 7 • "Scanning Software" on page 87.

■ A Guide to Each Chapter

Here is a brief description of what you will find in each chapter.

Chapter 1 • "What's Desktop Scanners: Image Quality Evaluation All About?"

Desktop Scanners: Image Quality Evaluation is based upon a previous series of books titled Reviewing and Testing Desktop Scanners. That series was written to help technical writers evaluate desktop scanners and write accurate articles about them. Along the way we found that many other people, from design engineers to marketing experts, from technical writers to novice scanner users, found the book useful. Since the previous editions were never "published" in the sense that you could buy them in the store, we kept running out of copies. In this book we've built upon those previous books and tried to address scanners and scanner technology from a wide range of viewpoints. While technical, the book is also written for the somebody who doesn't need to understand the details, but just the concepts. The book ranges from simple descriptions to detailed step-by-step analysis procedures.

Chapter 2 • "A Guide to the Book"

In this chapter you will find suggested reading for various people. You will also find a chapter-by-chapter description of the book. Some redundancy exists in the book, descriptions of the same thing may appear in multiple places. The reason for that is to make it easy to find things and to help each section stand on its own.

Chapter 3 • "Buying a Scanner"

So you want to buy a scanner? Buying a scanner today is easy. Figuring out which scanner to buy is not. Much of the information you will find in the store is incorrect and misleading—the curse of scanners today and a result of the rapid growth of scanner sales. Frankly, the information given has not kept up with the technology. What you really need is an expert to go along and help. In this chapter we try to be that expert. If you are in a hurry, jump ahead to "Questions You Should Ask Yourself" on page 20. You may also want to refer to Chapter 5 • "A Look at Scanners" on page 55.

Chapter 4 • "For the Technical Reviewer"

Really, this book is for you—the technical reviewer. Reviewing and writing about scanners is a challenging task. Even for the expert, keeping up with the trends and changes in scanners and how they are used is a tremendous job. In this chapter you will find some guidance on how to set up reviews, things to consider and information about new trends and new challenges.

Chapter 5 • "A Look at Scanners"

In this chapter you will find an introduction to scanners. What is a scanner? What types are there, and what are some of the advantages and disadvantages of each? What can scanners do? How do they work, and how are they changing? You will also find a brief introduction to image quality.

Chapter 6 • "Scanner Trends"

Scanner buyers can easily become overwhelmed by the endless spawning of scanner configurations, sizes and shapes, not to mention the proliferation of hybrid products that use the word "scan" in their advertisements. Which trends are significant and which are merely gimmicks?

Chapter 7 • "Scanning Software"

More and more, the software that comes with a scanner and its integration with the scanner hardware and target application are a key difference between scanners. A common misconception is that the scanner software is just a "driver" and that all the real work is done in an image editor after the scan.

Chapter 8 • "Scanner Gear"

Besides the scanner, what else comes in the box, and what accessories are available? Hardware interfaces; automatic document feeders; transparency adapters; scanning software; service, and support information; OCR software; documentation and image editing software are just some of the items scanner manufacturers are including with their scanners. Often, several different bundles are available. Also consider how the system is put together. Does the software represent a complete solution or an ad hoc collection of checkoff items?

Chapter 9 • "Setting the Controls"

Many scanner users rely on image-editing software to adjust the exposure after a scan. But for the best results, we recommend making these adjustments before the scan by using the scanner's controls. This chapter explains why and explains the controls.

Chapter 10 • "More on Image Quality"

Several factors determine whether or not you get the best possible scan from a given application. Some of these relate to how you use a scanner and others relate to how the scanner operates. A very important factor is how the scanner interacts with the software and the completeness of the whole scanner solution. This chapter examines these factors and how they affect the quality of a scanned image.

Chapter 11 • "Some Scanner Technologies"

Scanner development has not always evolved along the same path, so that different technologies have sometimes produced the same result. Understanding these different technologies with their advantages and disadvantages can help you in your scanner evaluation.

Chapter 12 • "Scanning Speed"

Although scanning speed is often used as the basis for comparison between scanners, it is only one small part of the time it takes to get a scanned image into your document ready for use. Better reviews will focus on the time taken to achieve typical tasks, not just the raw scan time. The only time when raw scan speed is of great importance is during preview scans, or possibly multi-page OCR jobs.

Chapter 13 • "Resolution"

The concept of resolution is probably the most misunderstood and misused specification applied to scanners today. The resolution of a scanner is most often discussed in terms of ppi or dpi (for example, a 600-ppi scanner). In fact, the relationship between the true resolution of a scanner and its ppi rating is tenuous at best—particularly for low-cost desktop scanners. This confusion is being further driven by unrealistic and inflated claims that provide no real information or benefit to the user. This chapter examines resolution and sampling rates, describes the limitations of typical tests for resolution, and offers a more accurate test that will measure the true optical performance of the scanner.

Chapter 14 • "Scaling and Interpolation"

Most scanning is not done at the scanner's optical sampling rate, but instead includes interpolation or subsampling to a higher or lower ppi. Typically, this is done to optimize a scan for a particular output device (printer or display) or to scale an image to a particular output size. We will use the term "interpolation" to mean the creation of images with a ppi different than the scanner optical sampling rate and for both increasing ppi above the optical sample rate and decreasing ppi below the optical sample rate. This chapter describes how scanners achieve interpolation and how to test for high quality interpolation. Interpolation quality is a very important aspect of scanned image quality and is often overlooked in scanner testing.

Chapter 15 • "Tonal Resolution, Density Range and Bit Depth"

Today, scanners are commonly specified with an increasing tonal resolution. Typically, this is specified as an increased "bit depth" as in a "30-bit color scanner." The bit depth or bpp specification is very similar to the specification of ppi in that it tells us something about the technology in the scanner, but nothing about the quality. In fact bpp, like ppi, is becoming meaningless. A better measure of tonal resolution is signal-to-noise ratio. A second specification often seen is density range (or dynamic range). Density range is a measure of how dark (dense) something is and is a specification more related to printing or pre-press work than desktop scanning. This chapter examines what these specifications mean to users and how can they be measured.

Chapter 16 • "Image Noise"

Image noise is a distortion or unwanted signal introduced into the captured image by a scanner. Image noise can take the form of random distortions (snow) or correlated distortions (streaks or patterns). Typically, noise is injected into the analog voltage signal captured by a CCD before it is converted to a digital number. That signal is quite small and susceptible to interference. Once digitized by the scanner analog-to-digital converter, an image is immune to the addition of noise. However, further processing such as sharpening can extenuate the impact of noise in an image.

Chapter 17 • "Uniform Illumination"

To produce consistent, high-quality scans, a scanner needs to have a light source that uniformly lights the original object during the scan. When illumination isn't uniform, lightness varies within a scan or between several scans. If the spectral output of the lamp changes, color in the scan can vary. For a discussion of the various light sources used in scanners, see Chapter 11 • "Some Scanner Technologies" on page 139. The lamp in a scanner is a critical part of achieving accurate color in the scanner. Refer to Chapter 19 • "Color Fidelity" on page 249 for a discussion of how lamps impact the color accuracy of the scanner.

Chapter 18 • "Color Registration"

Color registration error is misalignment in the scanner red, green and blue (RGB) channels. Color registration error will vary with the color separation technology used and may be quite different in the x and y directions.

Chapter 19 • "Color Fidelity"

The color accuracy of a scanner depends on many factors, including the scanner, but also including the original and the light source under which the original is usually viewed. Often more of a limit in color fidelity, when using a scanner, is the output device and how well the scanner and output device were matched.

Chapter 20 • "Scanning for Black and White Output"

While great growth has occurred in color scanning, the ability of a scanner to create black and white output is still quite important. Although high-quality color printers are quite affordable today, most of these printers are relatively slow. Many documents are destined for copiers for wide distribution, so many scans are created in grayscale (black and white). In addition, color image files are typically at least three times larger than a grayscale image file—further limiting the use of color scans. However, while most hardcopy output is still black and white, most originals being scanned are color. This chapter discusses evaluating the ability of a scanner to scan a color original for grayscale output. The related subjects, tonal accuracy, tonal resolution and ability to record shadow detail are discussed in Chapter 15 • "Tonal Resolution, Density Range and Bit Depth" on page 213 and Chapter 16 • "Image Noise" on page 229. Color balance of the scanner is covered in Chapter 19 • "Color Fidelity" on page 249.

Appendix A • "CIELAB to RGB Calculations and NTSC Equations"

This appendix contains a set of formulas to transform RGB to CIELAB (and XYZ) and back. Only a brief description and an equation set for RGB to CIELAB transformations are included. Thus, no discussion of the theory behind CIELAB or these transformations is included. The equation for the NTSC (National Television System Committee) system of color TV transmission signals is also included. A spreadsheet is provided on the CDROM which achieves many of these calculations.

Glossary

A list of common terms and definitions.

Chapter **3**

Buying a Scanner

So you want to buy a scanner? Buying a scanner today is easy. Figuring out which scanner to buy is not. Much of the information you will find in the store is incorrect and misleading—the curse of scanners today and a result of the rapid growth of scanner sales. Frankly, the information given has not kept up with the technology. What you really need is an expert to go along and help. In this chapter we try to be that expert. If you are in a hurry, jump ahead to "Questions You Should Ask Yourself" on page 20. You may also want to refer to Chapter 5 · "A Look at Scanners" on page 55.

■ What You'll See When You Walk into the Store

It used to be, when you wanted to buy a scanner, you went to a specialist and they helped you. Today, the cost of scanners has decreased to the point where you can walk into any computer store and find several different models. What you won't find, in most stores, is somebody with the expertise to help you understand exactly what scanner you need.

This is not intended to be a criticism of the good folks at your local computer store. You will find devoted individuals trying to provide the best service they can. But several factors conspire to make their job difficult:

- The cost of scanners is so low and the return to store sales representatives so small that it is not worth the investment of their time to really under-

15

stand scanners.

- Even if they wish to understand scanners, they are faced with two major problems:
  - Scanners are still evolving and are not a standard part of computers.
  - Most of the information available, even to sales specialists, is not very useful, or even correct.
- For example, the specifications most often quoted for scanners, ppi (or dpi) and bits per pixel (bpp) are:
  - Not applied in a standard manner (they mean different things on different scanners).
  - Have little or nothing to do with the real performance of the scanner.
  - Have little or nothing to do with what you need from the scanner.

The success of a scanner user depends on more than just the scanner hardware. The scanner will be used in a system and the components of that system often impact success more than the scanner itself. Today:

- There is an overemphasis on scanning hardware.
- There is too little emphasis on the importance of the scanning software—it is often considered just to be a generic "plug-in."
- Many of the claims made are just plain unsupportable—the goal is often to play the numbers game and claim a higher specification than the competitor, regardless of the reality of that specification.
- The printer and display play a critical role.

What you will find in the store:

- Lots of scanners ranging in price from under $100 to over $1000.
- Specifications called dpi, bits per pixel (also called Bit Depth) and lots of hype.
- Confusing claims that don't make sense.

For instance, you may find yourself asking:

How can this $200 scanner have better specifications than that $700 scanner?

There are several answers to this question:

- The specifications don't mean anything *(likely)*.

- The specifications are not really the same specifications *(very likely)*.
- One of the manufacturers is lying or misleading you *(quite possible)*.

Fine. All the specs are meaningless and may be incorrect. What should I do? Don't worry, all is not lost! Read on.

The two most common specifications—ppi and "bits"

Undoubtedly, when you walk into that store you will be faced with dizzying claims about scanner ppi (or dpi) and the number of "bits" a scanner has. These specifications mean little today and your best bet is to ignore them. However, if you want to know what they mean (or used to) look at "Pretending that the ppi and Bit Depth Specifications Mean Something" on page 36. If you are going to do this, it would also be a good point to take a look at "How Scanners Work" on page 64, "What is Resolution?" on page 173 and "Tonal Resolution" on page 213. Be sure to look at "Claims to Watch Out For" on page 36.

■ Ignore ppi and Bit Depth Claims

In fact, when buying a scanner, your best bet is to ignore ppi and bit depth claims and look beyond them to what your scanner can really provide in terms of productivity, support, ease of use and versatility. Bit depth and ppi, as they are used today, really mean nothing and really don't help you decide about a scanner. In fact, they will likely mislead you.

A big hint

If you cannot find any information *except* bit depth and ppi for a particular scanner, look for a different scanner! Better scanner manufactures are working hard to provide more information to show the real benefit of their scanner, beyond meaningless numbers. Note, even these better manufacturers will couch their claims in terms of ppi and bit depth because they realize people expect to see those numbers, but it will backed up with more complete information. Ask for it.

■ Technology Trade-Offs, You Can't Have It All

Despite what scanner manufacturers claim, you can't have it all. But you can make some informed decisions and get a good scanner that is appropriate for your tasks.

The art of engineering is the art of making trade-offs.

Scanner design is no different. There are some fundamental limitations to the technologies used in scanners that mean every function or quality of a scanner represents a trade-off with respect to some other function. In fact, the methodology used in a particular scanner may be reflected in the trade-offs made in that scanner.

For example, a scanner designed for high-speed document capture will likely not be optimized, or even usable, for imaging. The trade-offs result in a scanner that is better for document capture. At the same time, a scanner designed for high-quality image work may not be suitable for OCR.

Most desktop scanners today represent a compromise that presents the widest variety of capability for an acceptable price. However, it is important to realize there is no such thing as a free lunch or a scanner that provides everything for everybody. One might describe the task of the reviewer, or buyer, as one of evaluating how well the trade-offs used in a particular scanner best suit the customer's needs and expectations.

Light versus everything

One of the core limiters in a scanner is the amount of light available for imaging. Consider how a color scanner works. A light source illuminates an original, the reflected light is captured and separated into color information, converted to electrical signals and digitized to create the digital image. In fact, the amount of light available for imaging is a limit that drives almost all other design considerations for scanners. The more light available, the higher performance (speed and/or image quality) available. In addition, this available light can be used to achieve different performance factors. In one scanner, the light may be used to create very fast scans of black and white originals. In another, the light may be used to create high-quality images from transparent originals, albeit slowly. A well-designed scanner may be able to do both reasonably well.

From the standpoint of a reviewer or buyer, it is useful to consider how efficiently the light in a scanner is used. For example, compare two scanners with the same specification for sample rate, bit depth, and speed, but with different light sources. If one scanner has a lamp twice as bright as the other, then the scanner with the dimmer light source better have a more efficient color separation system, faster lens, or other compensating factor. Yet, in the typical case, the scanner with the dimmer light source will probably have noisier images (lower signal-to-noise ratio), even though the specifications would lead one to believe they are equivalent

A case study

Let us consider the case of a manufacturer with an 8 bpp scanner (24 bpp color) who wants to upgrade the scanner to 10 bpp (30 bpp color). To support the increased bit depth in the scanner, the manufacturer must improve the signal-to-noise ratio of the scanner by a factor of 4. There are a number of techniques that the manufacturer can use to achieve this. Table 3-1, "Techniques to Increase the Bit Depth of a Scanner," on page 20 illustrates this.

However, no single modification is likely to achieve the required improvement. The task of increasing the bit depth from 8 to 10 bpp rapidly becomes a complex set of trade-offs and changes throughout the system. Typically, increasing the bit depth will correspond to a significant increase in cost.

Similar arguments can be made for increasing sample rate (ppi). Again, light is a big limiter in this case. Consider that the light gathering area of a pixel for a 600-ppi scanner is 1/4 the size of a 300-ppi scanner. Again, for similar performance, a 4x increase in light is required (along with a 2x increase in data rate, better clarity optics, better alignment, etc.!)

■ Bit Depth Claims

How, then, can there be so many scanners claiming increased bit depth and/or sample rate combined with low cost?

Simply stated, the claims are unsupported by the actual performance of the scanner.

Table 5-4, "Importance of Scanning Capability for Different Types of Scans," on page 77, is helpful in comparing the various scanner specifications.

Hopefully, this little exercise has provided you with a healthy dose of skepticism about scanner specifications. The right way to buy a scanner is to evaluate what you need and go from there.

Table 3-1   Techniques to Increase the Bit Depth of a Scanner

Technique	Limits of this technique	Trade-off
Increase the brightness of the lamp 4 times.	Comparable to replacing a 100-watt lamp with a 400-watt lamp. This is unlikely to occur for cost reasons as well as for practical reasons (size and power). More typically, the trend is toward dimmer lamps for cost reasons.	Higher cost.
Increase the sensitivity of the CCD 4 times or more.	CCD manufacturers are making improvements in the sensitivity of CCD devices. However, much of that increased sensitivity is in the form of higher onboard amplification of the signal with accompanying amplification of noise sources.	Increases in sensitivity of this type are not useful in supporting the higher bit depth.
Increase the efficiency of the color separation 4 times.	Current color separation technologies range from 40% to 90% efficiency. An increase in efficiency of 4x is not possible as the technologies are more than 25% efficient to start with.	There are significant differences in color separation technologies.
Increase the amount of light passed by the optics (lens) 4x.	While theoretically possible, there are practical limits to how fast (big) the lens can be.	Increasing the aperture of the lens will have a negative impact on the clarity (resolution) of the optics.
Increase the exposure time (slow the scan down).	Again, there is a limit before the CCD becomes saturated or the scan becomes too slow to be useful.	Consider that most scanners are designed to use most of the dynamic voltage range of the CCD, so increasing the exposure 4 times will simply overdrive the CCD.

■ Questions You Should Ask Yourself

The first, and most important, aspect of shopping for a scanner is evaluating your own needs. In the next sections you will find a set of questions to ask yourself. For each question you will find a group of suggestions that will help you decide which type of scanner is best for you and what functions you should consider most carefully.

Why am I buying a scanner?

I really don't know, it just looks like a neat thing.

- Take a look at Chapter 5 • "A Look at Scanners" on page 55, especially "What Scanners Can Do" on page 62 and "Types of Scanners" on page 56, then come back here.

They are so cheap now, it just seems like the thing to do.

- Careful! Many of the very "cheap" scanners are just "cheap junk." You may have a very bad experience with them that will turn you off of scanners entirely, and that would be a shame because a scanner is a very useful tool.
- You can get a very nice scanner for just a few hundred dollars, but you can get junk too.
- Also, if you get a "free" scanner as part of a bundle, you will probably be disappointed. Don't let that turn you off on scanners entirely.
- Scanners are really cool things, with lots of possibilities. Have fun, explore and you will probably find you are using a scanner quite a lot.
- Demand quality and compare. Just because a scanner gives a recognizable image does not mean it is a comparably good image.

My children need one for school work.

- This is a common motivation and a good one. Look for a flatbed with easy-to-use software that is well integrated. Really look at the software—there are big differences. Get a demo if you can.

I want to copy important documents into my computer and then work on them. I'm really not interested in photos.

- You need a scanner that can do OCR and document management. Most flatbed scanners come with OCR. You may want to look for one that provides page analysis. Page analysis recognizes the contents of a page and preserves as much as possible. Look at "A New Scanning Interface—Task Automation Software" on page 91.

- Document management software, software that keeps track of things for you, can be quite useful. Be wary though, many scanners include what they call document management software, but they really don't deliver.
- Consider a scanner with an automatic document feeder (ADF). If you have a lot of documents, this can be a saving grace. But be careful—many times, an ADF may be listed as available, but may be very hard to get. The performance may be quite variable as well. See "What Accessories Do I Need?" on page 34.
- Also consider a sheet-feed scanner if desk space is a premium. Realize that you may not get the image quality out of a sheet-feed that you do a flatbed, and that the sheet feed is less flexible. Look at "Types of Scanners" on page 56. Also, if they are valuable documents, a sheet-feed scanner is more dangerous. Have you ever seen a fax machine "eat" the original?
- You probably don't need a high-end, high-resolution scanner.
- If you have a color printer, you can use a scanner for a color copier!

I'd like to create a web page for my friends and family, or maybe my favorite volunteer organization or church.

- You should probably get a flatbed scanner. Again, look for one with good software, support for web publishing and a simple interface.
- Look for a scanner that supports sRGB—a new standard that will make web images look better.
- For the web, you **don't** need "high resolution." Don't let somebody sell you a scanner based upon some very high "dpi" rating. First, it is probably false. Second, it is not needed.
- Pay more attention to color accuracy than resolution.
- Also very important is the scaling capabilities of the scanner. For the web, you want 72 to 75 ppi images. You need a scanner that can create this type of image quickly and with high quality. (See Chapter 14 • "Scaling and Interpolation" on page 197.)

I need it for my business. I want to make brochures, web pages, fax things, copy things, read documents, etc.

- You need a flatbed scanner. You should also plan on spending a little more money. Don't buy the cheapest thing out there. Your business and the way people see you will depend on these scanned images.

- Again, look for flexibility, support of standards and a high level of support.
- Consider a SCSI-based scanner instead of the cheaper parallel interface scanners. They are harder to set up, but the performance is much nicer, and you will probably have less printer problems. As USB and Firewire become available, those interfaces will be easier to use and faster. See "Which Interface should I use to connect my computer to my scanner?" on page 32.

I want to scan things, not photos. Like flowers, cloth, small art objects.

- Again, you need a flatbed, but you need a special one. Some flatbed scanners can handle 3-dimensional objects quite well, others cannot. Look at "Incident-Light Angle Changes and Multiple-Exposure Scans" on page 138.
- Another problem you face is color errors. Many scanners are optimized for scanning of photographic or printed dyes. When you start scanning other types of dyes, such as cloth dyes, or real objects, you may have problems. Take a sample of your original down and try it on the scanner first!

I've got a bunch of slides in my closet that I'd like to scan into the computer to make reproductions.

- You are one of the few people that really need high resolution (not ppi, resolution). You should look at a dedicated slide scanner.
- Keep in mind, a slide scanner, or slide and photo scanner, is a very limited device.
- You also need a photo-quality printer. Fortunately, there are now photo-quality inkjet printers for under $500. See "Do I need a new printer for my scanner?" on page 29 and "Scanners and Printers" on page 69.

Actually, I only have a few slides that I'd like to scan for the web.

- If you are not enlarging them greatly, and it is not your primary purpose, you can get transparency adapters for flatbed scanners.

- You still need high resolution and good tonal quality, so be prepared to spend a little more.

I'm a professional desktop publisher and I want to replace my older scanner or move scanning work in-house from the service bureau.

- It would be wise for you to look at other parts of this book. Also, talk to others with scanner experience and look for other sources of information.
- Spend more money. As most business people know, you tend to get what you pay for. You have the potential of saving lots, so some investment is worth it.
- Run, don't walk, away from the cheap scanners that claim high dpi and bit depth. The specifications don't mean what they used to and you will be disappointed.

Still, you can get very good scanners for under $1000, so go looking, but demand demonstrations.

- Look for scanners with more sophisticated scanning software. But don't be afraid of automation. Many of the automated exposure, gamma correction, white point adjustment and other automated tools are quite good and do a great job on 90% of images.
- Look for a scanner that performs scaling and tonal manipulation (gamma correction) in the hardware. Don't assume you can, or should, do it in an image editor after the scan. A good scanner can provide better results without ever using an image editor.
- Look for flexibility, larger bed sizes, transparency adapters and automatic document feeders.

I'd like to scan receipts and sale slips into the scanner and "auto recognize" them.

- If all you want is a computer copy of the receipt that you can read and print, say, for tax purposes, most basic scanners will do this. Simple document management software is a plus.
- If you are looking to have the computer automatically read the information off of receipts, you are asking a lot. Check with a specialist.

I've got lots (thousands) of documents to read and store.

- You need a dedicated document management scanner, or at least one with a robust, high-capacity automatic document feeder (ADF).
- Be aware that the low-cost, 10- to 20-page ADFs supplied for some scanners may not be very reliable or fast.

I'm an amateur photographer and I want to go digital.

- You need a photo scanner and a photo printer. Several digital photography systems are becoming available. Be aware, many of the terms used in photography, such as density, are used with scanners – but they may not be used correctly or in the same way.

Aren't scanners too hard to use?

They don't have to be.

- Much of the progress that has been made on scanners has been in the area of making them easier to use. Don't assume you need to be an expert to get good results.
- At the same time, you should consider more than just the hardware specifications. In fact, the hardware specifications should probably be one of the lower priorities in your decision. Look at the whole package instead.

Good scanners are designed to work for you, not the other way around.

- For instance, some scanners (and their software) will analyze whatever you put on the scanner bed and help make many of the decisions for you. They will recognize text and its format (columns, tables, font, etc.). They will also recognize pictures and adjust automatically for them.
- Scanners are getting much easier to use. That is why it is so important to look beyond just the specifications. Look at the solution provided, its completeness and how well thought out it is. Don't focus on traditional high-end numbers and tools. They are not where the excitement (or the benefit) is.

Scanners are now supporting some very easy-to-use features.

- In some scanners you can select text in the scan preview window, drag it to your word processor, and it will be converted to text and entered just as if you had typed it (probably with a few typos, too).
- In the same scanner, you can capture an entire page, format and all, and send it to your word processor as a formatted text, with pictures, heading, columns and all. Look at "Page analysis" on page 93.

How much should I expect to spend for a scanner?

With scanners, as well as anything else, you tend to get what you pay for.

- Quoting prices in a book is dangerous, particularly when talking about a product that has been falling in price as quickly as scanners. Still, at some point, the cost of the raw hardware will dictate a minimum cost for scanners. At the time of this book you could buy a quality scanner for under $500. Below $200 things get more questionable. Certainly if you spend less, you should expect less.
- Well-designed scanners, as they are driven to lower and lower cost, will make appropriate trade-offs. For instance, the speed may be slower, or the software less flexible.
- Above $500, you can find some truly great scanners that far exceed the capabilities of scanners costing thousands of dollars only 2–3 years ago.

Be cautious of deals that seem "too good to be true."

- They probably are!
- Also, if you see two scanners, one with a very low price and very high "specifications" and a second with the same or lower specifications and a higher price, tend to believe the high-priced scanner, particularly if the specifications you are looking at are dpi and bit depth. They are misused and mean little.
- Pay more attention to the package, support, completeness and the details of how a scanning system is put together than the specs.

What about speed? Don't I need a fast scanner?

In fact, the raw scan time is not that important.

- The time it takes to actually scan something is usually small compared to the rest of the job. For instance, if the scan takes 1 minute, but it takes 10 minutes to import the image into a word processor, place it, format it, do any touch-up, then saving 30 seconds on the scan (2x faster) is really not that important.
- Focus more on the time it takes to do a typical task. Some scanners support drag and drop and other features that allow you to achieve the task very quickly. Scan time is usually not that big a deal.
- Quality and reliability is also very important. A fast scanner that provides poor or unpredictable results is slower than one that takes longer, but gets the job done right, the first time and every time.
- Don't ignore scan time, but don't focus on the numbers like "time for a 300-ppi scan." These numbers probably have little impact on your real task speed. Refer to Chapter 12 • "Scanning Speed" on page 167.

Should I buy a digital camera or a scanner?

Both have advantages and disadvantages. The key difference is that scanners are good for scanning existing photos and all sorts of documents. If all you plan to do is capture *new* images, then a digital camera may be for you. Check out "Digital Cameras" on page 163.

I need portability more than image quality.

- Digital cameras make a lot of sense for those who need to capture a "snapshot" that will be sent digitally or used only on the web. For instance, real estate sales representatives, insurance agents and appraisers may find a digital camera very useful.
- If you find that you always take a picture, scan it and never look at the original again, a digital camera may be a good option.
- However, the quality of digital cameras still lags traditional photography greatly. Today, you can get a much better image out of cheap disposable camera and a good scanner.

■ Also consider using photo-CD services to create photo CDs from film. The cost is not high and the image quality much better than current digital cameras.

My primary need is to photograph 3-dimensional objects for the web.

■ If the quality provided by a digital camera is good enough for you, then this might be the best choice. Most digital cameras can provide decent quality at 640x480 for a computer screen.

■ Some scanners can also do a very good job of this. Consider beam splitting, single-exposure scanners first (refer to "Beam-splitting scanners" on page 157 and "Incident-Light Angle Changes and Multiple-Exposure Scans" on page 138).

■ If you need better quality than a digital camera provides, a normal camera plus a scanner is a better solution.

■ Refer to "I'm scanning for the web. What should I worry about?" next.

I've got original photos I want to reproduce.

■ You need a scanner. Digital cameras are not appropriate for this.

I've want to do OCR, fax, and document capture, too.

■ Again, you need a scanner.

I'm scanning for the web. What should I worry about?

In some ways scanning for the world wide web is simple. In others, quite difficult. For more information, refer to "Scanning for the Internet" on page 81.

Worry about color and how images will display.

■ One of the main challenges for images on the web is controlling how they will look on somebody else's computer. Look for scanners that support the new standard sRGB, which is aimed at helping assure consistency of image presentation.

■ In addition, color accuracy can be a problem. This is particularly important if you are selling something with a particular color. The color displayed on the web may not (probably will not) match the real item.

Don't worry so much about resolution.

- Images on the web are typically of lower quality and need smaller files— so they display faster. For this reason, you don't need a high-resolution scanner.

Do worry about scaling and file types.

- You do need a scanner that can create 72- or 75-ppi images well and makes it easy to control the number of pixels in the image. These parameters are important for good web images and minimal file size. Surprisingly, many scanners don't do this very well. See Chapter 14 • "Scaling and Interpolation" on page 197.
- The other important factor is the ability to create the right type of image file. Typically, you will want to use JPEG for photos, GIF for drawings or text, or maybe the new PGN or Flashpix formats.

You keep saying I don't need high resolution, but does it hurt?

- In fact, yes. Scanning at a high ppi causes huge files, can make Moiré worse, slows you down and fills up your disk. It also makes your printer go slowly.
- Also, because the specification, ppi, really doesn't relate well to true resolution any more, you probably aren't getting "high resolution" anyway.
- A good scanner will help you scan at the appropriate resolution for your task.

Do I need a new printer for my scanner?

To get the most out of your scanner, you may need a new printer.

- Only recently have printers, particularly low cost color printers, started to catch up with scanners in terms of printed image quality. For a long time, you could scan a beautiful image, but when you printed it, it didn't look so good. Often the scanner was blamed because it was the new thing. "That printer always works fine, must be the scanner. Maybe I need higher resolution" (*no*).

- Today (1998), you can get low-cost inkjet printers that provide photo-grahic or near-photographic quality. If you are expecting to be able to create "copies" of your pictures, you will likely need to have one of these new printers. A word of caution—"photographic quality" is not a very precise term. Get a demo.
- If your printer is more than a couple of years old, you may be disappointed.

If you have a good laser printer, you can probably print good black and white images now.

- Most black and white laser printers provide reasonable quality for images. For color images, inkjet printers currently provide better results.

For copies of text or drawings, most printers are sufficient.

- The place where printers have lagged behind scanners is in printing images, not text or drawings.

If I'm going to buy a printer and a scanner, how about an all-in-one instead?

The new all-in-one products have some distinct advantages.

- These devices typically have a printer, fax and scanner in them. This means they can be used as a copier, without using the computer.
- It used to be that the scanner or the printer in an all-in-one was not the latest or best. Today, they are quite good. They may lag slightly, but not much.
- One of the advantages of this type of system is that the printer and scanner are closely linked. This means the manufacturer can optimize them as a system and provide better results (not all manufacturers bother to do this).
- An all-in-one may be more cost-effective than buying the pieces. There was also a time when there was concern about reliability. This is not a problem now. See "All-in-one peripherals" on page 59 for more information.

There are some limitations in all-in-one products.

- You cannot replace a piece.
- You have to buy it all at once instead of a little at a time so the initial cost may be higher.
- You may have some contention issues. Can you print and receive a fax at the same time? Can you scan and print at the same time? In some products, you can do these things. In others, you cannot.

Be sure the scanner is color if you are interested in scanning with an all-in-one.

- Some all-in-one products have color printers, but only black and white scanners. It may not be obvious which is the case, so check.

How much memory and disk space do I need in my computer?

Images tend to take up a lot of room on the disk.

- For this reason, you may want to consider more hard disk space or a removable format such as Zip, Jazz or Syquest disks. If you do get an external, removable disk, it is probably not a good idea to get a parallel disk and parallel scanner (get SCSI instead). See "Which Interface should I use to connect my computer to my scanner?" on page 32.
- Remember, many images may not fit on a floppy.
- Frankly, you can never have too much disk space.

Memory, too, can be an important factor.

- Working with images also tends to take a lot of computer memory or be very slow. It is well worth it to invest in more memory for your computer. The extra memory will help in many ways, not just for scanning.
- You will see specifications for the amount of memory a particular scanner has. Those specifications are probably not very important. The amount of memory a scanner has depends on its internal architecture and doesn't necessarily imply faster or better scans.

The right scanner and software can make a big difference in the amount of
memory and disk space you need.

■ An important factor is how well the scanner and software help the user
  create images that have the appropriate settings. You rarely, if ever, need
  to scan at very high sample rates (ppi) *and* high bit depths. Good scanning software will help you pick the right settings or even do it automatically

■ Consider that some scanners require you to have as much memory as the
  biggest image you can scan. For instance, if you want to scan a 20-mega-
  byte image (not unusual), you would need 20 megabytes of memory free.
  These scanners are not well designed and should be avoided. A
  well-designed scanner will be able to capture very large images without
  holding them in memory.

Which Interface should I use to connect my computer to my scanner?

There are three primary interfaces used today and a fourth on the way. For
more information, see "Hardware Interfaces" on page 99.

SCSI, or Small Computer System Interface.

■ SCSI (pronounced "scuzzy," like "fuzzy") is a widely used interface that
  provides high speed and reliable connections. For the past few years,
  SCSI interfaces were considered the standard for scanners.

■ SCSI interfaces can connect up to seven devices to your computer, and
  many high-end computers have SCSI interfaces already installed. If you
  have one of those, a SCSI scanner is probably best. Be sure to check that
  the scanner you are considering is supported on standard SCSI interfaces.

■ If you do get SCSI, you can use this interface to connect external hard
  drives and tape drives, too. SCSI versions are more, but they are much
  faster and more reliable.

■ One of the problems with SCSI is that many new multimedia computers
  do not have it. That means you will have to buy a SCSI interface card
  (called a "host adapter") and install it. If the idea of opening your com-

puter makes you uncomfortable, consider a different interface or having a computer store install the SCSI card for you.

■ One other consideration is that many multimedia PCs have very limited expansion capability, and you may have difficulty adding a SCSI adapter to them.

■ SCSI interfaces can be very fast. Data transfer rates of 1.2 megabytes per second are common.

Parallel scanners

■ Due to the difficulties less experienced computer users had with SCSI interfaces, many low-cost scanners have switched to a bidirectional parallel interface. This allows the user to connect the scanner to the same port as their printer—making installation simple. In many cases, you can just plug the scanner in and it will work quite well.

■ The biggest problem with parallel interfaces is that they were never really designed to be used for input of data. They were designed to send data out—to printers. Consequently, incompatibilities between printers and scanners can arise. The best way to deal with this is purchase from a reputable manufacturer where support is available.

■ You may find that with a parallel scanner, you need to turn off bidirectional communications to your printer. This is inconvenient, but usually not a big problem.

■ Another problem with parallel interfaces is that they are also used by peripherals such as tape drives and external removable hard disks. Getting a printer, scanner, tape drive and external hard disk to operate on one parallel port is pretty unlikely.

■ The speed of a scanner on a parallel interface may be quite variable. Transfer rates on parallel may range from 100 to 800 kilobytes per second, depending on the configuration.

■ Frankly, use of parallel for scanners is probably a passing phase. Parallel will likely be replaced by USB or Firewire in the near future.

It is an interesting historical note that the first desktop scanner, the HP ScanJet, used a bi-directional parallel interface. In later years, that interface was replaced with SCSI because parallel was too slow and difficult to install, and the card was expensive. Now we find parallel back on many scanners because SCSI is difficult to install and expensive, and most computers come with bi-directional parallel interfaces.

USB or Universal Serial Bus.

■ The new USB interface started appearing on computers in 1997. USB is designed to be an easy-to-use, simple and cheap interface that can connect several peripherals to a computer.

■ One of the advantages of USB is the small flexible cables. Anyone who has wrestled with heavy SCSI or parallel cables will appreciate the small USB cables and connectors.

■ USB, while it had some teething problems, is a very promising interface, and you can expect many scanners to become available with USB.

■ If you are considering USB, check to see if your computer has it. You may also need to install some supplemental drivers if your computer was one of the first available with USB. Note, installing USB in an older computer can be quite difficult.

■ All in all, USB is likely to be a very popular interface for scanners. Data transfer rate on a USB interface is not high, but is quite acceptable for most low-end scanners.

1394 or Firewire.

■ This is a new interface starting to appear on computers in 1998. Like USB, Firewire uses small flexible cables in a daisy-chain fashion. Unlike USB, Firewire is extremely fast, so fast that it may replace IDE or SCSI for hard disk interfaces.

■ Firewire has been used in non-computer peripherals for some time. Digital video cameras and digital cameras are examples.

■ Firewire, once it becomes more widely available, will likely become a very popular interface for scanners.

■ A Firewire desktop scanner prototype was demonstrated at WinHec in the spring of 1998 (by Hewlett-Packard).

What Accessories Do I Need?

There are two primary accessories available for scanners, an ADF and an XPA or transparency adapter. For more information, refer to Chapter 8 • "Scanner Gear" on page 99.

If you plan on scanning lots of pages, you might consider an ADF (automatic document feeder).

- An ADF is useful if you want to scan multiple pages for OCR, fax, copying or for document storage. You don't want to trust an ADF for photos.
- Most lower-cost ADFs hold 10–20 pages and feed those pages in a scroll mode (like a fax machine). The reliability and ability of a low-cost ADF to feed lots of pages without jams is quite variable—test one. You also may have a hard time actually finding an ADF for a particular scanner.
- More expensive, 50- or 100-page ADFs are typically much more reliable and robust. They may cost nearly as much as the scanner.
- Some ADFs place the page on the scanner bed, then allow the scanner to scan normally, much like a high speed copier page feeder. These ADFs may be more robust and allow multiple scans of a single page, but are more expensive.

An XPA or transparency adapter allows you to scan transparent photographs at medium to low quality.

- Some scanners come with simple, passive (they use the scanner light) XPAs that allow scanning of 35-mm slides. Note, these scans are probably useful for small reproductions, or maybe the web, but they do not provide professional results.
- You can purchase active (they have their own light source) XPAs that allow scanning larger format transparent originals with higher quality. This may be the only option for large formats like X-rays or 4x5 photo transparencies. Be cautious, quality can vary.
- To get good results with a 35-mm slide or negatives, you should consider a scanner designed for that purpose. See "Film and photo scanners" on page 59.

For scanning overhead transparencies, such as you would use on an overhead projector.

- You can probably achieve acceptable results by just scanning the transparency directly, as if it were a normal page.

■ Claims to Watch Out For

The following specifications should be questioned:

1200-ppi (or more) scanner

At the time this book was written, the were **no** 1200-ppi flatbed scanners available. Specifications like this are typically referring to interpolated resolution of some sort. There are a very few 1000-ppi scanners available, typically at a cost of $3000 or more.

While you can expect to see scanners claiming 1200 ppi, most of those claims are based upon a maximum hardware interpolation. In the near future, expect to see "true" 1200-ppi scanners available. While these scanners probably actually capture 1200 pixels per inch, it is very unlikely that they will provide any real benefit. It is also unlikely they will meet the performance of dedicated 1200-ppi slide scanners (they do exist)

36 bit (or more) scanner

While there are many scanners claiming 30 or 36 bit capability, what that specification really means is very questionable. Often the 36 bits are not calibrated, or the signal-to-noise ratio does not support the bit depth.

■ Pretending that the ppi and Bit Depth Specifications Mean Something

PPI and bit depth used to mean something. For that reason and because buyers will undoubtedly run into ppi and bit depth claims, let us consider what you would need if the specifications were used appropriately (the way they once were). For more information on this, see "The Perversion of Specifications" on page 81 (and the rest of the book).

Once upon a time, these specifications were applied consistently and accurately, and you could infer something from them. For this discussion, let's go back to that time. Keep in mind, though, that even if used properly, these specifications are not all that important.

■ ppi Used as a Measure of Resolution

Remember—*resolution is the ability of a scanner to resolve fine detail in the original.* The number of pixels captured by the scanner is one of the limiters in resolution. In fact, ppi was once a good measure of resolution because the people designing scanners looked at them (scanners) as a system. They knew that if you increase the number of pixels captured, you must also increase the quality of the optical system to go along with the extra pixels.

Today, ppi is more of a marketing tool, a lever to convince people to buy a particular scanner.

What ppi would you need—assuming the claim were true?

In our pretend world, ppi, or pixels per inch, would tell you how well the scanner could resolve detail. That's because engineers and designers know that ppi and optical clarity should be related. In this world, the following guidelines would apply.

A quality 300-ppi scanner would work for:

- Scanning of printed photographs at 1:1 or up to 2–4x enlargement.
- OCR of normal sized text.
- Scanning of normal drawings, charts, logos and artwork.
- Scanning nearly anything for the world wide web (except scanning of slides).
- Archival and storage of simple documents.
- Making copies on your printer (color or b/w).
- Faxing.

A quality 600-ppi scanner is needed for:

- Enlargements of high-quality photographs beyond 4x, for instance, for poster work.
- Scanning of small originals, such as 35-mm slides, for web publishing.
- Scanning of small, high-quality original drawings for detailed reproductions or enlargements.
- OCR of very small text. Note: OCR of small text is quite challenging.

■ Scanning of large format transparent photographic originals (such as 4x5 and 2x2) Note: you also need transparent capability, high bit depth and a very low noise system for this application.

More than 600 ppi is required for:

■ Scanning of 35-mm slides and negatives for enlargement.
■ Little else. Most originals don't have the detail that would require more than the resolution a quality 600-ppi scanner can deliver.

Most people do not need more than 600 ppi.

In fact, very few uses of scanners require more than 600 ppi. Furthermore, most scanners claiming more than 600 ppi:

■ Are not really more than 600 ppi—they are using creative specifications.
■ Don't really deliver on improved resolution—even if the specification is true.

The reality of ppi claims

In fact, most ppi claims are meaningless today. The connection between optical clarity and ppi has been broken by those wishing to promote their products as "higher resolution." The good news is that most reputable scanners will deliver the resolution needed for basic users. But beware—you tend to get what you pay for. Cheaper scanners may not deliver what you need.

Reading ppi specifications

There are 3 (or 4) typical ways in which ppi is specified. The following table discusses what they are and what they mean. For more information see Chapter 13 • "Resolution" on page 173 and "Three types of ppi specifications." on page 178.

Table 3-2   Specifications and their Meaning (Not Much)

Specification	Meaning
Optical Resolution (ppi) Also Called "True Resolution"	The number of actual pixels captured per inch. If any specification is related to true resolution, it is this one. See "What is Resolution?" on page 173.
Hardware Resolution	Typically the Y direction (down the page) step rate of the scanner. Typically this is twice the optical resolution. This specification provides little or no information. See "X- and y-direction optical sampling rates" on page 177.
Maximum Resolution	Usually a very big number (like 9600), this specification relates the maximum number of pixels a scanner or software can create using interpolation. It is truly meaningless. The image processing software shipped with most scanners can do essentially infinite interpolation.

■ Bit Depth, Loosely Related to the Number of Colors a Scanner Can Recognize

The second claim you will see is a claim for the number of "bits" the scanner has. This refers to the number of bits of information captured per pixel. The minimum you will likely see is 24-bit, as in a "24-bit scanner." The maximum seen is probably 36 bits.

What do "bits" have to do with colors?

On the face of it, a specification in "bits" seems to have nothing to do with the number of colors captured by a scanner. In fact, the reason for this specification illustrates the technology in scanners. Inside a scanner is a device called an "analog-to-digital (A/D) converter." This device converts the voltage from the CCD to a number the computer can read. One of the specifications of an A/D is the number of bits converted. Thus, if a scanner has an 8-bit A/D and captures 3 colors (red, green and blue), then we call it a "24-bit" scanner (8x3=24).

Historically, this specification, like ppi, meant something.

This specification once meant something because the people designing scanners matched the A/D to the rest of the system. They would not put a more expensive, high-bit-depth A/D in a cheap scanner because they knew the extra bit depth was wasted.

Today, like ppi, the bit depth is more often a marketing tool used to attract customers to a particular scanner. What the specification does not tell you is the quality of the "bits" captured, or if they are even used!

What bit depth do you need—assuming it were true?

Again, let us assume, for a moment, that the specification for scanner bit depth reflected the real performance of the scanner. In that case, the following guidelines would be useful.

A quality 24-bit scanner will work well for:

- Scanning of photographic prints—for nearly any purpose.
- Scanning for OCR (you really don't need that much).
- Scanning for document management.
- Scanning of drawings or fine art.
- Most scanning for the web.

With a quality 30-bit scanner you get:

- The ability to scan poorly exposed images better (dark photos or those with light backgrounds).
- Slightly better scans of high-quality photos.
- Limited ability to scan photographic transparencies (like slides).

For this you need a quality 36-bit scanner.

- Scanning of high-quality photographic transparencies.
- Scanning high-quality originals for professional work.

It looks like 24 or 30 bits are enough!

In fact, for most people, a quality 24- or 30-bit scanner probably meets all their needs. This is one reason that manufacturers can get away with claiming high bit depths that are not really supported by scanner performance. Most 30- and 36-bit scanners today really perform like the 24-bit scanners of yesterday, and because a good 24-bit scanner meets most needs, most people are reasonably happy and don't realize they are not getting a "true" higher bit depth scan.

■ Reading Bit Depth Specifications

Sadly, it is nearly impossible to tell, from the box, if the bit depth claims are reasonable or correct. Some questions you can ask and things to watch for are:

■ You tend to get what you pay for. If a scanner has a high bit depth specification and an incredibly low price, the spec is probably wrong.

■ Read the specifications on the manufacturer's boxes or the manufacturer's literature carefully. Often specifications are shortened up in store literature. "36-Bit processing" may turn into "36-bit scanner" at the store.

■ Be careful about density range claims. Often they are not applicable. See "Density range" on page 215 for more information.

■ Look for other specifications, such as:

   ■ Signal-to-noise ratio (this is a better measure, but you may not find it).

   ■ Processing depth claims (manufacturers providing this type of specification probably approach the scanner from a more systematic view).

   ■ Calibration specifications, such as "30 bits per pixel, after calibration." Many of the low-cost scanners are quoting bit depth before calibration. Calibration reduces the effective bit depth.

Until better specifications, like signal-to-noise ratio, are adopted, bit depth claims are particularly useless and misleading. See "Bit Depth Claims" on page 214 for more information.

Chapter 4

For the Technical Reviewer

Really, this book is for you—the technical reviewer. Reviewing and writing about scanners is a challenging task. Even for the expert, keeping up with the trends and changes in scanners and how they are used is a tremendous job. In this chapter you will find some guidance on how to set up reviews, things to consider and information about new trends and new challenges.

■ The Challenge of Reviewing Scanners Today

Those faced with reviewing scanners today have a real challenge. They are faced with reviewing a myriad of scanners in a minimum of time. Reviews are often performed by teams of people, none of whom have the opportunity to see or use all the scanners. Often these teams are not located together and the actual text of reviews is written by people who did not test the scanners but received a set of reports.

Another problem is that scanners, even those with the same specifications or similar prices, are not similar in their performance. There is no standard test suite for scanners. Indeed, the specifications applied to scanners today are relatively meaningless.

Next in line is the fact that the uses of scanners vary dramatically. A given scanner may be used by two different people for two totally different tasks. Evaluating **every** scanner for **every** task is beyond the scope of anything but a book, and by the time the book came out, the scanners would probably be obsolete.

■ Changes in Reviewing Scanners

In the past (not that long ago), scanners were very specialized products and were reviewed by experts, for experts. Often reviews were performed by people who were experts in the use of drum scanners and professional publishing. Reviews were full of terms like "line screen" and "density range"—and the people who read the reviews knew what the terms meant and why they were important. Scanners were expensive, and reviewers spent a lot of time testing them.

Not so long ago, to those using scanners, the use of a scanner *was their job* or at least a very big part of it. They used the scanner daily and for a very focused purpose. Traditional DTP scanner users spent significant time understanding and learning how to get the best out of their scanner. They wanted *and needed*, high-end controls to manipulate scanners to get acceptable results.

Using the scanner was their job.

Scanner users of today

Today, scanners are everyday devices used by people who have never heard of drum scanners. There are dozens of scanners available, and the technical reviewer is faced with the task of reviewing all of them in a few days or, at most, weeks. The target audience for these reviews are different also, both in terms of needs and expertise.

For today's user, the scanner is a tool, not a job.

One of the biggest differences is that the users treat the scanner as a tool—something that is used in the course of their real jobs. Much like a printer, or a fax machine, the user has no desire, time or patience to become an expert. They need a tool that will help them achieve a task.

More often than not, today's users do not understand or need high-end scanning controls. The capability of scanners to provide good results automatically means that these controls are rarely needed. Users have no time to learn specialized software or the tricks of the scanning trade. What they need is a scanner and tool set that works well in their environment and gives good results quickly and easily. Keep in mind that scanning is an occasional but important task, and people cannot remember complex tasks when they use them only occasionally. What they want is the result. They do not want to deal with the process. Consequently, scanning software and interfaces should provide a proper amount of "hand-holding" to achieve a given task.

Sophisticated controls may be unnecessary

In fact, this may be one area where reviews and reviewers may be trailing users—the evaluation of scanning software interfaces. Reviewers who are experienced scanner users tend to look for sophisticated controls that existed in traditional scanning software. These high-end controls were once required to allow quality results to be achieved. However, they also required specialized knowledge and, more times than not, got the novice or occasional user into trouble. Scanning software today deals with the issues involved in getting quality scans without resorting to high-end controls. It is a challenge for those involved in reviewing (and designing) scanners to realize that the scanner user of today is much different than the traditional pre-press worker or graphic artist whose job revolved around scanning and document creation. Reviews that contain statements such as,

"The scanner did not provide high-end tools for professional work"

may be missing the point for the today's typical user. That reviewer may overlook the needs of the mainstream scanner user. These users can get what they would consider "professional results" without high-end tools. Often the availability of "high-end" tools which they don't understand, plus the perception that they need to use them, causes the average user more problems than it solves. The mainstream scanner user has no understanding of gamma correction tools, histogram tools, densitometers, or color separation tables. With a well-designed scanning solution, they don't need to.

Sophisticated results are required—automatically

At the same time, the results expected by the average user means that many of the functions the expert used to handle must be automated. While today's user may not understand gamma correction, they need it. If appropriate gamma correction is not applied, they will be disappointed in the results. And because they are not experts, they will not know how to fix it.

Today, thanks to advances in scanners, scanning software, system integration tools (OLE, TWAIN), better and cheaper color printers, and a much higher awareness of imaging, people who would not recognize a densitometer if they stepped on one are using scanners daily—with great results. Thus, when reviewing scanners, keep in mind that the user of three years ago is much different than the user of today—and scanners should reflect this.

Sophisticated controls can be useful

While they must not be required, sophisticated imaging controls are still important and useful for a significant class of users—those who want and need more control over their scanner. Refer to Chapter 7 • "Scanning Software" and Chapter 10 • "More on Image Quality" for more information.

■ Steps to a Successful Review

In this section we will talk about some of the steps you may follow to set up and perform your review. Clearly, you, the reviewer, have the best understanding of journalistic reporting, your goals and audience. Here we are just trying to help set up the scanner review by presenting a plausible set of guidelines that you can use. Much of the information here is expanded upon in other parts of the book and most of this information is common sense applied to the special subject of scanners. First, you may wish to review the section "Changes in Reviewing Scanners" on page 44 and "Some Guidelines to Consider" on page 52 (both in this chapter) and "Questions You Should Ask Yourself" on page 20 in Chapter 3 • "Buying a Scanner" on page 15.

Identify the type of review you are doing

Different reviews have very different requirements and expected outcomes. Scope the review and try to identify that what you want to do and the time needed to do it are appropriate. At the end of each section is an estimate for the time spent with each scanner.

First look.

First-look reviews are often based upon a preliminary unit or even just a press release and information package. Here are some thoughts.

- First looks will be based primarily on the information provided by the manufacturer. A first look may viewed by readers as just a press release about a scanner.
- If a scanner is marketed as a new type, or some new claim is presented, focus on that. If time is available, test performance of new claims.
- Even though the temptation is to group scanners based upon ppi and bit depth, try to avoid specification comparisons. There is little or no time to evaluate a scanner performance, and these specifications mean little.

- Be sure to read claims with care. In the current market environment, specifications are not used consistently, and subtle differences in the wording may be important. Just because the words "30-bit" appear, it may not mean the scanner is a "30-bit" scanner.
- **Time spent with the scanner:** 0 to 2 hours.

Simple review of single scanner.

In the review, a complete evaluation of a scanner is performed but probably not many analytical tests. Some things to consider:

- Evaluate all aspects of the scanning solution. Don't focus on just images, text or any single performance factor.
- Focus on task completion. Use the scanner to achieve the tasks claimed for the scanner fully. Include multiple scans per task—for instance, OCR of a multi-page document. Is it easy or hard? Can you combine the pages in one file, or do you have to created a separate file for each page.
- Spend enough time with the scanner to learn how that scanner works. Don't assume you know how it works just because you've reviewed scanners before. Changes in the way scanners are used are important and rapid.
- Require a minimum level of quality for a completed task. If the minimum level is not reached, then redo the task and include that redo effort in your evaluation
- Do more than one of each type of scan using different originals. Using different originals is very important to fully evaluate a scanner. Just because a scanner does poorly on one image does not mean it will do poorly on all images.
- **Time spent with scanner:** 3–5 hours of use time over several days.

Comprehensive evaluation of a single scanner.

This review will include in-depth analysis of the scanner performance using analytical tasks, as well as review of more important tasks for which the scanner is intended.

- This review includes all of the features of the simple review above but with the additional analytical evaluation of the scanner performance.
- You will need to identify appropriate test targets and testing procedures.
- Again, focus on task completion and quality.

- Plan for significant time spent with the scanner to assure the analytical tests are done in a consistent manner. Some scanners may not allow you to perform the analytical tests easily, so plan for some effort here.
- While analytical evaluation is important, don't overemphasize the analytical to the detriment of the a well-rounded review.
- **Time spent with scanner:** A comprehensive analysis can take a week of concentrated effort.

Roundup

In the roundup, a number of scanners are reviewed for a performance. The level of depth in a roundup can range from the first look to the comprehensive evaluations. Key factors to consider include:

- Ensure that you have a consistent test plan for all scanners.
- Spend up-front time planning for the review, and plan for troubleshooting time in the review process.
- Plan for some time to be spent reconciling differences in how the scanners operate. This will be important because it can be difficult to achieve consistent settings on all the scanners tested. For instance, some scanners perform auto-exposure for every scan, others do not.
- Classify what scanners you are reviewing. In the past, ppi, bpp and price have been used. None of these is a particularly good method today due to differences in how scanners are specified and what the specifications mean. The fact that these same criteria are what a potential user may consider illustrates one of the challenges faced in reviewing. The best method is to define a target market or audience and identify the scanners you believe those users would consider purchasing.
- Avoid using "default settings" because they do not exist. The default used for different scanners will be much different—so the "default" is really "inconsistent."
- **Time spent with the scanner:** Depends on the type of evaluation.

Other factors to consider

Create scripted procedures for specific tests.

For consistency and uniformity a scripted test plan is appropriate. Because the controls used differ from scanner to scanner, this can be quite challenging. The script needs to describe the activity, not the controls, because the controls will be different. It is important to understand the goals of each procedure so that the result, and not the steps, are evaluated.

Consider how the hardware interface may impact other functions on the computer.

Consider how the scanner (hardware) interface may impact other operations on the computer. For instance, if the scanner uses a parallel interface, do scanning and printing interfere with each other? Can you use the scanner to make a copy to the connected printer?

Invest in the appropriate training for testers.

It is unreasonable, due to differences in scanning interfaces, to expect an untrained tester to achieve the tasks set out in the test plan. The testers should have adequate training and access to expert help in terms of the goals of the test.

Design jury reviews carefully.

Jury review, where a group of people is used to judge the result of a scan, is a useful test that represents how people will view scanners. However, jury reviews need to be structured and controlled very carefully. Be aware that jury reviews are testing a system which includes the printer or display. The printer or display can introduce more error than the scanner for some images. When performing jury reviews, pay attention to items such as:

- Viewing environment. It needs to be consistent in terms of the lighting environment. Avoid rooms with windows.
- Color deficiencies in the jury.
- Be VERY clear in instructions.

Avoid open questions like:

- Which one is better?
- Which one is more accurate?
- Which one do you like better?

Instead, be very precise in your questions and the expected responses. For instance, instead of:

- Which image has better color?

Ask questions like:

- In which image is the color closer to the original? (Obviously the original must be provided.)
- Rank the images in order of color accuracy when compared to the original, from most accurate to least accurate.
- Rank the images in order of most lifelike color on a scale of 1 to 10, where 1 is "worst imaginable match to reality" and 10 is "the best imaginable match to reality."

An example test plan

The following is a simple test plan for a comprehensive review of a group of scanners. It is intended only as an example, and many of the details are missing.

Step 1: Identify the scanners to be tested.

The scanners to be tested fit the following characteristics:

- Price under $300 but over $150—including all cables and required accessories.
- Target market is the home user for home use, not business.
- Scanners must be user-installable.
- Only scanners introduced in the past 6 months will be considered.
- No pre-production scanners are to be considered.
- Scanners are obtained from retail market, not from the manufacturer.

Step 2: Develop a detailed test plan and realistic time line.

The review is a task-based review. Scanners will be rated on the quality resulting from each task as well as the time required to complete the task. Tasks will include:

- Installation of the scanner and all software.
- OCR of a simple page.
- Page replication of a complex page which includes: multiple columns, color graphics, headers and footers, and a color image. The task is to replicate the page inside a word processing application. Color is to be maintained.
- Fax using fax modem of a colored legal document, such as a birth certificate.

- Simple copies, both color and b/w, using a system printer.
- Replication of a color image on a b/w printer.
- Scan of several images for a web page. In the web exercise, include scaling images for various target width and height.
    - For instance, take a particular original and scan it for a 300x200 pixel image on a web page. Do not use the web creation software to scale the image, use the scanning software to create the correct image size.
- Creation of a "computer scrapbook" of children's elementary art work (refrigerator art).

Step 3: Train the testers appropriately.

The goal of the review is to evaluate both the learning curve and the trained productivity of the scanners. To this end, the review will:

- Include performing each task more than once with different users, some more experienced and some less. The first task is intended to measure the ease of use for a new user. The second, how well the scanner works for a more experienced user. Realize that users are "new users" only once.
- There will be a cooling-off period of one week where the tester does not use the scanner. This is intended to measure retention of scanning tasks and models real use of scanners.

Step 4: Perform analytical measurements of scanner performance.

Each scanner will be analytically evaluated for:

- Resolution (MTF).
- Scaling capability.
- Image noise.
- Tonal accuracy.
- Color fidelity.
- RGB misregistration.
- Task speed.

Clearly, many of the tasks above need to be further defined. However, this can illustrate some of the planning that must be used to achieve an accurate and representative review.

■ Some Guidelines to Consider

Here are some general guidelines you may wish to consider. Some of them may seem obvious, but it does not hurt to reiterate.

- Be prepared to revise and retest if something is not going well or doesn't make sense.
- Make sure appropriate communication avenues exist between testers and writers. Open discussions are very valuable.
- Question the traditional specifications; many of them are being misused today.
- If you are going to do analytic tests, prepare for significant work.
- Spend the up-front time to set the process up carefully. It is well worth it.
- Spend the time to learn about scanners. Again, it is well worth it.
- Obtain quality originals, and treat them with care.
- Also, test with typical originals for your target audience.
- Don't fall into the trap "image quality is easy to evaluate, just look at the image."
- Check for color deficiencies in testers.
- Don't focus too much on the numbers—or particular failure.
- Realize that any scanner can be made to look bad and that all scanners will make color errors. If a particular scanner does poorly on a particular color, that does not mean it will do poorly on all colors.
- When somebody tells you something is always true, or false, for all scanners, doubt.
- Scanners are used as part of a system to achieve a task. Consider including performance of typical tasks in your reviews. If you do measure the time and effort it takes to perform a series of tasks:
  - Require acceptable output. Often the "task" is performed, but the result is not something anybody would accept. If you can't get an acceptable result without multiple tries, then include those multiple tries in the time to completion and the rating of the scanner.
- In the case of OCR, define the goal and include time used in correcting format and recognition errors. Use people of similar skill to achieve format corrections.

- Consider having both novices and experienced scanner users perform the tasks. You may find a novice can achieve a particular task faster than an expert, because the novice has no preconceived notion of how to do it.
  - The expert may spend time "fixing" things that aren't really broken or overriding automatic settings because they worked poorly in the past.
  - On the other hand, the novice may run into a roadblock that only an expert could fix.
- Approach the tasks with an open mind to new ways. The way scanners work is changing. If you try to achieve a task the way you did on a scanner just two or three years ago, you may be missing the biggest advances in scanners.
- Consider contacting the scanner manufacturers for expert assistance or to answer questions. In today's retail environment, misinformation often prevails. While it is valuable to emulate the customer experience, one of the goals a review should have is to correct common misconceptions.
- Live with the scanners for a while. Use them daily if possible. You may find a really slick interface with lots of "controls" becomes cumbersome, or that a simple interface becomes limiting. Remember, scanner users will use the scanner for more than the few hours the reviewer has.
- Examine the software carefully. Look for integrated installs, consistency and completeness.
- Consider jury reviews, but if you do, design them carefully. Refer to "Design jury reviews carefully." on page 49.
- If you see something that doesn't make sense, then it is probably wrong. Specifications that seem too big to be real probably are. If a scanner you expect to do well does particularly poorly in a specific task or test, contact the manufacturer and question the viability of the test.

■ Testing and Reviewing an All-in-One Scanner

From a reviewing standpoint the tests and evaluation of the scanner portion of an all-in-one product are essentially the same as a stand-alone scanner with the exception of special tests for device contention (what happens if you try to scan while a document is printing?) Also, the integration of the scanning function with the other functions in the device are an area of interest. For example, does a copy require data transferred to the host and back to the printer or can it go directly from the scanner to the printer?

■ Testing Digital Cameras

This book does not address testing of digital cameras, but many of the concepts could be applied. Special attention should be given to de-mosaic artifacts and colorimetery as well as how well the camera captures natural colors. It would be a good idea, when performing color accuracy tests, to use a controlled viewing booth and controlled conditions—then compare to standard film. Information about digital cameras is scattered about in the book, so refer to the Index.

Chapter 5

A Look at Scanners

In this chapter you will find an introduction to scanners. What is a scanner? What types are there, and what are some of the advantages and disadvantages of each? What can scanners do? How do they work, and how are they changing? You will also find a brief introduction to image quality.

■ What is a Scanner?

A color desktop scanner is a device that captures an image of an object and converts it into a digital light-intensity map for computer processing. The object might be a physical article, a photograph, a transparency, or a printed document. The result is a two-dimensional map of pixels, the smallest elements of a scanned image. In this map, each pixel holds an intensity measurement corresponding to the reflectance (for paper) or the transmittance (for transparencies) of the object at the physical location represented by that pixel.

Wow! If you didn't know what a scanner was before, the description above probably didn't help! Let's try to simplify it a little.

In the most general sense, a scanner is a device that allows you to put a image of something into your computer. Once you have that image, you can do many things with it.

Like a camera

In some ways scanner works like a camera connected to a computer. Like a camera, a scanner captures a black and white or color image. In a scanner the image is made up of a bunch of very small elements called "pixels." Each pixel contains the color or value of a very small part of the image. Pixels are used in other devices, like computer displays. If you have a computer display with 640x480 resolution it means your computer display is 640 pixels across by 480 pixels tall. When you put all the pixels together, side by side, you see the entire image.

A scanner captures each pixel as a number which tells the computer the color or intensity of that pixel. Scanners capture pixels with as many as 36 bits to describe the gray levels or color gradations, whereas a camera captures an image on film. Film offers many shades, so we call it "continuous tone." Unlike a camera, which captures an image on film, a scanner captures an image and stores it in a computer file where it can be used over and over, modified or sent to somebody else.

Like a fax

People may not realize it, but a fax machine has a scanner in it. In fact, many fax machines today come with "scan back" capability, which allows you to use them as a simple scanners. If a fax is like a scanner, then it makes sense that a scanner is like a fax. In fact, you can use a color scanner, combined with the right software, as a fax machine.

Like a copier

A flatbed scanner looks a lot like a copier, and, combined with the right software and a printer, a scanner can act as a copier. If you have a color printer, then the scanner and printer can be used as a color copier.

■ Types of Scanners

There are three basic types of scanners; handheld, sheetfed and flatbed. In addition, there are some special versions of these scanners, including photo scanners, slide or film scanners and products called all-in-ones, which combine a scanner with other functions, such as a printer and fax. Each has advantages and disadvantages.

Handheld scanners

Handheld scanners are small devices that the user slides or rolls across the original. Better handheld scanners have wheels that measure the motion as the user moves them or even provide some feedback (resistance) to keep the user from moving them too rapidly. Handheld scanners provide some level of portability and functionality for a very low cost. Typically these scanners can be used to scan originals in strips about 4 inches wide. These strips can be reintegrated using special stitching software provided with the scanner. Handheld scanners are typically of the lowest cost and poorest quality of any scanners.

Advantages.

- Small size.
- Low cost.
- Somewhat portable (can be carried and connected to a laptop computer).

Disadvantages.

- Image quality is often poor and uneven.
- Variations in the motion cause stretching or tilting of the image.
- Stitching of images may not be very effective.
- Must be tethered to a computer, limiting portability.
- Require a very steady hand. Particularly if images are to be stitched together, it is important that the motion between the two scanned strips be identical. Otherwise one image may be stretched compared to the other and may not stitch well.

Handheld scanners are becoming of less interest as the cost of more capable sheetfed and flatbed scanners comes down.

Sheetfed scanners

Sheetfed scanners have a slot into which a page or picture is fed. As the page moves through the scanner, an image is captured. Fax machines are the most common version of a sheetfed scanner. The optical imaging element of a sheetfed scanner can be either an optical reduction sensor or a contact image sensor. Refer to "Optical Reduction or Contact Image Sensor Scanners" on page 139.

The quality of sheetfed scanners can vary dramatically—from consistent with a fax machine to special, high-quality photo scanners. Some sheetfed scanners can be detached and used as page-wide hand scanners.

Advantages.

- Small size. Some fit between the keyboard and the monitor.
- Ability to be integrated into other devices, such as keyboards and all-in-ones Products.
- Low cost.
- Some sheetfed scanners can be detached and used as page-wide hand-held scanners for bound originals.

Disadvantages.

- Usually limited in image quality.
- Typically not appropriate for delicate or important originals.
- Only one scan can be done of an original, unlike a flatbed scanner that can perform multiple scans of the same original.
- Cannot scan bound or large objects (except as mentioned above).

Flatbed scanners

This is the most versatile and most common type of scanner. A flatbed scanner resembles a copier in that it has a document glass on which you place the original and a carriage which moves across and scans the original. Unlike a copier, the scanner sends the image of the original to a computer where further processing can be done. Some scanners perform sophisticated image processing internally, and consequently operate much faster and with better results. Most of the information in this book is focused on flatbed scanners.

Advantages.

- These are the most versatile scanners. With a flatbed you can scan a wide variety of originals and objects.
- These scanners do not physically move the original, so they are safe for delicate originals.

■ Multiple scans of the same original are possible. This can vastly increase the available image quality and the ability of the scanner to capture complex pages.

■ Large scanning area combined with multiple scan capability means several originals can be placed on a flatbed and scanned in a minimal amount of time. This is especially useful for document creation.

Disadvantages.

■ The large footprint is often a problem. People are unhappy about devoting a large space for a device used occasionally.

■ Flatbed scanners cannot be stacked, and placing items on top of them is not very convenient.

■ The cost of a flatbed is higher.

Film and photo scanners

This is a specialized scanner designed to scan 35-mm slides, negative film strips, or standard size photos. Some perform all three types of scan, others do only one or two. For more information, refer to "Slide or Film Scanners" on page 161 and "Image Quality Requirements for Scanning Transparent Originals." on page 124.

Advantages.

■ These scanners are optimized for this specialized format and may deliver much higher quality than a transparency-equipped flatbed.

■ Photo scanners can be integrated into computer, much like a disk drive.

Disadvantages.

■ Quality photo and film scanners are more expensive and not as versatile as flatbed scanners.

All-in-one peripherals

A new and growing product category is the multifunction or all-in-one peripheral. Typically, this product includes some combination of a scanner, fax, printer, and copier. Initially, these multifunction products represented a combination of functionality, typically of one-generation-old technology, i.e., last year's printer with last year's scanner. They were created by combining already-existing products and were called "multifunctional" devices.

Today, new versions of these products are available, often called "all-in-one" products. The key difference is that some of these devices are designed from the start as all-in-one devices. They are not an *ad hoc* combination of existing devices. For more information refer to "If I'm going to buy a printer and a scanner, how about an all-in-one instead?" on page 30 in Chapter 3 • "Buying a Scanner" on page 15.

Advantages.

- Cost effectiveness. The consumer has to buy only one device. While that device is more expensive than any one or two of its components, it is usually cheaper than the sum of the pieces.
- Natural synergy. Combining a printer and scanner gives you a fax and copier.
- Space efficiency. The all-in-one products are typically smaller and more compact than the combination of separate devices.
- Optimization. All-in-one devices may be optimized for typical tasks, thus working better together than independent peripherals.
- Installation is easier for one device than for several.

Disadvantages.

- Shared downtime. If one breaks, they are usually all out of service. This problem is minimal, as most of these products today are very reliable.
- Device contention. Scan and print at the same time? What if a fax comes in during a print or scan?
- Older technology? Often the base technologies in these products are one generation old. The trend toward purpose-designed products is alleviating this somewhat.
- Lack of flexibility or upgrade options. When all the peripherals are tied together, one single peripheral cannot be upgraded.
- Higher initial cost. Can't piece it together. Have to buy it all at once.

Digital cameras

With the recent arrival of digital cameras, users are asking how scanners compare to digital cameras. Let us consider that from two standpoints, technology and use. Technically, digital cameras and scanners are quite similar in concept to scanners, but quite different in execution. Table 5-1, "Technical Comparison of Scanners and Digital Cameras," lists some of the technical differences. Table 5-2, "Comparison by Use of Scanners and Digital Cameras," compares the two product types from a use standpoint .

Table 5-1   Technical Comparison of Scanners and Digital Cameras

Scanner	Digital camera
Uses a high-intensity artificial light source to illuminate the original	Uses natural or scene light augmented with a flash
Captures one "raster" line of the original at a time, combining them to form an image	Captures an entire scene in one shot with a low number of pixels
Has fixed focus and limited depth of field	Has variable focus and focal length
May use one of a number of color separation technologies	Typically uses transmissive filters in a mosaic (CCD-based consumer products)
Uses a liner (or trilinear) CCD to capture 2500 –5000 pixels per raster line, but millions of pixels per image	Uses a square CCD array to capture several hundred thousand pixels per image. Digital cameras may claim "a million pixels," but they are counting red, green and blue CCD sites added together. They currently do not have a million of each color
Typically transfers the image to the host computer immediately (often several megabytes per image)	Must have onboard storage capacity to store a number of images (10Kb to 1 Mb total)
Has reached the point where technology is not a fundamental limiter	Still fundamentally limited by the technology of CCD arrays

Table 5-2   Comparison by Use of Scanners and Digital Cameras

Scanner	Digital camera
Is most useful capturing already existing hardcopy art (photographs, drawings, small objects) or information (text, documents)	Is most useful recording the actual scene (replacing traditional photography)
High-quality capability today (desktop publishing to professional publishing)	Is an emerging technology that is growing in capability and quality, but still quite limited
Widely available and low cost	Expensive
Appropriate for OCR and document management	Inappropriate for document management, due to limited resolution

In summary, digital cameras and desktop scanners are somewhat overlapping and somewhat complementary technologies. As digital cameras become more cost-effective and achieve higher quality and as more original art is captured in or converted to digital form, the role of digital cameras will undoubtedly grow. However, given the amount of hardcopy original information that exists and the continued use of paper, it is unlikely that digital cameras will replace desktop scanners in the near future. For more information on the technology of digital cameras, see "Digital Cameras" on page 163.

■ What Scanners Can Do

With a desktop scanner you can capture an image of something and save it as a file in your computer. Some scanners can even capture images of small three-dimensional objects as an alternative to photo reproduction. Once captured, the image can be stored in a database, used to make copies, faxed over a phone line, used for web page creation or included in electronic communications. If the image is of text or a document page (such as a page of a report that contains graphics or drawings), it can be processed into text or integrated with other information to create new documents. Some scanners even retain the formatting of the page—the column layout, tables and images—giving you an electronic copy of the page.

Table 5-3, "Some Examples of Scanner Uses," on page 63 list some of the things you do with your scanner. If your scanner is well designed and has good software you can do all of these things without being an expert.

Table 5-3   *Some Examples of Scanner Uses*

Desktop Publishing (DTP)	Desktop scanners are useful for business and desktop publishing (DTP) applications in which the quality of the image is the primary consideration. But keep in mind that although some desktop flatbed scanners have the capability to scan common 35-mm slides, most don't have the capability to scan high-quality 35-mm slides for commercial printing.
Document Management	Most scanners, with the appropriate software, offer document management—a database created from scanned images such as newspapers, magazines, memos, and reports, all indexed and instantly accessible. Some scanners are available with an automatic document feeder (ADF), which allows you to scan many documents at once.
Text (OCR)	When you scan text, you capture it as a graphic image in your computer. Although you can't edit this image or search it with key words, you can process the scanned image using optical character recognition (OCR) software, which reads the document and translates it into computer-editable characters. This enables you to edit, search, and retrieve the words as you would any other text file.
Copying	With copying software and a color printer, many scanners offer the ability to make convenience color copies—bringing this higher-end capability to the average user's desktop. Even with just a black and white printer, a scanner provides limited copying capability for the small or home office.
Transparencies	With a transparency adapter, which is available for many desktop scanners, you can import images from photo transparencies, usually from 35-mm slides up to 8.5-inch by 11-inch transparencies. Just because a transparency adapter is available for a particular scanner does not mean that the scanner can perform quality scans of transparent originals (particularly small ones like 35-mm slides). See the sections on "Requirements for Transparent Originals" and "Film Scanners" in Chapter 8 • "Scanner Gear" on page 99.
Internet	A new and growing area for scanners is electronic communication using the Internet. Using a desktop scanner, people can easily include images, text and other information into web pages or email. Some scanners provide web authoring tools, and many office tools allow web authoring straight from a word processor or presentation package.
Electronic Information Distribution	Another new application for scanning is widespread electronic document distribution. This can take the form of a network connected scanner or a scanner connected to a fax broadcast system. One use is in companies that need to send regular updates to outlying offices, such as insurance or sales offices.

■ How Scanners Work

A desktop scanner uses a light source, a color-separation method and a charge coupled device (CCD) array to collect optical information about the object scanned and transform that information into a computer image file. For a more detailed discussion of scanner technology, including flatbed, sheetfed, digital cameras, and drum scanners, refer to Chapter 11 • "Some Scanner Technologies" on page 139. Here is a brief discussion of some of the parts and aspects of a scanner.

CCD.

A CCD captures, stores and transfers the photoelectrons created by a photoreceptor such as a photodiode. The photodiode is located right next to the CCD. Working together, the CCD and the photoreceptor measure incident light and convert the measured value to analog voltage. The CCDs in a scanner are arranged in an array.

A CCD records lightness as intensity, which is proportional to the number of photons captured per time period. Intensity is the amount of light reflected or transmitted by an object; black is the lowest intensity and white is the highest intensity. This means that the CCD response is related linearly to the amount of light that is reflected or transmitted by the object.

When you put an object on the scanner copyboard or glass surface and start the scan, the light source illuminates a thin horizontal strip of the object. The reflected light is captured by the CCD array and converted from an analog voltage to a digital value by an analog-to-digital converter. Figure 5-1 shows a raster line and a CCD array.

Y-direction sampling rate.

The CCD captures the whole horizontal strip, called a "raster line," in one step. During the exposure of each raster line, the scanner carriage (optical imaging element) is mechanically moved a small distance. The distance the carriage moves during the exposure determines the *y*-direction (down the page) sampling rate. Thus, a 1/800-inch movement is equal to an 800-ppi *y*-direction sampling rate.

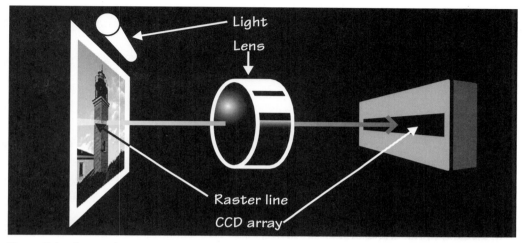

Figure 5-1 Raster line and CCD array

X-direction sampling rate.

The width of the copyboard divided by the number of usable CCD elements in the array determines the *x*-direction (across the page) sampling rate. This is typically expressed as a 300-, 400-, or 600-ppi sampling rate.

In a 600-ppi scanner that is 8.5 inches wide, there are 5,100 (600 ppi x 8.5 inches) usable CCD elements in the array. The array is physically smaller than 8.5 inches wide so the optical system focuses the light down to the proper size using reduction optics—something like a microscope in reverse.

PPI and resolution.

Usually, the "resolution" quoted for a scanner is really its sample rate (ppi). In fact, this is an imprecise use of the term. At one time, it was probably appropriate to equate ppi and resolution. However, this is no longer true. The trend is to increase the ppi of scanners to claim a higher specification without any real improvement or benefit. In fact, a higher ppi may be a detriment to the user!

Today, ppi is an almost meaningless specification.

It's something like looking at the top number on the speedometer of a car and concluding how fast the car is. There may be a relationship between the speedometer and top speed, but not a strong relationship. Probably a car that has a speedometer that goes to 300 kph is faster than a car that has a speedometer that stops at 150 kph—this is a big difference. But the same cannot be said about two cars whose speedometers stop at 160 kph and 180 kph, respectively. PPI for scanners is similar—except that even extreme differences, like 600 ppi and 300 ppi, may mean little. For more information on ppi and resolution, refer to Chapter 13 • "Resolution" on page 173.

Bit depth and reality.

When the analog voltage from the CCD is converted to a digital number, the measurement of bpp comes into play because the digital-to-analog converter has a certain number of bits. The number of bits from the analog-to-digital converter for each sample determines the scanner's number of gray levels. Theoretically, an 8-bit sample represents 256 gray levels or 2^8 possibilities. For a 24-bit color scanner, each pixel is represented by three 8-bit samples for 2^{24} different colors. Figure 5-2 illustrates pixels in a 4-bit scanner.

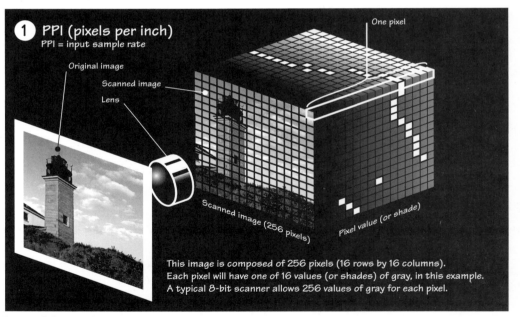

1 PPI (pixels per inch)
PPI = input sample rate

Original image

Scanned image

Lens

One pixel

Scanned image (256 pixels)

Pixel value (or shade)

This image is composed of 256 pixels (16 rows by 16 columns).
Each pixel will have one of 16 values (or shades) of gray, in this example.
A typical 8-bit scanner allows 256 values of gray for each pixel.

Figure 5-2   Pixels in a 4-bit scanner

Bit depth and density claims

Theoretically, an 8-bit scanner can see 256 levels, so the smallest reflectance it can see is 1/256, or 0.4% reflectance. The density of this lowest count would be $\log_{10}(1/.004) = 2.41$. In reality, scanners cannot capture density changes at the level you would expect based upon bit depth because there is noise in the system that creates limitations.

For a 10-bit scanner there are 1,024 theoretical levels, so the smallest reflectance it can theoretically see is $1/1024 = 0.000977$, or about 0.1%. The theoretical best density would be $\log_{10}(1/.000977) = \log_{10}(1,024) = 3.0$. But again, image noise and surface reflection limits the actual density.

Some manufacturers base density specifications on the theoretical limit at a certain density. For example, a 36-bit scanner has a theoretical density limit of $\log_{10}(4096) = 3.61$, but few, if any, really deliver this. These specifications are probably not representative of a scanner's performance since density is limited by noise, stray light and surface reflection.

In addition, density specifications should include a spectral specification, such as status-T density. The spectral portion of density specifications is often ignored in scanners. Today, much like ppi, bit depth is a meaningless specification for three reasons.

Insufficient signal-to-noise ratio

In most scanners, the signal-to-noise ratio does not support density claims based upon bit depth. If a 10-bit scanner has noise equivalent to the bottom 4 bits (16 counts), then the real performance of the scanner is more like a 6-bit scanner. See "What Do You Get for Your 10 (Or 12) Bits?" on page 126.

Most users don't need extreme density range or bit depth.

Most users and most originals have no need for density ranges beyond about 2.0, which would correspond to about 8-bits per pixel per color. In fact, the benefits from a 10-bit scanner are more related to the quality of tonal transformations, like gamma correction, than they are the increased density ranges of the scanner.

The extra bits are used for PRNU, not for the Image.

Often the extra bits are used for photo response non-uniformity (PRNU) or dark signal non-uniformity (DSNU) compensation, not for image capture. In essence, these bits are used to correct for imperfections in the scanner, not to capture information in the image. For more information about PRNU and DSNU, see Chapter 10 • "More on Image Quality" on page 121.

Today – bit depth claims, like ppi, are used as a marketing schemes to make a scanner appear more capable.

In fact, the claims are often misleading. It is very easy to install a higher-resolution A/D converter in a scanner and claim higher specifications with no benefit to the user—and in fact, no real increased value.

■ An Intro To Image Quality

Image quality has a large number of factors. Unfortunately, image quality for a scanner is often reduced to two meaningless numbers, ppi and bit depth. In fact, many factors contribute to the quality of an image, and different images have different requirements.

A different view of image quality

Traditionally, when people talk about image quality, they "picture" a pretty image, a lovely face, a beautiful scene or a profound one. From a scanner standpoint, image quality is a much broader concept and a much more mundane one.

For instance, have you ever considered the "image quality" of a fascimile? A fax is not something most people would associate with a quality image, yet a fax is an image, and its quality can vary.

A scanner is a device that captures an image. That image could be of almost anything, and it could be used for almost anything. An image of a page of text may be used for OCR, or fax, or a copy. If the image is intended as an archive of an important document, the quality had better be good. Consider a fingerprint or an X-ray. These are areas where image quality can affect life. Image quality can also be quite subjective—the same image may have different quality for different users.

Because image quality can mean such a wide variety of things, there is no one test that can be used to determine the image quality of a scanner. This book takes the tack of testing many performance aspects of a scanner and trying to relate those components to particular needs and tasks and to qualities of an image.

Image quality has a number of components, such as resolution, scaling, tonal resolution and color fidelity, each of which can be tested separately. The image-quality components that are important to you depend on what you are scanning and your application for the scanned image. Not all scanners perform well in all categories and not all categories are necessary for all applications. For example, line drawings need high resolution while color photos need tonal and color accuracy. Table 5-4, "Importance of Scanning Capability for Different Types of Scans," on page 77 lists the scanning features for each category and rates the importance of those features for different applications.

One obvious way to test image quality is to compare the object with the printed output of the scanned image. But the printer you use may have more impact than the scanner on the quality of the printed image.

A printer's capability (or lack of it) may even conceal the differences between quality scanners.

Given these variables, no single test is the final measure of a scanner's image quality. But the tests we recommend to evaluate the different aspects of image quality offer these advantages:

- Fair, repeatable and quick comparisons of each scanner's performance.
- Attention to all the variables in the scanning process.
- Help finding the right scanner for the user's application.

■ Scanners and Printers

Probably the biggest impact on scanning has come from the introduction of low-cost, high-quality printers. So it is important to understand how scanners and printers work together.

This section deals with printer dpi and scanner ppi and how to relate them. But good scanners do this for the user, so you probably don't need to understand this in detail today. Just look for a scanner that handles it for you, and use it. Avoid scanners that require you to understand this.

Scanners treat an image as an array of pixels. The value of each pixel captured by a scanner represents one of many shades of gray or color (millions). Traditionally, printers print dots and the value of each dot is a choice of black or white, or one of a few colors. Comparing scanner pixels with printer dots, you see that a scanner pixel contains much more information than a printer dot.

For a black and white laser printer, the value represents either a black dot (the smallest element of a printed image) or white paper. For most color printers, the value represents one of a handful of solid color dots or white paper. As printers have progressed, the traditional description has changed somewhat. Today some business or home printers are able to print a variety of dot sizes or, in the case of color printers, mix different colored inks to create intermediate shades of dots. Instead of just a single cyan, magenta, yellow and black, some printers have more than one intensity of cyan or magenta or may be able to print various intensities of those inks by varying the dot size. These changes have greatly improved the quality of printed photographs on low-cost printers. In addition, there is a class of printers such as dye-sub and thermal wax that can print true multilevel pixels. Still, for most printer applications, the printer is more of a limitation than the scanner when printing scanned photographs.

Using the right sampling rate

Sampling rate is not the same as resolution.

Because printer dots and scanner pixels contain very different amounts of data, it is important to understand their relationship. Typically, people make the mistake of matching scanner ppi and printer dpi. Only in certain cases is this really appropriate.

Sampling rate is the number of samples, in ppi, that are created by a scanner per linear distance. The sampling rate you use in a scan is dictated by your object, your application for the scanned image, and your printer. Sampling rate is not the same as resolution.

Resolution is the degree to which a scanner distinguishes detail in an object; it is affected by sampling rate but also by other aspects of a scanner such as lens quality, filter quality and the motion of the carriage. For more on sampling rate and resolution, see Chapter 13 • "Resolution" on page 173.

A further distinction is made between sampling rate and optical sampling rate. Sampling rate is the number of ppi created by a scanner and may include interpolation (mathematical estimation of more pixels) and subsampling (throwing away some pixels). Optical sampling rate is determined in the *x*-direction by the CCD array and magnification of the optical system.

Depending on whether the object is a line drawing or a photo print, the information content in the scan can vary in the amount of spatial detail. Also, depending on your application and printer—for example, if you are reducing the image size or printing on a low-resolution printer—it might be less important to reproduce detail as sharply as in the original. Simply put, the required sample rate depends on what you are scanning and your printer.

User guidelines for scanners often relate sampling rate to printer resolution. Only some of these guidelines apply to desktop scanners; whereas the others apply to high-end image editing systems that would only result in overkill for a desktop printer. An example of this is the scanning rule that says scan at twice the line screen of your printing process. Some desktop printers claim a line screen of 133 lpi. So, using this rule you would have to scan at 266 ppi. In reality, this sample rate produces files larger than needed and slows the printing process significantly with little or no improvement in image quality. The much simpler rules given here are more efficient.

What ppi do you really need?

This is where traditional scanner reviews don't pay enough attention to user needs. Users don't want or need to understand ppi and dpi. Good scanning solutions will help the user achieve the appropriate results without this understanding. As a reviewer, however, it is important to understand the relationship between scanned ppi and printed dpi. To do so you must consider the type of image being scanned and the desired result.

Scans of text and line drawings.

Scanning text and line drawings, and printing text and line drawings on a black and white printer, are both bilevel processes. In each case, either a black dot or a white dot is scanned or printed, and a scanned pixel is lined up with a matching dot on the printer.

A scan of text or a drawing is detailed compared to a continuous-tone photo image. Images in text and drawings change from one place to the next—from ink to no ink or from black to white—much more abruptly than images in photos, producing what is called a "sharp edge." The detail and the sharp edge should be scanned at high sampling rates.

> **The rule for text and line drawings is:**
> Scan with a sampling rate equal to the dpi of the printer, up to but probably not more than 600 dpi. Consider that there may be little or no image quality benefit going over 600 dpi for desktop printers, even those that claim 1200 dpi, because printers typically cannot print a 1-dot-wide line or space. In addition, file size for 1200 dpi is 4 times larger than 600 dpi and may create memory overflow problems in a printer.

Note: for OCR scanning of text, refer to the section on OCR in this chapter for information about sample rate.

Sub-sampling—scanning at less than an optimum sampling rate—can cause objectionable "jaggies" and loss of detail, whereas oversampling—scanning at more than the optimum sample rate—just wastes time and file space. (Jaggies are the stairstep effect that appears in diagonal lines or curves when reproduced digitally.) You gain nothing by scanning at a sampling rate higher than the dpi rate of the printer.

Scans of color drawings.

Color text and drawings also produce sharp edges and need high sampling rates. In addition, you need a full-color scan to capture all the color information. This means you create huge files and the consequent system bottlenecks. One solution is to scan color drawings as black-and-white drawings, then trace and colorize them using separate image-editing software.

Another solution available in some scanners and from some third-party image editing software is to choose the color-drawing image type. The full-color scan is converted to a drawing with only a few colors. This creates the color information by assigning similar colors to one value. The result is smaller files and easier image editing. Although this conversion to a color drawing is prone to error and may need some cleanup, the image file is probably closer to the output you want and needs less work than the image editing option.

Scans of photos.

Continuous-tone images (such as photographs) can be color or black and white. These images are less detailed and need lower sampling rates than text and drawings, regardless of the printer. In addition, most printers must halftone or dither to achieve a "continuous-tone" appearance. This means they "spread" the image data from one scanned pixel over many printed dots. See "Halftoning printers" on page 75.

> **The rule for photo prints is:**
> Scan at 100–200 scanner pixels for each printed inch.

For low-end, 300-dpi printers, scanning at 100 ppi is usually enough. For 600-dpi printers, 150 ppi is usually enough. Treat the newer photo quality inkjet printers much like 600-dpi laser printers. These printers are able to print limited-depth pixels, so they can use the extra information, so scan at 150 ppi. Refer to "Photo-quality inkjet printers" on page 74.

In some cases, for high-quality photographs that contain lots of fine detail, you may see a slight improvement by scanning at 200–300 ppi when printing on

600-dpi laser printers or on newer photo-quality multilevel inkjet printers. For high-end image setters (super laser printers that create camera-ready art) 200 ppi is enough. However, for best results when working with a press, contact the printer to find what they feel is best for their process.

Although scanning at more than 200 ppi rarely improves same-size images, the higher rates are useful for scaling (enlargements). For example, to enlarge an image to 200% using a base 150-ppi scan, the scanner would actually operate at 300 ppi. From the user perspective, all they would do is choose 150 ppi and 200% scaling. The scanner software sets the scanner at 300 ppi (150 times 2) but the image file is labeled a 150-ppi file. Quality scanning software should insulate the user from this detail. When reducing, you use proportionately lower sampling rates. See Chapter 14 · "Scaling and Interpolation" on page 197 to learn more about scaling.

Photo transparencies.

Continuous-tone images in photo transparencies such as 35-mm slides and larger format transparencies can contain more detail per unit area than photo prints.

> **The rule for photo transparencies is:**
> Scan at 100–300 scanner pixels for each printed inch, but not more than 2000 ppi or the scanner's maximum interpolated sampling rate.

Since most transparencies are enlarged for final reproduction, the scanning software will adjust the sampling rate of the scanner so that there are 100–300 scanned pixels for each printed inch. For example, if you are scanning a transparency and intend to print it using a 400% enlargement on an offset press, the scanner would operate at 800 ppi (200 scanner pixels per printed inch times 4x). Most scanning software does this automatically when you specify a sample rate and a scale factor. Common 35-mm slides may contain less detail than high-quality 35-mm slides or larger format transparencies, so you can scan the common 35-mm slides at 150 scanner pixels per printed inch. For most originals, 200 scanner pixels per printed inch works well. Only for high-quality originals with lots of detail is scanning at above 200 scanner pixels per printed inch needed.

Remember, we are talking about scanned pixels per printed inch, not scanner ppi. If you are printing a 2x enlargement of a 5-inch image and want 200 scanned pixel per printed inch, then scan at 200 x 2, or 400 ppi. Again, the software should do this for you. For more information see Chapter 14 · "Scaling and Interpolation" on page 197.

A simple rule-of-thumb used by one scanning expert

> **For text and line art:**
> Scan at 1 bpp, but at the same ppi as your printer is dpi. Note, for 1200-dpi printers you probably don't need to scan at 1200 ppi.

> **For photos**
> Scan at a higher bit depth (at least 8 or 24), but don't scan at the printer dpi. Since a scanner pixel contains much more information than a printer dot, you should be scanning at less then the printer dpi—1/4 to 1/3 the printer dpi will often work well.

Dye-sub printers

Photo prints and transparencies can be printed in high-quality photo-realistic color using commercial dye-sublimation (dye-sub) printers. While dye-sub printers produce photo like printed images, there are drawbacks such as ink expenses, special paper, and accessories. Also, dye-sub printers are unable to generate the sharp edges needed for text and drawings.

When scanning a photograph to be printed on a dye-sub printer, you may consider scanning at the printer ppi rating. For instance, you may consider scanning at 300 ppi for a 300 ppi dye-sub printer. Keep in mind, however, that in many cases lowering the scan sample rate to 200 ppi will significantly reduce the file size without much impact on the printed result. This happens because all the detail in the typical photograph (reflective) has already been captured by a quality 200-ppi scan.

Photo-quality inkjet printers

A new class of inkjet printers specifically designed to provide "photo-quality" prints is now available. These printers use a combination of multiple dye loads (more than just cyan, magenta, yellow and black), variable dot sizes, and dithering to provide more colors and better images. These printers may not provide "dpi" specifications because dpi is not a useful measure for these printers. From a scanning standpoint, these printers fall between dye-sublimation printers and 600-ppi halftoning printers because they act like a limited bit depth continuous-tone printer: They are printing pixels. When scanning for these printers, consider scanning at about 150–200 pixels per printed inch. Treat them as more like a dye-sub printer than a dithering printer. However, is it unlikely that exceeding 200 ppi is of benefit for these printers when prints are viewed at normal distances. When comparing images printed on these printers, always consider images from a normal viewing distance. While close examination may show subtle differences between 200- and 300-ppi scans, these differences are likely not apparent at normal viewing distances.

Halftoning printers

Why printers use halftoning

Typical color scanners produce 3 bytes (24 bits) of data for each pixel. A typical color printer, either laser or inkjet, needs only 3 bits to describe a color dot. For the scanner, each of the 3 bytes describes the intensity level (1 of 256 possible levels) of each of the three red, green, and blue (RGB) color channels. For the printer, each of the 3 bits describes the presence or absence of each primary color: cyan, magenta, and yellow (CYM). When all three primaries are present, some printers automatically swap them for a fourth primary: black.

The 3 bits per printed dot allow for the eight possible colors generated from mixing the primaries. These eight colors are the primaries (CYM); the secondaries, created by mixing three primaries (RGB); the two extremes of white (no ink) and black (all the primaries mixed together; or a fourth primary, black ink). Compare this total of eight printer-dot colors to the more than 16 million possible scanner-pixel colors on a scanner. To reproduce the larger number of colors in the scanned pixels, each scanner pixel must be spread out among several printer dots.

Halftones and dithering

Most printers, from electronic laser printers to commercial offset presses, produce these many shades of gray and color using halftones through a process of dithering. A halftone is an image representing continuous-tone information: the image is shown as spots of different sizes to create the appearance of different intensities. Dithering is creating these spots (called "halftone dots") by combining the printer dots in a halftone cell.

Types of dithering

A printer halftone cell is the equivalent of the halftone dots produced by traditional halftone screening. A laser printer can produce 65 shades of gray from black to white using a halftone cell of 8 x 8 printer dots. Each 8 x 8 cell produces one halftone dot. This is called an "ordered dither." It's sometimes clustered into a traditional-looking halftone spot on PostScript printers and sometimes dispersed in what is called a "Bayer dither."

A diffusion dither, made by randomly placing the individual printer dots, produces a more desirable result by eliminating the often-visible halftone dots. This is called "error diffusion" or "scatter." Some large commercial printers use a similar halftone method called "stochastic screening." Diffuse dithers produce better images when they are printed, but photocopiers have trouble reproducing the small dots in a diffuse dither. As a result, ordered dithers are better for documents that will be photocopied. Figure 5-3 shows the relationship between pixels and dithers.

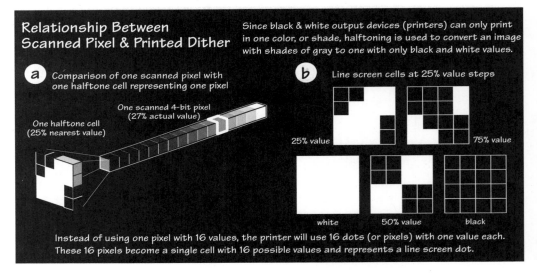

Figure 5-3   Relationship between scanned pixel and printed dither

Table 5-4 Importance of Scanning Capability for Different Types of Scans

	Scans of color photos	Grayscale scans of color photos	Scans of black and white photos	Scans of transparencies	Scans of color drawings	Scans of black and white drawings	Scans for OCR	Scans for document management
Resolution	low	low	low	high (small objects)	high	high	medium	low
Scaling	medium	medium	medium	high (small objects)	critical	critical	medium	low
Color fidelity	high	low	low	(see photos)	high	low	low	low
Grayscale accuracy	high	high	high	high	medium	medium	low	low
Dropout colors	low	critical	low	(see photos)	critical	low	medium	low
Uniform lighting	high	high	high	(see photos)	medium	medium	medium	low
Shadow detail	high	high	high	critical	low	low	low	low
Image noise	high	high	high	high	low	low	low	low
Color registration	low	low	low	medium	high	low	low	low
Scanning speed	medium	medium	medium	medium	medium	medium	high	critical

low: the feature is **not important** for this type of scan
medium: the feature is **important but not primary** for this type of scan
high: the feature is **very important** for this type of scan
critical: the feature is **extremely important** for this type of scan

Chapter 6

Scanner Trends

Scanner buyers can easily become overwhelmed by the endless spawning of scanner configurations, sizes and shapes, not to mention the proliferation of hybrid products that use the word "scan" in their advertisements. Which trends are significant and which are merely gimmicks?

■ How Scanners Are Changing

Scanners of yesterday and today

Scanners were first used to import graphics for desktop publishing (DTP). Today they are common in office environments, where typical applications include everything from traditional DTP to copying, faxing, electronic document distribution (email) and sharing information on the Internet. Today, anyone who uses a computer can probably use a desktop scanner for added productivity and more effective communication.

In addition, more and more people are buying scanners for their homes. They use the scanners to make greeting cards, send pictures of the kids to friends and family, create albums, store important family documents and for children's school work.

Another way scanners have changed is in the way users interact with them. In the past, scanners were specialized devices that required expert knowledge to use them effectively. Today, scanning is becoming much simpler and more straightforward. Where in the past users had to understand ppi, bit depth, and specialized image manipulation tools, today scanners come with software that allows the user to get good results without understanding these archaic terms and technologies.

■ Scanner Trends

Scanning has moved from the arena of graphic arts and sophisticated desktop publishing to more of an everyday business application. A number of positive trends are driving this movement:

- Imaging and the Internet. The rapid growth of the Internet and the use of images on the Internet have made people realize the value of visual communication. Why describe in text a product, concept or your personal life when images do so much more for so much less?
- Increased system performance. A few years ago, computer systems greatly hindered the ability to integrate imaging into communications. Today's faster and bigger multimedia computers are able to handle scanned images for use in everyday communication.
- Availability of image-capable color printers. One of the biggest limiters to using images in business or personal communication was the fact that there was no simple way to print scanned images with sufficient quality. With the introduction of color printers that can provide acceptable, even photo-realistic images, scanning is much more usable.
- Increasing awareness of scanning. Continued integration of scanning into the everyday office workflow has dramatically improved the awareness of scanning as well as the information available on what can be achieved with scanners. Today, people know what scanners are and have some idea of what they can be used for.
- Integration of scanning into other products. An increasing number of all-in-one products—products that integrate printing, scanning, copying and faxing in one device—are appearing. A more traditional name would be "multifunctional devices."
- Decreasing price. Dramatic decreases in prices continue. Scanners that perform well are available in all price ranges. It is important to note, however, that many of the claims for performance are misleading.

The Perversion of Specifications

There are also some negative trends that are impacting the industry:

- Misleading specifications. Currently scanners tend to be "spec'd" in terms of bpp and ppi (or dpi)—neither provide any information about the actual quality of the scanner. Often scanners with the same bpp and ppi specifications (for example, 30 bpp and 600 ppi), are priced at a factor of 2 or more apart. The user attempting to identify which scanner will meet his or her needs is misled or misinformed by the specifications.
- Incorrect specifications. In addition to being misleading or confusing, some manufacturers simply misstate their specifications to look like the better value. For example, a scanner mat claim 1200 ppi optical "resolution" at a very low price. First, that specification means nothing to the user. Second, it is incorrect (at the time this book was produced, there were NO scanners available under $10,000 that provided 1200 ppi optical resolution).

Trends in applications and standards:

- In addition to trends in hardware, integration from an applications standpoint is impacting scanning. For example, OLE and TWAIN allow integration of images directly into end-user applications.
- Introduction of new color image standards like sRGB and FlashPix file format and standard page description format languages such as Adobe PDF are creating the ability to communicate electronically and with high fidelity.
- Software for scanners is becoming both simpler and more sophisticated at the same time, providing easy-to-use interfaces and exceptional results without requiring expertise from the user.

■ Scanning for the Internet

Scanning for the Internet means giving special attention to graphic file formats, resolution, color and bit depth, and compression routines. One of the primary difficulties of scanning for electronic presentation on a computer monitor is knowing the characteristics of the display where the image will be viewed. For instance, if you scan for a particular computer screen at a gamma 1.8 and the image is viewed on a screen that has a gamma of 2.4, the image will appear too dark.

sRGB standard

A new standard has been developed to provide a simple solution to this issue. This new standard, sRGB, is being supported by many of the major manufacturers in electronic communication, including Hewlett-Packard and Microsoft. The sRGB standard is simple, yet robust. It is not a complex color management system, but rather sRGB specifies the tri-stimulus values, gamma compensation (gamma 2.2) and illumination source for images. For further information on sRGB, refer to specifications for the standard, which can be found on the Internet.

Images and documents that are created to the sRGB standard will be displayed with more accuracy and fidelity, even on systems that do not adhere to sRGB. This is because the system is designed to work well on typical computer monitors and printers. In addition, if a system, driver or application supports sRGB, even better rendering can result.

With sRGB it is reasonable to expect that documents containing color images will be more portable and provide more fidelity on more systems. The sRGB standard requires no special knowledge or involvement from the user, making it simple and effective.

Graphic file formats

GIF.

The two most commonly used graphic file formats on the Internet are GIF and JPEG. GIF, or Graphical Interchange Format, is a bitmap graphic. All graphical web browsers display GIF graphics, which are stored in a compressed format that saves space. The type of compression that GIF files use is "lossless," which means that in the process of compressing and decompressing, the graphic is not distorted. This is especially important for line drawings, where even a small amount of distortion could change the graphic. Unfortunately, GIF images are limited to 256 colors, which means that the quality of scanned images is often unacceptable.

JPEG.

JPEG, or Joint Photographic Experts Group, is becoming a more common file format that web browsers recognize. JPEG files use a different type of compression called "lossy." With this compression process, the graphic can become distorted or degraded. The amount of this distortion depends on the amount of compression you use. The higher the compression, the more the distortion. JPEG files have an advantage over GIF files because JPEG files store 24 bits of color information per pixel, allowing over 16 million colors, as compared to GIF's 256 colors. JPEG format works best for photographs with a continuous range of colors. It is not as good with black and white photographs or line drawings. JPEG is particularly poor for text compressing, introducing blockiness or fuzziness.

PDF.

The Adobe Page Description Format or PDF file is a very powerful addition to electronic communication. PDF files provide a robust and high quality compressed representation of a complex page for electronic communication. By using the PDF format, with the widely available free viewer software, the user knows that the page he or she sends is received uncorrupted.

Resolution and color

While it's true that computer monitors are lower in resolution than printers (72 or 75 ppi vs. 300–600 dpi), the fact that they are pixel-based devices (they can display 256 or more colors per pixel) means that for images, they are often better than printers. In fact, an image displayed on a high color or "true" color display will typically look much better than that same image printed on a typical office printer. The key factors impacting how images look on a computer display are:

- The gamma of the monitor and the gamma correction used in the scan.
- The bit depth (number of colors) the monitor has.
- Matching the sample rate (ppi) of the scan to the display ppi.
- Compression algorithms used.

A key advance in this area is the sRGB standard being adopted by industry leaders.

Gamma.

Most PC monitors have a gamma of 2.2 or above. Thus, an image that is scanned with a gamma compensation of 1.8 or below will appear too dark. Macintosh monitors are 1.8. So if you are scanning for a Macintosh monitor, use 1.8. If you expect the image to be displayed on a PC monitor, 2.2 is better. Incidentally, 2.2 will work well for most inkjet printers too, so it is a good all-around choice. The new sRGB standard uses a gamma of 2.2. For more information see "Gamma compensation and tone mapping" on page 133, Chapter 15 • "Tonal Resolution, Density Range and Bit Depth" on page 213 and "Gamma correction (compensation)" on page 113.

Bit depth.

No matter what you do for the scan, if there is a 256-color display at the other end, the image will suffer. For this reason, GIF is not a good format for images as mentioned above. GIF only supports 256 colors, so images stored as GIF will suffer no matter what the computer on the other end supports. If the computer on the other end has a high color (16 bit) or true color (24 bit) monitor, and your image is stored as JPEG, the image will look pretty good, assuming gamma and scaling are appropriate. See Chapter 15 • "Tonal Resolution, Density Range and Bit Depth" on page 213 for more information.

Sample rate.

People often scan at a sample rate too high for a monitor, or they scale the image after scanning and introduce scaling artifacts. This is a very common problem in web design because people will import an image, then use the handles in the web creation package to make it fit in the spot they want.

A much better solution is to figure out how big you want the image to be (probably in pixels), then set the scanner scaling and cropping such that the original scan is the right size. For instance, if you wanted the image to be a little less than a full screen, you would select the image and scaling in the scanning package to give say, a 600 x 400 pixel image. Again, avoid scaling after the scan. If you must scale the image after the scan, use an image editing package that does a better job of scaling rather than the publishing package (which are typically poor). See Chapter 14 • "Scaling and Interpolation" on page 197 and Chapter 13 • "Resolution" on page 173.

Compression algorithms

As mentioned in the previous section, GIF is a good choice for line art or images with fine detail. For photographs, JPEG is better because GIF would limit the palette to 256 colors. Also, for JPEG, you should try a number of compression levels, examining the resultant image until you get an image that is a good trade-off for image quality and file size. Note that the more fine detail in a photograph, the less compression you can use for JPEG. This is because JPEG is a frequency domain compression algorithm that works by throwing away the high frequency part in the image (for example, fine detail like the lines between the bricks in a brick house or the limbs in a tree).

Remember, once you store an image as a JPEG compressed image, the detail is forever gone. So if you are experimenting with JPEG compression to see what level is best for a particular image, make sure to store the intermediate test images in different files, not the original. If you overwrite the original, you will have lost its original detail

Figure 6-1 shows loss of image quality due to overcompression in JPEG. The image on the right was saved with the lowest possible quality and highest possible compression.

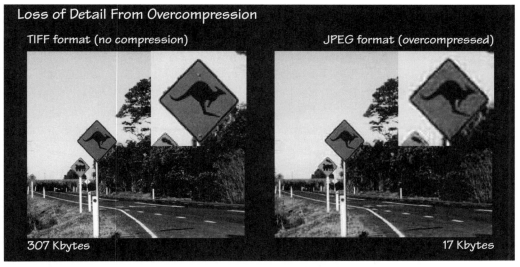

Figure 6-1 Image quality loss due to overcompression (color)

Chapter 7

Scanning Software

More and more, the software that comes with a scanner and its integration with the scanner hardware and target application are a key difference between scanners. A common misconception is that the scanner software is just a "driver" and that all the real work is done in an image editor after the scan.

■ Scanning Software

Scanners come with scanning software, often called a "scanner driver." Calling the software a "driver" is really misleading—it is much more and can make or break a scanner. The quality, ease-of-use and integration of the scanning software is a key factor in how well the solution works. Scanning software is discussed throughout this book, but some important considerations include:

- Integration of the software with the scanner. Is the software well focused and directed or is it generic software that supports a number of scanners? In the latter case, it probably does not support them well.
- Complex or simple. Many scanners come with software that provides the appearance of being sophisticated—by providing lots of tools or controls. Yet the scanner user probably does not understand or need these controls. Furthermore, often the controls do not operate well so they are

more of a distraction than a benefit. Unfortunately, the presence of more controls is often assumed to mean more capability in a scanner.

■ Usable controls, or just controls? Again, in an effort to provide the appearance of quality, many scanning software packages provide lots of controls. In fact, even an expert user may not be able to use the controls if they are not well designed and effective.

■ Integration with standard interfaces—does the scanner support standards such as TWAIN and OLE? A well-designed scanner might allow insertion of images directly into documents using OLE, eliminating the need to save an image in a file and import it. If the scanning software works well, the use of an image editor is not required.

■ Changes in Scanning Software

In fact, much of the advancement in scanners has been in the software. In the past, scanner "drivers" were used to capture the image and then the image was corrected, adjusted, cleaned up, scaled or otherwise manipulated in an image editor. Use of the image editor was required to correct for errors in the scan or to manipulate the image for further use. In essence, the image editor was required to fixup the scan because the scanning software did not provide usable results.

Yesterday: The image editor was required to fixup the scan because the raw scan was not good enough.

Today, good scanning software should eliminate the need to use the image editor except for creative process or to eliminate defects in the original. A well-designed scanner is really a solution that provides a quality image in the appropriate form directly. For most people, using the image editor is (or should be) an unnecessary step. Unfortunately, some scanning software forces you to scan from inside an image editor, adding unnecessary steps.

Today: The image editor should be needed only for creative purposes—to add something to an image or correct for defects in the original, not to correct for scanning errors.

In order to be effective, scanning software must be well integrated with the hardware, the operating system and the everyday tasks the user performs. It should not force a user to operate the scanner in a manner inconsistent with his or her goals. See "A Scanning Solution or Pieces of a Puzzle?" on page 90.

■ Evaluating Scanning Hardware and Software

Should the scanning software and hardware be evaluated separately or together? This seems like a simple question but, in fact, some reviews have treated the two separately. This was partly because a number of vendors used the same software (from an independent company) and partly because of the view that scanning software was just a "driver" and that the real action happened in an image editor. Consistent with the view that a scanner is a tool to be used, a complete review of the scanner must include an integrated look at the software tools included and how well they integrate.

Even today there is great disparity in the integration of hardware and software, or of different scanning tasks. See "A Scanning Solution or Pieces of a Puzzle?" on page 90.

Proprietary vs. third-party scanning software

Some scanners have proprietary software that controls the scanner. Other scanners use third-party software that may or may not work well with a given scanner. Third-party software developers usually don't have the resources to tailor the software to a specific scanner. As a result, third-party software tends to treat scanners as generic devices and uses only the most basic functions in most scanners.

An example.

Consider a scanner with more than 8 bits of tonal resolution. That scanner may need software that downloads a nonlinear tone map to the hardware to use the higher-bit tonal resolution. Third-party software usually doesn't do this because each scanner needs different formats and commands for tone maps, and many can't even use them at all. In this case, third-party software doesn't give you the benefit of the scanner's higher tonal resolution.

Another example.

As another example, many third-party software packages allow you to choose one of only a few sampling rates—75, 100, 150, 300 and 600 ppi. But some scanners can scan well at any sampling rate. Again, the software doesn't complement the scanner.

Integration for the best solutions.

Thus, the best solution will be integrated scanning software, allowing the user to achieve many tasks easily and without confusion. This is most likely to come from scanner manufacturers who treat the scanner as part of a system and part of a process—not as a separate component to be plugged into the computer.

■ A Scanning Solution or Pieces of a Puzzle?

Most scanners come with a variety of software that included: scanning software, OCR, an image editor, a copy utility and maybe some simple document management software. Often, the software included is part of a checkoff list that is compared for completeness. Scanners that had "better" software included were rated higher. Also, some scanners are integrating functions and it may not be clear that all the functions are included if you look only at the list of packages included. Refer to "A New Scanning Interface—Task Automation Software" on page 91.

When evaluating a scanning solution, look beyond the pieces of the puzzle to questions such as:

- Is the software install integrated or does the user have to separately install five packages?
- Is it clear what software is used to do what?
- Does the software work well together, or is it a hodgepodge of the cheapest software available at the time?
- Does the included software actually match what the literature says, or has it changed? If what is in the box does not match what is written on the outside, don't expect the scanner to deliver on other promises.
- How are the various pieces supported?
- Is the software complete and up to date or is it an older, unsupported version.
- Look for innovation based upon what the tasks are. For instance, scanning business graphics works better if a colors are "snapped to" spot colors rather than treated as a photographic image.

■ A New Scanning Interface—Task Automation Software

A new class of software has appeared with some scanners—software which analyzes the object or objects on the scanner, determines what they are and what processing is required, and performs that processing. In some cases, the scanning hardware has been optimized to help achieve this by providing different views of an image from one scan (see "Dual image processing" on page 135).

This type of software may recognize that the page on the scanner has text, an image and a drawing, select them and present the page to the user in a way that makes sense. In this case, the users may select the text and indicate that they want the text exported to a word processor. The scanning solution would then perform OCR on the text and import it into the word processing program. If the user selected an image on the page, the scanner would send an appropriately exposed and scaled color image to the target application. Any number of transforms could be used, each designed to provide the appropriate result (see "Image Transforms" on page 93 and "Advanced Image Processing" on page 132).

The key factor here is that the scanner no longer requires the user to identify the objects on the scan bed and determine what needs to be done. Now the scanning solution helps the user by making the obvious choices—in essence, helping the user achieve the task. This is critically important for today's user who really does not want to deal with scanning as an expertise, but as a step.

A comparison to printer drivers

Consider, for comparison, a user printing out a page from a word processing program. The page may include many different types of information—normal, bold and italic text, an image, lines in a table, a graphic or drawing and headers or footers. When the user prints the page, they don't need to specify each type of data and how the printer should handle it—or rather, that specification is implicit in the page. The page is replicated automatically.

Scanning should be no different. The scanning solution should recognize all the different elements and treat them appropriately. To date, that ideal has not been reached, and the user may have to override and specify some items, but the trend is there and the goal makes sense.

Is it perfect?

An obvious question with this type of software is, "What if it makes a mistake?" In fact, recognizing all the aspects of a page correctly, 100% of the time, is beyond the current state of the art of scanning. For that reason, the automated software must be coupled with an easy-to-use interface that allows the user to override and correct for mistakes. Again, it should be natural and easy.

■ Ease of Use

"Ease of use" is a term applied all too frequently, and all too inaccurately, throughout the computer world. Have you ever seen something advertised as "hard to use?" Of course not, every program is "easy to use." In fact, many are not and the term means different things to different people. Ease of use can vary dramatically, on one scanner, depending on the task. Some scanners make OCR very easy to perform, but images are difficult. Capturing an image at the original size may be easy, but enlarging or reducing it may be difficult.

Easy to use may mean automated.

For some users, automation may be the key. For instance, a scanner that auto-selects, auto-types, auto-exposes and simply sends the image to a target application with no user intervention may be just what is needed. A scanner that provides an interface that is simple and familiar, for instance, a copier application that looks like the front panel on a copy machine, may provide the familiarity and ease of use needed for occasional users. Drag and drop is another example.

Easy to use may mean semi-automated.

In some cases, tools that automate only parts of the task may be ideal. For instance, if clicking on a photo causes the photo to be selected and auto-exposed, that may be easier than having to manually select the image and push an auto-expose button.

Easy to use may be a wizard that guides the user.

A very popular addition to many software packages are wizards or experts that guide a user through a series of more complex steps. These can be for training or for repeated use. Unfortunately, many wizards become devils when used—don't assume a scanning wizard is good!

Easy to use may mean manual tools.

Finally, easy to use may mean that the software does not perform any automated function but provides simple, clear and effective tools with real-time feedback. This is for the more expert user or more complex tasks.

■ Image Transforms

Scanners capture images. What becomes of that image depends greatly on the task at hand and the type of image being captured. The following sections discuss some of the major transformations that can be applied to an image and the requirements of the image to be processed. For further information, refer to Chapter 10 · "More on Image Quality" on page 121, Chapter 9 · "Setting the Controls" on page 109 and Chapter 5 · "A Look at Scanners" on page 55.

Page analysis

Page analysis is not really a single image transform but a collection of transforms applied to a complex page. Some scanners will recognize and retain the format and content of a page and store the page in a form that retains much, if not all, of the format. Images will be treated as such, drawings converted to bitmaps or vector formats and text converted to an editable form, including tables and columns. While page analysis is still not perfect, much of the reformatting and touch-up that was once required is now automated. Note that while page analysis and conversion may cause the scan to go slower, the task—capturing a formatted page in editable form—is much faster because much of the manual format and correction process is eliminated.

Image auto-type

Auto-type is the process of evaluating the image and determining its important characteristics. Included are:

- Identify the size and extent of the image.
- Determine if the image is color or black and white.
- Determine if the image a spot-color image, like a logo, or a natural image, like a photograph?
- Determine if it is negative or positive.

The goal is to perform those automated steps that can be done so that the user does not have to.

Image auto-exposure and gamma compensation

Here the image content is analyzed, and exposure settings are picked for the image. In addition, any gamma compensation required for output may be applied. Challenges to auto-exposure are:

- Images with white background and dark foreground (such as skiers on a ski slope).
- Images that were poorly exposed in the original.
- Images where only a small part is important, and the rest of the image can be degraded.

Auto-exposure routines may work well on some images and poorly on others. In reviewing a scanner, include poor-quality originals to see if the scanner can compensate for them.

Spot color

Business graphics, such as corporate logos or graphs, are typically made up of just a few solid colors. One problem with scanning these is that a constant color in the original will often come out of the scanner as a range of colors. Some scanners can recognize this type of image and "snap" to a few colors to more accurately represent the original. This is also called "pallet optimization" or "color reduction." If a scanner provides for spot color, evaluate how well it does. The quality of edges should not degrade, and the uniformity of the colors should be high.

Special requirements for spot color.

Business graphics can be a particularly difficult original to scan correctly and can result in very large files. This is because the color requires high bit depth, and the sharp edges require high sample rate (ppi). Good spot color routines, combined with raster-to-vector conversion address this problem.

Raster-to-vector conversion

Scanners capture raster images called "bitmaps." In a raster images a line is represented by a series of pixels arranged in the image. If the line is long and wide, it may require many thousands of pixels with color information for each one. In a vector image, that same line can be described by a start point, stop point, width and color—a much simpler and more compact representation.

To illustrate this, imagine drawing a line on a piece of paper by making a small dot, picking the pencil up, moving a small distance and making another dot, over and over again. Compare that to drawing a line, as you would normally do it, by putting the pencil down, drawing to the end of the line, then lifting the pencil.

An additional advantage to a vector image is that it can be scaled with little or no corruption. Scaling a bitmap image can cause significant image quality artifacts. Chapter 14 • "Scaling and Interpolation" discusses scaling further.

Some scanners include raster to vector conversion.

However, the manner in which it is accessed is quite different. Some scanners allow saving in a vector format directly from the scanning software. Others require you to scan the bitmap image and process it with a separate program. The quality and reliability can vary dramatically as well.

OCR

Optical character recognition (OCR) is the process of converting an image of text to editable characters. The requirements for scanning text for OCR are somewhat different than line art or photos. Remember, in OCR, the scanner is sending an image of the text to the OCR software, and the quality of that image is important! In an ideal world, OCR of a complex page (with multiple columns, tables, images, callouts, drawings, headings, etc.) would consist of recognizing the format as well as the content. The user would end up with a page that looked just like the original, but was editable. While that goal has not yet been achieved, some scanners are attempting it.

For OCR to work well, the following image characteristics are important:

- Letters should be complete and separate. Descenders (parts of the character that extend below the line) should be attached and separate from letters on the next line.
- Opens or closes cause problems. Opens occur when a letter is not complete. For instance an "O" looks like a "C" or an "o" looks like an "e." Closes are the opposite, when the opening in the character gets filled in, so "C" looks like "O."

- Adaptive thresholding. OCR packages typically work on binary (B/W 1-bit) data, which is created by thresholding a grayscale or color image. If the threshold is not chosen well, the text may be too dark or too light.
- Background colors, gradients, etc. Many pages have background colors, even a color gradient. A single threshold will not work well for this type of page. More sophisticated scanners specially process the image to remove this type of background.
- Format. Pages are often multi-column or include tables and callouts. Some scanners recognize this type of formatting and pass the page on to the OCR package. Some scanners just prevent mixing of different columns; others preserve formatting and pass information on to the OCR package to allow the page to be reformatted like the original.
- Images. OCR of pages with images or drawings combined with text pose a special problem. Quality scanners will recognized photos and drawings and process them differently than the text to preserve the quality of the image. OCR packages may or may not accept and use this type of information.
- Small text. Scanning above 300 ppi is rarely of any benefit, except for very small text. High sample rates on normally-sized text just slow the process.

In terms of the image quality parameters discussed in this book, OCR has the following needs:

- Resolution. The resolution of the scanner (ability to resolve detail) is rarely a limit in an OCR scan of normally-sized text. For small text, 6 pt and below, higher resolution and higher sample rate (ppi) may be required.
- Sample rate. A quality 300 ppi scan is sufficient for normally-sized text. Below 300 ppi, the accuracy of the OCR will suffer.
- Scaling quality. Quality of scaling routines are very important for OCR. Scaling routines that introduce jaggies, cause opens (breaks in characters), loose or separate descenders (parts of letters that extend below the line) and so on, can have a significant impact on OCR. These defects appear to OCR packages as features of the character.
- Tonal uniformity. This is very important as small changes in the apparent lightness of a page can cause significant changes in the contrast of thresholded characters.

- Color accuracy. Rarely a consideration for OCR.
- Grayscale scans of color originals. Very important for OCR because colored text is common. Scanners that have dropout colors may not do well for this type of text.

Challenges and limitations of OCR

Despite great advances, OCR is still limited:

- Accuracy. For good originals, OCR accuracy of about 95% is common. This is sufficient for most purposes, but spell-checking and further editing is still needed.
- Complex pages. Still a difficult task for scanners and OCR. Pages with "fancy" graphics and layouts that a person would find very easy to read can be totally misread by OCR packages.
- Lower-quality originals. Pages such as second- or third-generation photocopies can be very difficult for OCR, even though a person can read it easily. A page a person has trouble reading is assuredly a problem for OCR!
- Document feeders. On a hardware note, many scanners are available with ADFs. On the face of it, this would appear good. However, the quality and reliability of ADFs vary dramatically. Often an ADF is supplied as a "checkoff" item at the lowest possible cost and may not work well. ADFs are not typically included in reviews, but they should be.

8 Chapter

Scanner Gear

Besides the scanner, what else comes in the box, and what accessories are available? Hardware interfaces; automatic document feeders; transparency adapters; scanning software; service, and support information; OCR software; documentation and image editing software are just some of the items scanner manufacturers are including with their scanners. Often, several different bundles are available. Also consider how the system is put together. Does the software represent a complete solution or an *ad hoc* collection of checkoff items?

■ Hardware Interfaces

Currently three interfaces are used for scanners: SCSI, bi-directional parallel and USB. In the past, some monochrome scanners used serial interfaces. On the horizon is a new interface, Firewire. For more information, see "Which Interface should I use to connect my computer to my scanner?" on page 32.

SCSI

SCSI (pronounced "scuzzy," like "fuzzy") stands for Small Computer Systems Interface and is the most prevalent interface for higher and mid-range scanners. SCSI interfaces provide high-speed and reasonably simple installation. High-performance computers often come with SCSI interfaces, and SCSI is the primary interface for Macintosh computers. SCSI is well suited to scanners because of the large amount of data created by scanning.

Advantages to SCSI.

- High performance—1 megabyte per second or greater (yet most computers currently cannot sustain this rate of transfer for large amounts of data.)
- Readily available—standardization means that most scanners will work with most SCSI interfaces.
- Often present in higher-end computer systems.
- SCSI provides for up to seven devices on one bus, allowing other uses for the SCSI bus, such as tape drives, CDROM drives and hard drives.

Disadvantages to SCSI.

- SCSI is not the lowest cost interface nor are the cables cheap.
- SCSI is not typically pre-installed in the new multimedia computer systems. Thus, the user must install a card in the computer.
- Many of the new multimedia computers today have several interface cards installed, so that there may not be a open slot for the SCSI card.
- Availability of interrupt request lines (IRQs) in the computer. Again, with many new multimedia machines, there are no (or very few) interrupt request lines (IRQs) available for installation of the SCSI card.
- A SCSI interface must be terminated (electrically). This is a challenge. However, it is somewhat lessened by the introduction of automatically terminating scanners.

What should be in the SCSI box?
If a scanner is a SCSI device, the following items should be included:

- SCSI interface card.
- SCSI cable.
- Terminator (some scanners have internal and/or automatic termination).

Today, the trend is to leave this stuff out so the scanner can be advertised at a lower price.

Parallel interface

Due to difficulties with installing SCSI in new multimedia computers as well as cost, there is now a number of scanners that connect to the computer using bi-direction parallel interfaces.

Advantages to parallel.

- Nearly every computer has a parallel interface, eliminating the need for installation of the interface card.
- Hardware installation requires only plugging in the scanner.
- Cost is minimized because no card is required.

Disadvantages of parallel.

- Speed. Parallel interfaces provide data transfer rates of 150–800 kilobytes per second, with slower being more common. This can slow the scans dramatically.
- Compatibility. Because of the parallel interface advantages, more and more peripherals are using parallel connections. Unfortunately, the parallel interface was never intended as a multi-device, data-input port. Conflicts between scanners, printers, tape drives and zip drives are common.
- May require installation. If contention with other devices occurs, the only fix may be to add a second parallel interface to the computer. In that case, SCSI is a better one to add.
- For scanners, parallel interfaces are more of a quick fix than a complete solution and will probably disappear.

USB (Universal Serial Bus)

This new interface holds significant promise for scanners. The USB or Universal Serial Bus, is now appearing on most new computers. USB is a much more robust solution than parallel and provides significant installation enhancements with respect to SCSI. USB is probably not going to become prevalent until the widespread use of Windows® 98, due to difficulties with driver consistency and hardware compatibility prior to that time.

USB advantages.

- Standard interface that is included on most new computers.
- Plug and play—no addressing or other installation is required.
- Sufficient speed—at least for moderate scanning. Probably not appropriate for high-speed or higher-end scanning in which large files are passed.
- Low cost.
- Daisy chain—more than one device can be installed.
- Small, simple cables.

USB disadvantages.

- USB drivers are not standard on Windows® 95.
- Not available on all computers—particularly older computers and low-cost computers.
- Speed is limited.

1394 or Firewire

This is a new interface which may start to appear on computers in 1998 and become supported by devices in 1998 and 1999. Like USB, Firewire uses small flexible cables in a daisy-chain fashion. Unlike USB, Firewire is extremely fast, so fast that it may replace IDE or SCSI for hard disk interfaces. Firewire, once it becomes more widely available, will likely become a very popular interface for scanners. A Firewire prototype scanner was demonstrated at WinHec in 1998 (by Hewlett-Packard). Unfortunately, in spring 1998, a key hardware manufacturer delayed introduction of Firewire support in computer chipsets.

Firewire advantages.

- Small flexible cables.
- Very high speed.
- Daisy chain—more than one device can be installed.
- Firewire has been used in non-computer peripherals, such as digital video cameras and digital cameras. Thus, the hardware has existed and has been tested for some time.
- Plug-and-play capability.

Firewire disadvantages.

- Not yet available (1998).
- More expensive than USB.
- Key hardware developer delayed introduction (1998).

■ Accessories—ADFs and XPAs.

Several add-on products are available for scanners, including document feeders and transparency adapters. How useful these products are depends on how the scanner is used. Also refer to "What Accessories Do I Need?" on page 34 in Chapter 3 • "Buying a Scanner" on page 15.

Automatic document feeders

Many flatbed scanners have automatic document feeders (ADF), available for an extra cost. Some sheetfed scanners provide for multiple document feed, while others provide only single-sheet scanning. In the case of flatbed scanner, the capacity, speed and reliability of the ADF varies greatly. Unfortunately, the quality of the ADF is typically not reviewed. This is unfortunate because the performance of the ADF may vary greatly.

ADFs are of most interest to users wanting to do large amounts of document scanning for applications such as OCR, fax, document capture, forms entry and document archive and retrieval. You don't want to trust an ADF for photos. Most lower-cost ADFs hold 10–20 pages and feed those pages in a scroll mode (like a fax machine). The reliability and ability of low-cost ADF for feeding lots of pages without jams is quite variable. You also may have a hard time actually finding an ADF for a particular scanner. More expensive, 50- or 100-page ADFs typically are much more reliable and robust. They may cost nearly as much as the scanner. Some ADFs place the page on the scanner bed, then allow the scanner to scan normally, much like a high-speed copier page feeder. These ADFs may be more robust and versatile, but are rare.

Transparency adapters

Many flatbed scanners come with or can be equipped with an optional transparency adapter which allows the scanner to scan transparent originals and occasionally negatives. There are two types seen, a passive XPA, which utilizes the lamp in the flatbed scanner, and an active XPA, in which a supplemental lamp is installed above the scanner bed.

The passive type provides limited quality—quite acceptable for some work, not for others. However, it is of very low cost. (Note, the passive type is a patented technology available only on certain Hewlett-Packard scanners). Active transparency adapters can provide better quality and the ability to scan larger originals.

For more information on the image quality requirements for scanning transparent originals see "Image Quality Requirements for Scanning Transparent Originals." on page 124 and "Comparing transparency adapters to dedicated slide and film scanners" below.

Requirements for overhead slides (foils)

Scanning an overhead transparency like those used on an overhead projector can often be done by simply placing the overhead on the scanner. You will get better results if you use a scanner with a backlit XPA, but many transparency adapters do not allow scanning of full-size pages (8.5x11 or A4).

Comparing transparency adapters to dedicated slide and film scanners

A special class of scanners is optimized for scanning photographic transparent originals and negatives—film scanners. When considering the differences between dedicated slide scanners and transparency adapters for flatbed scanners, consider the following factors in the Table 8-1

Table 8-1   *Differences Between Slide Scanner and Flatbed Transparency Adapter*

Slide scanner	Flatbed with transparency adapter
Optical resolution is sufficient to capture all the detail in even high-quality slides.	The optical resolution (MTF) of the scanner may limit the detail. For amateur slides, a high-MTF scanner will provide acceptable results. Low-cost scanners will probably not provide acceptable results.
Tonal resolution, signal-to-noise and optimization are designed for scanning 35-mm slides.	Most flatbed scanners will be quite limited in this regard, particularly low-cost scanners that provide low light levels.
A slide scanner must measure only the amount of cyan, magenta and yellow dye in the slide to re-create the image. This is a simpler problem and may provide better optimization for that particular media.	Flatbed scanners must be optimized for a wide variety of originals and thus may not be quite as optimal for this special case original.
This scanner is usable only for the specific task of scanning slides. (Some slide scanners may allow scanning of negatives and color reflective prints up to 5x7.)	The flatbed is a much more flexible device, providing quality scanning from a wide variety of originals and media. Also, applications other than imaging are supported.

■ Software in the box

Scanners typically come with sets of software called "bundled" software. Often, in an attempt to provide the appearance of a complete or high-quality solution, unrelated software packages are just thrown in. Scanners have even come with games! Be sure to refer to Chapter 7 · "Scanning Software" for more information.

When reviewing a scanner, consider the following:

- Whether the software is an actual solution or a bunch of pieces. Well-thought-out scanners will provide software that works together to solve the problems faced by the customer.
- Compare installations. Are five different installations required, or is some level of integration achieved?
- Does the software work together, or does the user have to approach different scanning tasks in different ways?
- Is the software included just to fill a set of checkoff items for reviews?
- Is the software full-featured, limited edition, shareware, or demonstration only versions and is it from reputable vendors?

■ Bundled Software

Typical software that might be included with scanners is:

- Scanning software (often called the "driver").
- Image-editing software.
- OCR software.
- Special capability for page processing, such as page decomposition and OCR conditioning software (HP Accupage is an example).
- Desktop organization or management software.
- Copier software (to allow using a scanner and printer as a copier).

■ Service and Support

Getting help from the scanner manufacturer can be just as important as evaluating the scanner specifications. Although they might look similar, not all scanner support services are created equally. For example, a toll-free 800 number might seem thrifty until you actually use it and are kept waiting 30 minutes or longer. Or that 800 number may be "toll free," yet play a recorded message saying all agents are busy and that calling a regular long-distance number will give you better service.

The following sections summarize the service and support that manufacturers may offer and suggest questions to determine the support program quality. Make sure you test each of the services that are advertised when evaluating a scanner's support plan.

Warranty period and repair or exchange

- What is the warranty period?
- Does the warranty include shipping and handling?
- If servicing is required, how long does it take? Some manufacturers provide overnight warranty replacement.
- Do you need to register the scanner to qualify for the warranty?
- Do you need the original sales receipt?
- What are the out-of-warranty repair costs?
- Can you buy an extended warranty or special long-term support plan?

1-800 Or regular long-distance numbers

- Does the manufacturer offer a toll-free number? If so, what is the average response time? Many manufacturers provide 1-800 numbers as a marketing gimmick. The lines are always busy or may only allow users to record a message—better service may be provided by a toll call that is answered!
- What is the quality of the support personnel answering the phones?
- What are the telephone support hours?
- Ask the same questions for regular long-distance numbers. You may find that paying for the call yourself actually saves you time and gets you answers faster than the toll-free number.

On-line support

- Does the scanner manufacturer have an Internet email address for receiving questions?

- Does the manufacturer provide an electronic bulletin board service (BBS)? How many dial-in numbers are available or will you often hear busy signals?
- Does the manufacturer provide support information on America On-line (AOL)? CompuServe? How often is the information updated?
- Does the manufacturer have a world wide web home page that has scanner support information? How often is it updated? Is the information useful?

Faxback services

Faxback services use documents created by the scanner manufacturer and usually contain the newest troubleshooting information or scanning tips. Users can receive a document index and request specific documents to be faxed back to them. How many documents are available, 3 or 50? Some manufacturers may claim a faxback service, yet the sparse content might not be worth the trouble. Ask how often the information is updated. Look at an index and some sample documents. Is it useful information?

■ OCR/Text Scanning

The OCR capability of scanners different. Some scanners provide very basic OCR packages that have you scan the text as an image or picture, then send it to the OCR package. Others provide software that preconditions the image for OCR, as well as software that helps the user through the OCR task.

Reviews of OCR capability in scanners should consist of more than just a casual check to see if it is in the box. For example, some scanners

- Precondition scanned text by removing background colors on the page, thus providing a higher-quality image to the OCR package, resulting in fewer errors.
- Analyze and preserve page layout information, such as columns, tables and paragraph formats.
- Recognize and handle images differently to provide better renditions of the entire page instead of just the text. See "Page analysis" on page 93.

■ Documentation

While documentation and other information sources are rarely given more than a check box in a review, they can make a tremendous difference in how successfully a user installs and uses the scanner.

Out-of-box experience

Today, with all the software bundling, a scanner might come with multiple user manuals and installation guides, plus warranty information, packing lists, quick cards, coupons, and various product advertising. What confusion when the box is opened! How well does the scanner manufacturer help the user know where to start and which document needs to be read first?

Attractive and efficient

While color and graphics can make a paper-based document more inviting, check for usability. Does it have a good table of contents and a thorough index? Is the page layout easy to scan for information? Is the document complete and consistent? Some manufacturers provide manuals from older products and may or may not include an errata sheet. Are the software, the on-line help, and the paper documentation localized (translated into the local language)? Does a color scanner's documentation give examples printed in color?

On-line or paper or both?

More manufacturers are cutting costs by supplying their previous paper-based documents as on-line, portable documents. This is not necessarily a drawback for the scanner product. What may be more important is whether the user can get started easily and know that on-line information is there if needed. So reviewers should look for enough paper documentation to get the user up and running. Once the user is started, there should be enough documentation (either on-line or hardcopy) available in a usable format to answer the user's questions and help get the scan. The on-line help system for the scanning software should be examined for consistency and clarity.

Chapter 9

Setting the Controls

Many scanner users rely on image-editing software to adjust the exposure after a scan. But for the best results, we recommend making these adjustments before the scan by using the scanner's controls. This chapter explains why and explains the controls.

■ Overview

A scanner collects more information about an image than it passes on to the image file. That information is available during the scan and not after the scan. In addition, image editing after the scan can introduce irreversible transformations (see Chapter 10 • "More on Image Quality"). By setting the controls before the scan, you avoid the irreversible transformations that are inevitable during image editing, and the resulting scan is a more accurate reproduction of the original.

■ Overuse of Controls

Before discussing the controls in particular, realize that the controls provided in scanning software can be overused. Most, such as white point and color adjustment, are intended to modify, in a slight way, the image captured—perhaps to remove a tint from a photograph. Others, such as gamma compensation, should be used only once. They are intended to compensate for other devices like printers or displays. If these controls are applied more than once, unintended and irreversible effects may occur. One control that is often overused is sharpening!

If your intent is to dramatically modify the image, then scan it with controls set to capture it optimally (including gamma compensation and such), then perform the major modifications in an image editor.

■ Sampling Rate

Most scanners offer controls for adjusting the sampling rate. On some scanners, you can select the output device you are using and the kind of image you are scanning, and the software automatically chooses the best sampling rate. Some even do this automatically. The guidelines below might be helpful. These guidelines are detailed in "Using the right sampling rate" on page 70.

- Set the sampling rate before you begin scanning, not after the scan is finished.
- Remember that if the sampling rate is too low, the scanner doesn't capture enough information. If it is too high, the image files are unnecessarily large and processing takes longer.
- For text and line drawings, scan with a sampling rate equal to the dpi of the printer, up to, but not more than, 600 dpi.
- For continuous-tone images in photo prints, scan at 100 –200 scanner pixels for each printed inch.
- For continuous-tone images in photo transparencies, scan at 100 –200 scanner pixels for each printed inch, not more than 2,000 ppi or the scanner's maximum interpolated sampling rate

■ Color

The color controls enable you to adjust the hue and saturation. Hue is the color mixed from red, green and blue. Saturation is the amount of color in a specific hue. Some scanners offer a separate control for each of the three colors; other scanners offer a color palette combining all three colors in one control.

The hue control can be used to create a mood. For example, increasing the red content usually creates a warmer picture. Adjusting the hue can also compensate for lighting or exposure errors or compensate for different printing processes. Increasing color saturation can cause skin tones look unnatural!

■ Automatic White Point

Some scanners will examine an image for an apparently white region and automatically adjust hue so the region is recorded as white. This automatic white point is usually active only when a color control is active.

■ Exposure Controls

Tone maps, automatic exposure, and brightness and contrast are the exposure controls on most scanners. Some scanners also have highlight and shadow and emphasis controls. These controls are tone maps that remap the intensity levels of individual samples to make details in the image more apparent. As with other controls, you get better results by setting the exposure before you scan than making these changes afterward with image editing.

On the following pages, we explain the exposure controls and how to use them to your advantage.

Tone maps

A tone map is a function that remaps the values of the input samples to the value of the output samples. The purpose is either of the following or a combination of both:

■ To shift the samples to a different intensity level so that details are more apparent.

■ To stretch the output over a larger or smaller intensity spectrum so that adjacent gray levels in the input have more contrast in the output.

Figure 9-1 shows a neutral tone map with 1:1 mapping (which does not change the image at all) and a tone map that enhances shadows in an image. Tone maps are required to get the benefit from 10-bit scanners as discussed in "What Do You Get for Your 10 (Or 12) Bits?" on page 126.

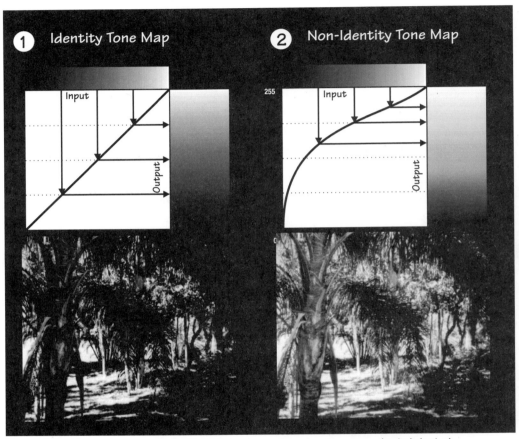

Figure 9-1 Neutral tone map (left) and shadow-enhancing tone map (right) (color)

Advantages of tone maps.

■ The important information in an image can be enhanced at the cost of losing portions of the intensity spectrum that hold less important information.

Disadvantages of tone maps.

■ The output has fewer gray levels than the input, and some detail may be lost. This is less of a problem for 10-bit scanners.

■ When you use a tone map to shift all the samples to a higher or lower value, clipping may result. Clipping is the assignment to a cutoff value of all the samples that are above or below that cutoff in the input. For example, if a tone map shifts the values higher by 35 counts, then all samples with an input value between 220 and 255 have a value of 255 in the output. Any input detail in that portion of the intensity spectrum is lost.

■ When you use tone maps to stretch a portion of the input over a larger output, quantization results for another portion of the spectrum. Quantization is the assignment of two or more adjacent input levels to the same output level. Any detail that was between those adjacent input levels is lost when this is done with an 8-bit scanner. With a 10-bit scanner, less information is lost. See more information about tonal accuracy in Chapter 15 • "Tonal Resolution, Density Range and Bit Depth" on page 213.

Gamma correction (compensation)

Gamma correction, which is really just a special kind of tone map, is a common and important function in scanners. It is referred to as "gamma correction" because a special tone map called a "gamma curve" is used. A gamma curve is the mathematical function $y = x^\gamma$ that describes the nonlinear tonal response of many printers and monitors. The compensating function is $y = x^{1/\gamma}$. A tone map that has the shape of this inverse function cancels the nonlinearities in printers and monitors. Figure 9-2 shows a tone map that compensates for the gamma-shaped, tonal response of an output device.

People often think that gamma compensation is performed to correct an error in the scanner but, in fact, gamma compensation is done to pre-compensate an image for the non-ideal response of display devices such as printers and monitors. If you do not gamma compensate a scan, then the image will appear

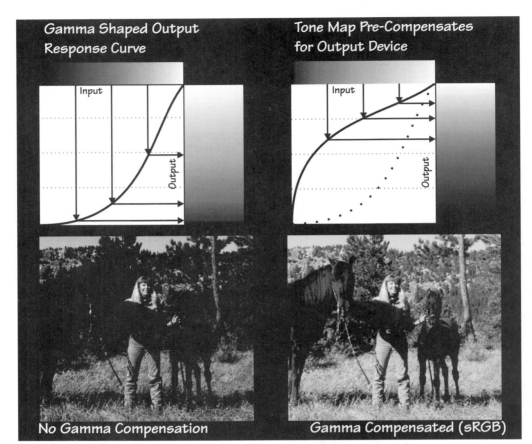

Figure 9-2 *Gamma-compensating tone map and example images (color)*

quite dark when displayed or printed.

Histograms

Another useful tool with tone maps is a histogram, a bar graph for variables measured at the interval and ratio levels. A histogram quickly tells you the relative distribution of information at different intensity levels and where on the intensity spectrum the information is located. For instance, a histogram of an image shows how many samples are located at each intensity level.

If most of the image information is located in a certain intensity area, that area can be stretched out so that the contrast is higher. If one end or the other of the histogram holds little or no information, that portion of the input can be deleted, and the remaining information can be stretched out over the entire intensity spectrum. Histogram tools usually have slider bars that allow you to set the end points. We have used histograms many times in the tests in this book.

Highlight and shadow

The highlight and shadow controls enable you to choose the lightest and darkest portions of an image and automatically create a tone map that uses those limits. The tone map stretches the image information over the entire spectrum for the output and, in this way, increases the contrast. In Figure 9-3, the darkest portion of the image has an intensity of 110, and the lightest portion has an intensity of 215. Thus the input ranges from 110 to 215, and the output ranges over the full scale from 0 to 255.

Highlight and shadow controls are useful because they allow you to set the exposure based on the content of the image. You can choose the part of the image you want as the highlight and the part you want as the shadow. Anything in the image that is brighter than the selected highlight is clipped to white, and anything in the image that is darker than the shadow is clipped to black, leaving the selected shades between white and black well exposed.

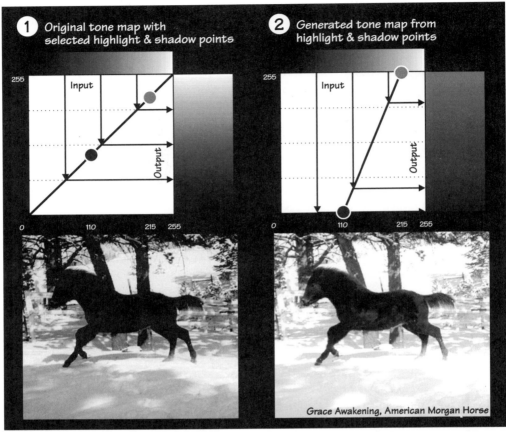

Figure 9-3   Highlight and shadow (color)

Automatic exposure

Most scanners offer automatic exposure to create a tone map based on the content of the image and provide a balanced, high-contrast scan. Sometimes automatic exposure allows you to specify a small portion of the image for which you can optimize the exposure. The automatic exposure is based on that portion of the image alone. This is useful when you want proper exposure of a particular part of the picture, such as a person's face.

More and more common are scanners that always automatically expose an image based upon the area of the image selected. This eliminates the need for the user to adjust exposure settings or invoke autoexposure routines.

Brightness and contrast

The brightness control enables you to shift the whole image to a lighter or darker setting. If the image information is located mainly in the darker areas, shifting to a lighter area makes the details more apparent. But when you use the brightness control to shift everything to a lighter area, all the detail that was in the light areas is lost through clipping.

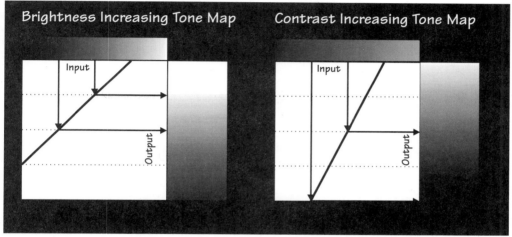

Figure 9-4 *Brightness tone map (left) and contrast tone map (right)*

If two samples are only one gray level apart, they may not be readily apparent to our eyes. The contrast control enables you to accentuate details by increasing the contrast between adjacent gray levels, making them more apparent. Figure 9-4 shows how the brightness and contrast controls shift the tone map. Note that highlight and shadow, and automatic exposure, unlike brightness and contrast controls, create tone maps with limits set according to the content of image.

Emphasis

Brightness and contrast are linear controls; an emphasis tone map is a combination of these two. The emphasis control enables you to change the brightness and contrast selectively for different intensity portions of the image. If most of the image information is in a small portion of the intensity range, a higher contrast is used in that range, and a lower contrast is used in ranges that don't hold as much information.

The emphasis control usually supplies a tone map with two or three push points that you can move with a mouse. This allows you to create a custom tone map to fit a specific application. An emphasis tone map is shown in Figure 9-5.

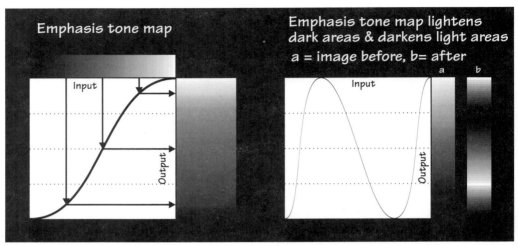

Figure 9-5   Emphasis tone map

■ Other Controls

Sharpening

The sharpening control enables you to enhance detail in an image by increasing the contrast between adjacent pixels. Whereas a tone map works on all the samples in an image by transforming one value into another, sharpening looks at the adjacent samples in an image to find the relative difference in value. If one pixel is light and an adjacent pixel is dark, the sharpening control lightens one and darkens the other, this way increasing the difference between them.

For example, sharpening brings out the outline of objects in the image such as a building against the sky. Sharpening can also be used to compensate for poor focus in a photo. Sharpening tends to extenuate noise in the image. Oversharpening is a common mistake. In Figure 9-6, too much sharpening was applied in an attempt to overcome the softness in the image due to clouds.

Figure 9-6 *Oversharpening (color)*

Preview scans

Previews enable you to create an image file with a low sampling rate for viewing on a computer monitor. With a preview scan you can identify and choose the image for the final scan. You can also use a preview scan for cropping and scaling.

Since the sampling rate of a preview scan is low, it's much faster than a final scan. Some scanners have only grayscale preview scans while others have full-color preview scans.

Interactive preview.

A timesaving feature of some desktop scanners is the interactive preview, enabling you to apply tone maps, color correction, cropping, and other software functions to the existing data from a preview scan and see the results immediately on a computer monitor. The settings you use for the interactive preview are then used for the final scan. If you adjust the controls on the interactive preview, which you can do quickly, you have a much higher chance of getting the final scan right the first time. Interactive preview is useful only if it is accurate (e.g., it matches the actual scanned result).

Zoom.

The zoom feature enables you to magnify and view on a computer monitor a portion of an image for a preview scan. Zoom is useful for precise selection of an area for a final scan. It is also useful for adjusting the exposure based on a small but important portion of the image, a function that is available only in scanners with interactive preview. Note, some zoom commands just enlarge the existing preview limiting their usefulness. Good ones re-scan to show more detail, but a slow scanner may hinder that.

Preview window.

In some scanners the size of the preview window on the computer screen can be enlarged, providing a larger preview image and easing image selection and manipulation.

Automatic image type and automatic image locate.

More sophisticated preview routines will identify the type of the image on the scanner and make automatic selections of the images. In some scanners, multiple image areas may be recognized and selected automatically. For example, in a scan of a complex page there may be text regions, color images, drawings or charts. Some scanning software will identify these different regions and determine their type, the appropriate sample rate (ppi), and so on. This allows the user to select the area(s) of the page to scan by simply clicking on them. This eliminates the need for the user to select an area, set the image type, set the ppi or set the exposure.

■ Trend in Controls

The trend in scanner controls is toward simplicity and automation:

- Scanner users are less interested in imaging and more interested in task. They use the scanners as a simple tool to achieve a goal, not as a primary function.
- Scanners and scanning software are more able to make optimal choices for users and automate their tasks.
- Scanner users are less sophisticated in terms of imaging – they do not know what terms like "density," "gamma," and "sample rate" mean— nor do they need to. They want a quality scan with minimal effort.

As scanners move into the home, the needs and expectations of users change as compared to business use.

Chapter 10

More on Image Quality

Several factors determine whether or not you get the best possible scan from a given application. Some of these relate to how you use a scanner and others relate to how the scanner operates. A very important factor is how the scanner interacts with the software and the completeness of the whole scanner solution. This chapter examines these factors and how they affect the quality of a scanned image.

■ Scanning with Default Settings

In the past, a common practice has been to scan at default exposure settings and then attempt to adjust the exposure using image-editing software like Adobe Photoshop. This was particularly true when scanners were reviewed.

Why default exposure settings are used when testing scanners

Sometimes default exposure settings are used when testing scanners because:

- It's hard to get the same exposure for scanners with different characteristics and different user interfaces.
- In a review, different users perform scans on different scanners. Using default exposure settings means different scanners are operated in a consistent way, regardless of whether it was optimal for a scanner.

Why scanning with defaults can result in misleading tests

However, using defaults is not optimal because:

- Defaults don't allow a scanner to show off its best scan. You won't get optimal exposure for any application with any scanner using defaults.
- Some manufacturers pick defaults to optimize results with industry-standard images such as the Kodak musicians image or GATF images. The scanner may work well using default settings with these images, but this has little relation to how well the scanner works with other images.
- The term "default settings" is misleading. What is the default setting on a scanner that automatically exposes every image? Is it a default to scan with no gamma compensation (gamma 1.0) or with a standard gamma (such as sRGB).

The tests we recommend in this book help prevent these problems by compensating for exposure. Still, it's important to test with several different exposures so you can evaluate how well the controls work and how easy they are to use.

Why users sometimes scan with default settings

In the past, users often scanned with defaults because:

- On many scanners it is hard to set exposure. The image had to be scanned, examined using an image editor, re-scanned, and re-examined again and again before you get acceptable results. Might as well start with defaults in this case.
- The exposure controls on some scanners are hard to understand or are very limited.
- More advanced users may not trust automatic exposure settings.

This is becoming less of a problem as scanners and scanning software improve.

Why scanning with defaults is not optimal for users

Previously, users adjusted exposure, scaling, or sampling rate after the scan because many early scanners did not provide tools that were easy to use or that allowed the user to capture the optimal image during the scan. So these adjustments were required after scanning. While adjusting the image after the scan may work, it is not optimal because it does not take full advantage of the scanner hardware and software. For example, on a 30-bpp scanner, the extra image information is not passed to the computer, so that image information is available only for transformations made in the scanner itself. Many of the transformations in the scanner are irreversible and cannot be fixed after the scan. Irreversible transforms are discussed later in this chapter.

More common today are scanners that perform much of the image processing automatically, including automatic exposure, automatic color adjustment, gamma compensation, filtering, and other complex tasks. This is in response to today's scanner users who have neither the time nor desire to become image experts. Today scanner users need scanners that will help them achieve their tasks with a simple and effective interface.

Default or auto-exposure from a testing standpoint

From a testing and reviewing standpoint, a number of factors must be considered when considering scanning with or without default settings.

- In some performance tests, specific settings are required—or the effects of automatic exposure must be compensated for in the test.
- In scanners with automatic exposure controls, it may not be possible to defeat these controls so the test must be designed to be exposure-independent.
- Reviewers may find that software that works very well for users does not support specialized scans for testing. Often reviewers will interpret this software as limiting, whereas a user may interpret it as very easy to use.
- An important aspect of reviewing scanners is to understand the user experience. Thus, both specific performance directed testing and user-directed testing are required.
- It is not safe to assume that "default" settings will be identical (or similar) and produce identical results from different scanners.

■ Irreversible Transformations

During a scan and during any postscan image editing, an image goes through a series of irreversible transformations. Each time the image goes through an irreversible transformation, information is lost that can't be recovered. Since scanners apply some irreversible transformations during a scan, applying additional irreversible transformations after the scan further degrades the image. The goal is to minimize the number of irreversible transformations an image goes through by doing as many as possible during a scan. Using default settings is not the way to do this.

Examples of irreversible transformations.

- An image is scaled down from 300 ppi to 100 ppi. While you can scale back up to 300 ppi, the lost information can never be recovered.
- An image is mapped from 30 to 24 bits in a scanner, losing several bits of information on the way. Again, the lost information can never be recovered.
- A grayscale image is thresholded to create a black and white image. Once thresholded, the image can't be changed back to grayscale.
- Tonal transformations, such as gamma compensation, are applied to the image. Tonal transformations may eliminate image information.

The best scanner is one that has good image processing capability and allows you to do as many irreversible transformations as possible during the scan. The scanner has the best image information on which to base those irreversible transformations.

■ Image Quality Requirements for Scanning Transparent Originals.

First, it is important to note that for the purposes of this discussion, "transparencies" means photographic originals such as 35-mm slides, 2x2, 4x5 and larger transmissive originals and negatives, not overheads or foils used on an overhead projector in business presentations. The two most important requirements for scanning transparent originals are:

- Optical resolution of the scanner—note that this is the MTF of the scanner, not the ppi rating. See Chapter 13 • "Resolution" on page 173.
- Tonal accuracy—bit depth, signal-to-noise ratio and linearity. See Chapter 15 • "Tonal Resolution, Density Range and Bit Depth" on page 213.

This is because:

- Transparencies are typically much more detailed and will be enlarged significantly. That enlargement has already been performed, to a great extent, in the case of reflective prints. Thus, scanning transparencies requires a much higher resolution (MTF) and sample rate (ppi) for quality scans.

- Transparencies have a much greater dynamic range (range from light to dark) and more detail in the shadows than reflective prints. As such, they are much more demanding from a signal-to-noise and tonal resolution standpoint. See Chapter 15 • "Tonal Resolution, Density Range and Bit Depth" and "Tonal requirements for transparent originals" on page 126.

- Transparencies, especially color negatives, have a fog density or background density that exists for every image. In other words, film that is 100% exposed is not 100% transmissive in the transparency. Thus, some of the dynamic range of the scanner is used to remove or compensate for base film density.

- In the case of color negatives the orange base film must be removed—a special case that is not typically supported by scanners. Note that changing a color negative into a color positive is not a simple invert!

Resolution requirements for 35-mm slides

Can a flatbed scanner with a transparency adapter be used for 35-mm slides? In fact, quality 35-mm slides can contain spatial detail smaller than can be resolved by a typical flatbed scanner. While quite pleasing and usable images can be captured with a quality flatbed scanner, they don't compare to scans of the same slide using a 35-mm slide scanner. For this reason most flatbed scanners claim FPO or "for position only" capability for 35-mm slides. This means that the scanned image is used only as a place-marker during page layout and higher quality image is substituted later. Less reputable manufacturers ignore this limitation and make claims based upon the ability of the scanner to scan the slide as opposed to the acceptability of those scans. With the increased use of desktop printers and computer displays for viewing, many scanners with high MTF (resolution) can create quite acceptable images from 35-mm slides. Again, the key is the MTF of the scanner, not the ppi rating. Remember that resolution refers to the ability of the scanner to resolve fine detail and is not just the ppi rating of the scanner. See Chapter 13 • "Resolution" on page 173.

Resolution requirements for larger transparent originals

As the size of the transparency is increased, a quality flatbed scanner becomes more able to resolve the detail in the original. Again, this is a trade-off with the higher image quality expected by users of large format photographic transparencies (typically professional photographers). In this case, the limit is probably more often the true pixel depth and signal-to-noise ratio of the scanner than the resolution.

On the other hand, excluding traditional drum scanners, there are few, if any, specially built scanners designed just for large format transparencies. So this is an area were a quality flatbed scanner can provide a real lower-cost alternative for desktop publishing professionals. Still, the image quality requirements for this type of work are clearly beyond the ability of many flatbed scanners, even those claiming high resolution and bit depth—so be careful!

Tonal requirements for transparent originals

Another feature of the photographic transparency is an increased tonal range. Whereas reflective photographs rarely have densities greater than 1.5, and where a density of more than 2.0 is nearly impossible, quality transparent originals regularly exceed densities of 2.0. While a reflective original may often include a peak reflectance of 80% or greater, transparent originals often have background densities significantly higher than this. This means that a scanner must be able to resolve very subtle differences in shades in the original. Stray light and signal-to-noise ratio are really the key factors here. See Chapter 15 • "Tonal Resolution, Density Range and Bit Depth" on page 213.

■ Condition of the Object Being Scanned

Image quality is affected by the quality of the original. For example, poorly exposed photographs or drawings with dirt or scratches give poor scans. Often people try to improve the scans by increasing the ppi—but that just shows the scratches and dirt more!

■ What Do You Get for Your 10 (Or 12) Bits?

Desktop scanners claiming 10 bits or more of tonal resolution per color are becoming common. Users and reviewers want to know about the cost and benefits of these scanners and of scanners 10 bits or more. Be sure to read "Misleading bit depth claims in digital compensation scanners" on page 132. The questions we answer here are:

- What do 10 bits give me and do I need it?
- How do I use a 10-bit scanner?

Advantages

There are two primary advantages of a scanner with more than 24 bpp of data. In order of importance, they are:

- Improved tonal manipulations such as gamma compensation and exposure compensation.
- Improved shadow detail, particularly for scans of transmissive originals.

Tonal transformations in a scanner

When scanned, an image must go through a number of tonal transformations (a tone map). A tone map is a function that maps the digital input to a different output value, shifting the intensity of some or all of the samples. It's essentially a lookup table in the scanner that maps the digital input RGB signal to the output RGB data stored in the computer. The most common tonal transformation is gamma compensation, but others include adjusting contrast and brightness, highlight and shadow, or using a special tone map such as "lighten midtones" or "enhance shadows." See Chapter 9 • "Setting the Controls" on page 109 for more examples. Those transformations are performed for two reasons:

- Gamma compensation, which is precompensation of the image for downstream processing, such as compensation for printer or monitors (displays). Monitors and printers do not have a linear response in terms of reflectance. So if a grayscale is printed or displayed it will appear too dark in the shadows and midtones. To compensate for this effect, scanned images are pre-compensated so that when displayed or printed, they appear correctly exposed. The term "gamma compensation" is used because the mathematical function defining the tone map is a gamma curve. Figure 9-2 on page 114 shows gamma compensation.

■ Other tonal manipulations are performed in a scanner to adjust for the exposure of the image or to process the image for other uses such as OCR.

Tone maps for 10-bit scanners

The use of tone maps is very important in scanners with more than 24 bpp because while the scanner can produce 10 or more bits of data per color, most applications, such as word processing and desktop publishing (DTP), accept only 8-bit data. A tone map converts the data from the 10-bit scanner into 8-bit data.

In a 24-bit scanner, the tone map often causes quantization because fewer than 256 input values are being mapped into the 256 output values. (You're trying to fill 256 buckets with fewer than 256 rocks so there are some empty buckets.) The left side of Figure 10-1 shows a gamma compensation tone map applied in an 8-bit scanner. Notice that in the darker areas of the image, the 24-bit scanner (8 bits per pixel per color) causes quantization because there are not enough input values to completely fill the output values.

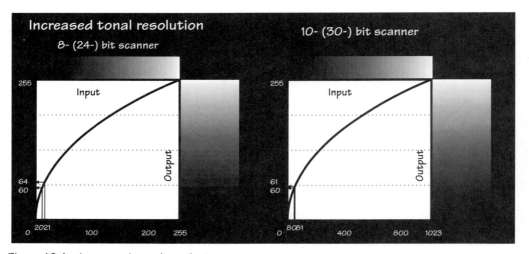

Figure 10-1   Increased tonal resolution

Consider, in Figure 10-1, the input values of 20 and 21 counts. They are mapped, through the gamma curve, to 60 and 64 counts, respectively, and the output values 61, 62 and 63 are empty.

For the same case with a 10-bit scanner (shown on the right in Figure 10-1):

■ The input values of 80 and 81 (corresponding to 20 and 21 in the 8-bit scanner) are mapped to 60 and 61, resulting in a more fully populated output image.

■ The 10-bit scanner produces a better image. Instead of 256 possible input values, there are 1024, enough to fill all the 256 output values.

One of the most important considerations for a 10-bit scanner may be how easy or hard it is to create the tone map to convert from 10 bits to 8 bits. A 10-bit scanner with well-designed software does this automatically when you set the exposure controls or use automatic exposure. You must have software that is designed to work with the 10-bit scanner to get any benefit from the added tonal resolution.

When you use 10-bit scanners that aren't well designed, you have to understand tone maps well enough to create 10-bit to 8-bit tone maps yourself. Most users do not, and should not, need to understand tone maps to get a better image from a 10-bit scanner.

■ PRNU and DSNU

There are two characteristics of CCD arrays in scanners that need compensation: dark signal non-uniformity (DSNU) and photo response non-uniformity (PRNU). DSNU is the pixel-to-pixel variation in a CCD's voltage when no light is incident on it. PRNU is the pixel-to-pixel variation in a CCD array's response to a fixed-intensity light. How well a scanner compensates for these characteristics affects the quality of the scanned images. Poor PRNU or DSNU will cause vertical streaks in the image as shown in Figure 10-2 on page 130.

The effects of both DSNU and PRNU are fairly consistent during a scan, although they change slightly as the temperature of the CCD element changes, and they may also change from scan to scan. To compensate for DSNU and PRNU, the scanner measures these values and applies compensation factors, either digitally or by varying analog reference voltages during the scan. Compensating individually for each CCD element is preferred.

Dark signal non-uniformity (DSNU)

A CCD element with no light shining on it should be at zero volts. In reality, CCD elements have leakage current (dark voltage) that causes non-zero voltage even when no light is shining on the CCD element. The amplifiers in CCD arrays also have non-zero offset voltages (voltage remaining at the amplifier's input terminals when no output voltage is present).

Dark voltage and offset voltage appear as a DC offset voltage at the analog-to-digital converter and may be slightly different for each CCD element. If it's not compensated for, the DC offset voltage produces artificial lightness or streaks in dark areas of the scanned image. Not all scanners compensate for dark voltage for each CCD element; instead they use a less effective, average fixed compensation for all CCD elements.

Figure 10-2   Image streaks from poor PRNU or DSNU (color)

Compensation for DSNU

For a scanner to compensate for dark signal non-uniformity a short scan is done with the scanner's light off or blocked. During this scan, any CCD voltage measured is dark voltage. Since dark voltage is a DC offset, it can be added to or subtracted from the voltage recorded from each pixel during the scan.

Scanners that keep the light on probably don't measure dark voltage before each scan but do so only once when you turn them on. The scanner uses that dark voltage in all subsequent scans, and because of changes in the temperature of a CCD element, the compensation factors may not be accurate for the later scans. Some new scanners may monitor DSNU and recalibrate when needed. Scanners that measure dark voltage before each scan by turning off or blocking the light probably have slightly better dark-voltage compensation. Very low-cost scanners may not do DSNU compensation at all.

PRNU

CCD elements aren't identical in their response to light. Two different CCD elements exposed with the same intensity light output two slightly different voltages. This is called "photo-response non-uniformity" (PRNU) and a scanner has to compensate for it. Ineffective PRNU compensation causes vertical streaks in the image.

A scanner measures PRNU in a test scan of a built-in, calibrated target strip. The output of each CCD element is compared to the expected voltage for that target strip.

Since PRNU is a gain factor, its compensation is more important than for dark voltage. (An average value doesn't work well because PRNU is multiplied instead of added or subtracted.) After the scanner measures PRNU and DSNU, it compensates with either a digital value or analog voltage.

Digital compensation

For digital PRNU and DSNU, the analog CCD voltage is converted to a digital value before the compensation is applied. Compensation for DSNU is computed by adding or subtracting a small number from the digital pixel value. Compensation for PRNU is computed by multiplying the digital pixel value by a gain factor.

Digital compensation can be done by the scanner or by the computer, but it introduces quantization as a result of the integer mathematics used for the compensation. The quantization causes slight errors in the recorded digital values and may increase vertical correlated noise. It also tends to decrease tonal resolution because some of the bits needed for tonal resolution are used up in the compensation. Quality scanners will provide extra image processing bit depth to eliminate the math quantization in digital compensation.

Analog compensation

Analog compensation for PRNU and DSNU has to be done in the scanner, not in the computer. For analog compensation, the DC ground point and DC reference voltage of the analog-to-digital converter are adjusted for each pixel to compensate for DSNU and PRNU variations before the CCD voltage is converted to a digital value. This eliminates the effects of quantization, but it needs more sophisticated analog and digital electronics (for example, an analog-to-digital converter with high-speed programmable offset and gain.) Analog compensation is performed on small signals, so noise isolation in the electronics is very important.

In a scanner with analog compensation, none of the captured digital data is used for scanner PRNU and DSNU compensation. Thus, a scanner with a 10-bpp per color A/D converter can provide full 30-bit calibrated data. Note that it is still necessary to test the signal-to-noise ratio of the scanner to evaluate the quality of the image data.

Misleading bit depth claims in digital compensation scanners

When DSNU or PRNU compensation is done digitally, it will effectively reduce the image bit depth in the scan. In essence, some of the bits of the image are used to compensate for DSNU and PRNU compensation. In this case, some of the reported bit depth is actually used to compensate for imperfections in the scanner and cannot be attributed to image data. Unfortunately, it is usually not possible to determine if claims for bit depth are for scanners that have been compensated or not.

When evaluating the bit depth of a scanner:

- Ask the manufacturer if the bit depth claims are for compensation or if PRNU and DSNU are applied to the claimed bit depth. If the latter, then consider that the extended bit depth is not available for image data.
- A 30-bit scanner with digital compensation must have an A/D converter of more than 10 bpp per color. If not, some of the claimed 30 bits are used only to compensate for imperfections in the scanner.
- It is best to evaluate bit depth in terms of signal-to-noise ratio and tonal resolution as discussed in Chapter 15 • "Tonal Resolution, Density Range and Bit Depth" on page 213.

■ Advanced Image Processing

Many scanners include hardware or software for advanced image processing. Some of the image processing that can take place in the hardware includes:

- Sharpening or filtering.
- Gamma compensation or tone mapping.
- Interpolation and scaling.
- Color correction and NTSC transformations (3x3 matrixing).

■ Dual image processing.

While all of this image processing can be done in software, scanners that include it in hardware provide some important performance benefits. First, the hardware is typically much faster at this type of processing than corresponding software processing. Second, often this processing greatly reduces the amount of data that must be transferred to the host computer. This can have a profound effect on speed. Finally, often the scanner has, internally, much more image data to work with so the result of image processing is improved. A good example of this is 10- or 12-bpp per color scanners that perform tone mapping and gamma compensation to on the full bit depth data, but output only 8 bpp per color.

Most scanners do not have high-speed microprocessors, and any hardware image processing is done by dedicated and custom-designed image processing chips.

Sharpening or filtering

Often an image looks better if it is sharpened. On the other hand, Moiré may be reduced by appropriate filtering. The method used for filtering or sharpening may range from simple one-dimensional moving averages to very sophisticated two-dimensional convolution processing kernels. Scanner manufacturers can provide information about what kind of advanced filtering may be implemented in a particular scanner.

Gamma compensation and tone mapping

Gamma compensation, which is a special kind of tone mapping, is a very common process used on scanned images. In fact, for display on the Internet and for standards such as sRGB, gamma compensation is required. If gamma compensation and tone mapping are performed inside the scanner, the results are often better because the scanner has richer data to work from. See "What Do You Get for Your 10 (Or 12) Bits?" on page 126 and Chapter 15 • "Tonal Resolution, Density Range and Bit Depth" on page 213. Figure 9-2 on page 114 shows gamma compensation.

Interpolation or scaling

Nearly all scans include some form of interpolation or scaling. Scanners with high-quality image processors can often achieve superior results more quickly than scanners that must rely on software scaling. For example, consider a black and white drawing (1-bpp image) that is to be enlarged. If enlarging the image is done in software, then the calculations are based upon the binary (1-bpp) data, because that is all the software has. If the same image were to be scaled inside the scanner, the enlargement can be performed on full 8-bpp (or higher) data, before conversion to the 1-bpp format has been done. The scaling, if well implemented, will be of higher quality just because richer data was used in the calculations. The only way the same quality could be achieved in software would be if full 8-bit data, 8 times as much, were sent to the computer. Since drawings are typically scanned at 300 or 600 ppi, increasing the amount of data sent by 8 times is a significant problem. Consider that a full page scanned at 600 ppi, 1 bpp, is about 4 megabytes. The same page at 8 bpp is over 32 megabytes. See Chapter 14 • "Scaling and Interpolation" on page 197 for more information.

3 x 3 Matrixing

Color errors resulting from deviation from spectral sensitivity in the scanner such as instrument metamerism are nonrecoverable, as explained in Chapter 19 • "Color Fidelity" on page 249. These errors can't be corrected once they are introduced.

But with a simple 3 x 3 matrix multiplication on the RGB data from the scanner, you can compensate for differences in color-matching functions in scanners, printers, and monitors and for different viewing conditions. 3 x 3 matrixing takes an RGB_{in} tri-stimulus value and creates a new RGB_{out} in which the new values are weighted combinations of the original ones. For example, you might create a G_{out} that is a combination of 15%, 90%, and -12% of the R_{in}, G_{in}, and B_{in}. The weighting factors you use depend on the scanner's color-matching functions and the color-matching functions of the output. Mathematically, you do this with a matrix multiplication of the RGB input vector by a 3 x 3 matrix, as shown in the following equation. The coefficients determine how much of the input color component is added or subtracted to produce the output color component.

$$\begin{bmatrix} R_{out} \\ G_{out} \\ B_{out} \end{bmatrix} = \begin{bmatrix} a_{rr} & a_{rg} & a_{rb} \\ a_{gr} & a_{gg} & a_{gb} \\ a_{br} & a_{bg} & a_{gg} \end{bmatrix} \begin{bmatrix} R_{in} \\ G_{in} \\ B_{in} \end{bmatrix}$$

Some of the uses of 3 x 3 matrixing include:

■ Compensation for differences in the color-matching function in scanners, printers and monitors, and in the CIELAB standard observer model.

■ Calibration for scanners, printers and monitors.

■ Transformations between RGB and other color models such as NTSC.

■ Changes in the hue and saturation of RGB data to compensate for errors, for color calibration or to produce special effects.

Several factors limit the use of 3 x 3 matrixing:

■ It is computer-intensive, needing 9 multiplications and 9 additions per pixel. Without hardware acceleration added to the scanner (or your computer), it can be prohibitively slow.

■ It needs all three color components (R, G and B) for each pixel to be available at the same time. This limits its use in three-pass and some one-pass, three-exposure scanners.

Because of these limitations, 3 x 3 matrixing is not universally available in color scanners. You should be able to get information about this from the scanner manufacturers.

Dual image processing

An example of a high-performance image processing capability recently introduced by one manufacturer is Dual Image Processing.[1] In dual image processing, more than one view of a page is captured by the scanner during one scan. For example, the scanner may capture one color image at low ppi and a second, black and white image, at high ppi, all at the same time. The scanning software can then analyze the image(s) and use the appropriate view for different purposes, eliminating the need for repeated scans. The black and white view may be used for OCR, for instance, and the color view for an image.

Other advanced forms of image processing may be included in scanners. Contact the manufacturers for further information.

[1.] Hewlett-Packard patented

■ Calibration

One of the difficulties of using color or grayscale scans in documents is that color or tonal accuracy of the final output is often not predictable—the printed output does not look like the original or may vary from printer to printer or display to display. This is a particular problem for the Internet.

Fortunately, standards are becoming available meaning that users can scan images and add them to documents with predictable results without special calibration or tuning.

Types of calibration

Four common types of calibration are sRGB, screen calibration, system calibration, and closed-loop calibration. sRGB, while new, is the most important for most users and will limit the need for most other types because an sRGB-calibrated image will look good on most systems, even if the system has not been fully optimized for sRGB.

sRGB

sRGB is a new standard which promises to provide quality results with low complexity. The sRGB standard provides a color space (tri-stimulus) definition and defines a default gamma compensation of 2.2. The goal of sRGB is to provide a consistent and good-quality display on monitors and printers without the use of special calibration routines or special software. sRGB does not attempt to control color rendering or performance, but specifies a defined image space so that applications can make appropriate transformations into device space—assuring a good-quality display or printout. The intent of sRGB is to solve 80% of the problem by providing good quality easily, not to provide perfect color matching.

Before sRGB, the color space and gamma compensation that had been applied to an image was often unknown to the application. In fact, answers to simple questions such as, Has gamma compensation been applied? were unknown. The burden was left on the user to determine if adjustments in an image were required and how to apply them.

sRGB is designed to work well with typical computer displays and printers, so good results can be expected even with non-sRGB devices.

Screen calibration

Screen calibration helps ensure that the scanned image, when viewed on the screen, is close to correct in terms of tonal response (lightness and darkness). Screen calibration rarely compensates for color errors.

Screen calibration can be rudimentary and non-standard, or it can be a sophisticated special-purpose system. Most scanning applications and image-editing software allow you to specify a gamma value for display on a monitor. Sometimes you have tools to roughly measure the gamma on the monitor by interactively reviewing test patterns and selecting matching patterns.

More limited systems assume that you know the gamma of your monitor. The most sophisticated systems include a measuring device and software that accurately compensate for the monitor.

System calibration

System calibration attempts to calibrate the whole system (typically a scanner, monitor, computer and printer). There are a number of system calibration packages, most targeted to a particular computer platform and for use in high-end (professional) systems.

sRGB is in fact, a system-level calibration technology, except that it extends beyond a given system to cross-system uses.

Closed-loop calibration

Closed-loop calibration is available only on a few scanners, and it calibrates a particular desktop publishing package, scanner, printer, photocopier, and so on, to work together. The results of closed-loop calibration are better than the more generic calibrations. But because it's so specific, any changes in the process or changes to hardware devices, even changing the toner in the printer, may mean that you have to recalibrate. Also, closed-loop calibration is not practical for images that are printed or displayed on multiple systems.

Closed-loop calibration works by processing a standard test target generated by the scanner or software as if the target were an image in a document. This includes all the steps an image in a document goes through: printing, copying and duplication. After processing, the target is scanned, and the scanning software evaluates the errors introduced by the process. Subsequent scans are automatically adjusted to pre-compensate for those errors.

■ Incident-Light Angle Changes and Multiple-Exposure Scans

When you scan three-dimensional or textured objects, the incident-light angle has to be the same for all exposures: red, green, and blue. If the incident-light angle is not the same for the three exposures, the resulting image has colored fringes or shadows caused by the different illumination angles. This problem occurs with colored-light-source and on-chip, color-filter scanners because both have slightly different angles for the three colors. Incident-light angle is typically not a problem for three-pass, white-light-source scanners or for one-exposure scanners. Refer to Chapter 11 • "Some Scanner Technologies" on page 139 for more information about the scanner technologies that have this problem and what it means when scanning three-dimensional or textured objects. (See Figure 11-12 on page 159).

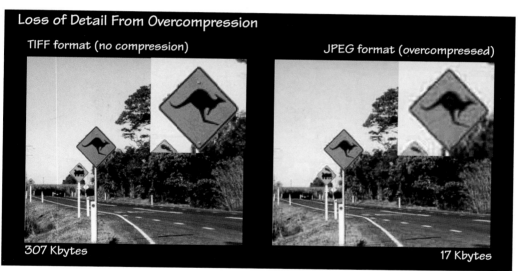

Figure 6-1   Image quality loss due to overcompression

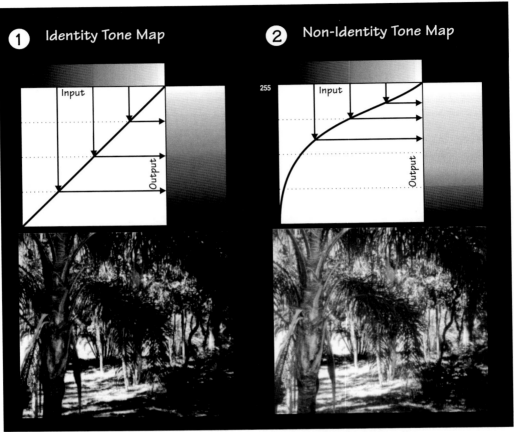

Figure 9-1   Neutral tone map (left) and shadow enhancing tone map (right)

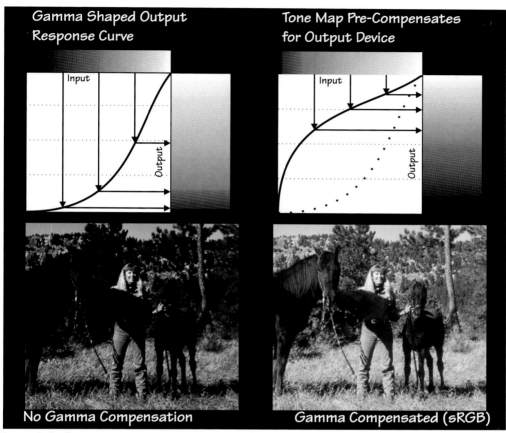

Figure 9-2 Gamma compensating tone map and example images

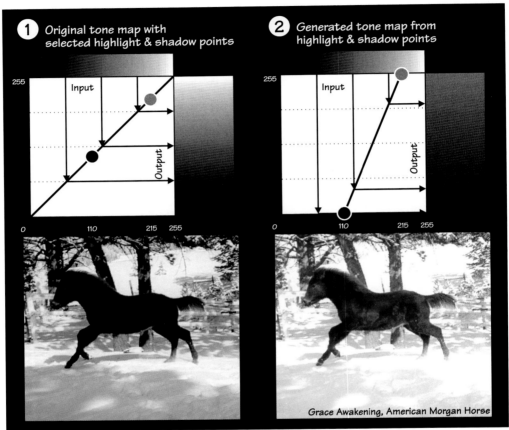

Figure 9-3 Highlight and shadow

Figure 9-6 Oversharpening

Figure 10-2 Image streaks from poor PRNU or DSNU

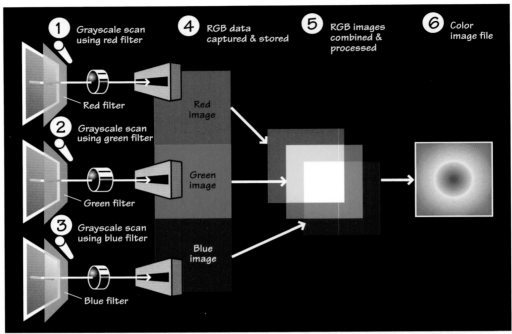

Figure 11-3 Manual filter-placement scanner

Figure 11-4 Example image from manual filter placement

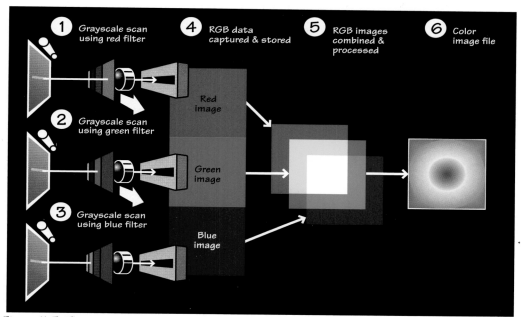

Figure 11-5 Three-pass scanner with filters in optical path

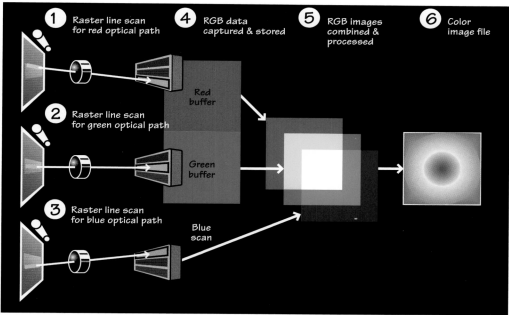

Figure 11-6 On-chip color filter scanner

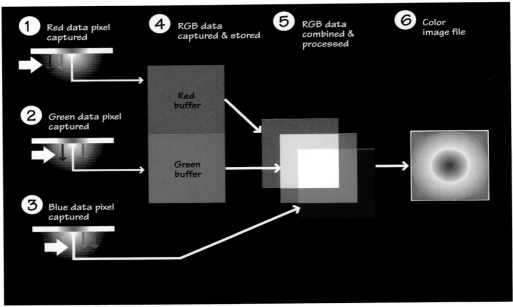

Figure 11-7 On-chip color filter scanning sequence

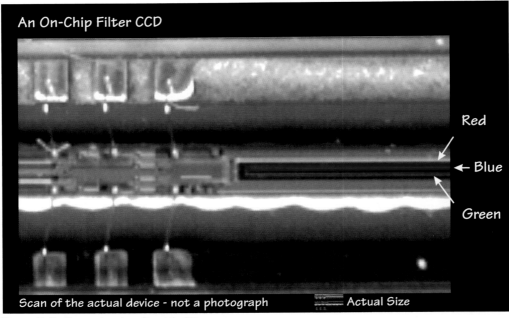

Figure 11-8 Scan showing On-chip filters

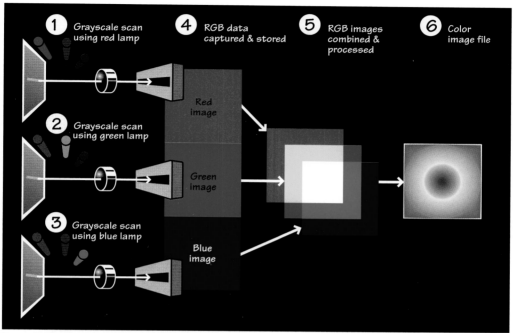

Figure 11-9 Three-pass scanner with colored-light sources

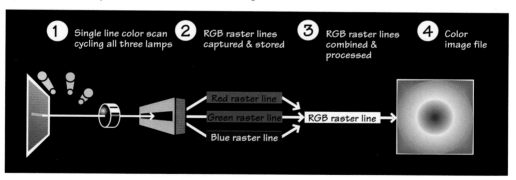

Figure 11-10 One-pass scanner with colored-light sources

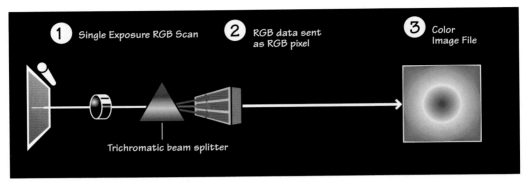

Figure 11-11 One-pass, one-exposure scanner

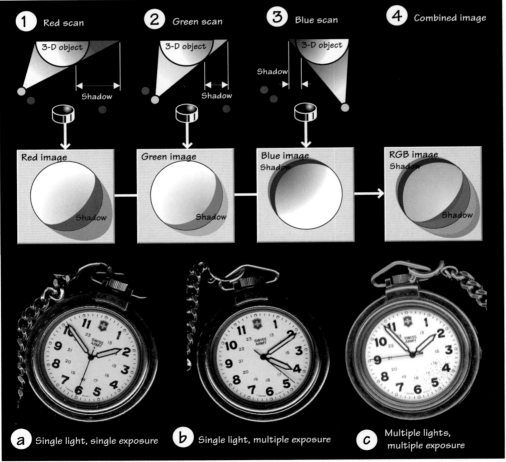

Figure 11-12 Incident-light angle changes on scans of three-dimensional or textured objects

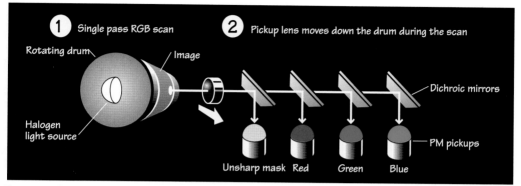

Figure 11-13 Typical flying-spot, drum scanner

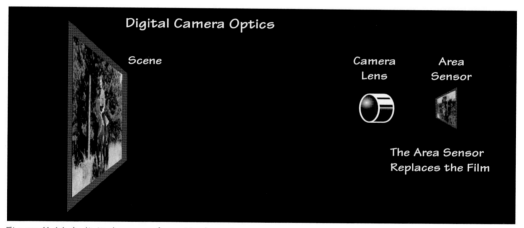

Figure 11-14 A digital camera's optical system

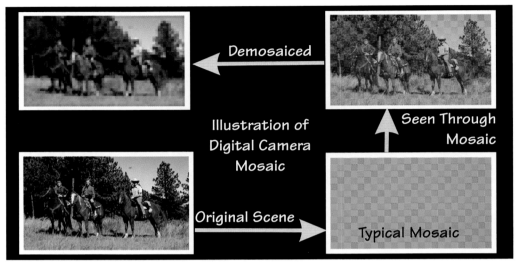

Figure 11-15 A digital camera mosaic

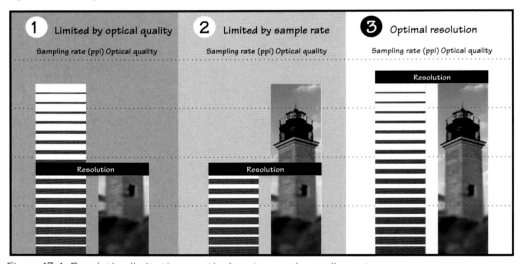

Figure 13-1 Resolution limitations: optical system and sampling rate

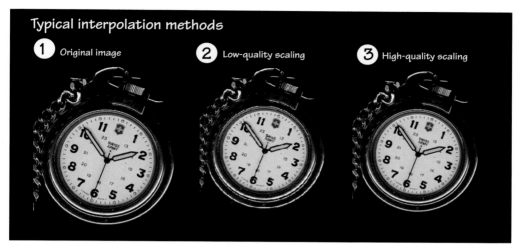

Figure 14-2 Comparison of two kinds of software interpolation

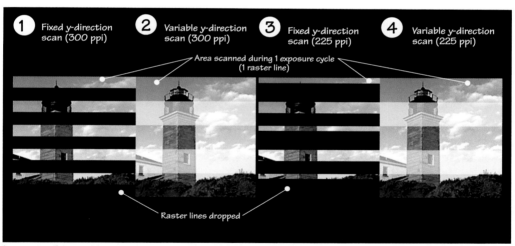

Figure 14-5 Variable y-direction sampling rate and line dropping

Figure 19-3 A tale of two lamps

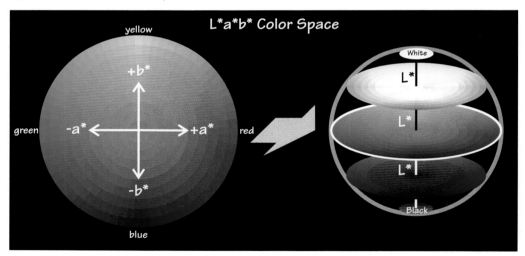

Figure 19-4 CIELAB color model

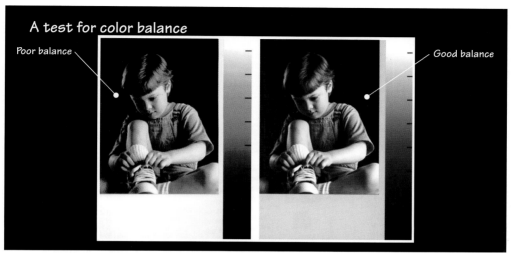

Figure 19-5 Black and white photo and gray target scanned in color on two scanners

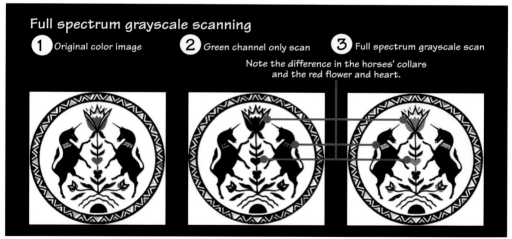

Figure 20-1 Full-spectrum, white light (right) and green channel only (left)

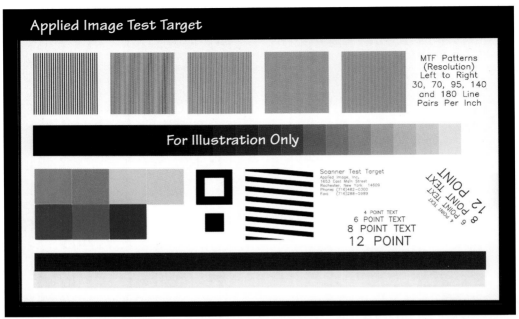

Figure A-1 Applied Image Test Target (color). For illustration only - this printed image is not appropriate for testing

Chapter 11

Some Scanner Technologies

Scanner development has not always evolved along the same path, so that different technologies have sometimes produced the same result. Understanding these different technologies with their advantages and disadvantages can help you in your scanner evaluation.

■ Optical Reduction or Contact Image Sensor Scanners

Scanners can be built using either optical reduction or contact image sensors. Typically, higher-quality scanners are optical reduction scanners, and lower-cost ones are contact image sensor.

Optical reduction scanner

In this scanner, the image of the object is reduced using a lens, to be captured on a much smaller device, typically a CCD. Most flatbed scanners, film scanners and drum scanners are optical reduction scanners. Figure 11-1 on page 140 shows an optical reduction scanner.

Optical reduction is almost always used in flatbed scanners. However, some very low-cost flatbed scanners are appearing with contact image sensors. Any scanner that uses a linear CCD sensors must use reduction optics as the CCD arrays are much smaller than a page (1–3 inches).

Advantages of optical reduction scanners.

The advantage of optical reduction scanners is quality. These scanners use lenses and mirrors to image the object on a high-quality, small sensor. Advantages include:

- High-quality optics can be used to achieve sharp image.
- The cost and quality of the optics can be tailored for the particular application.
- Light-gathering optics focus light from a large area down to the small sensor, improving speed and signal-to-noise ratio.
- The depth of field of this type of scanner is quite good, meaning textured or wrinkled objects remain in focus.
- High-quality linear CCD arrays can be used as sensors.

Disadvantages of optical reduction scanners.

- Size. Optical reduction requires a long focal path. While the optical path is typically "folded" to reduce the size, there is a limit to how small they can be made.
- Cost. The added optical system, mirrors and the structure to hold them add cost.

- Lack of ruggedness. Optical reductions systems are more easily damaged.

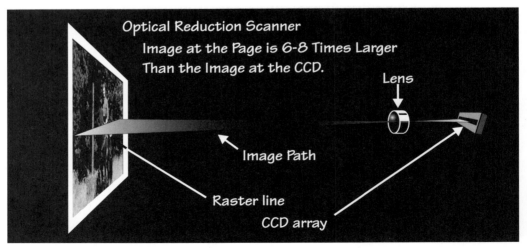

Figure 11-1   Optical reduction scanner

Contact image sensor scanner

A contact image sensor (CIS) scanner uses a special sensor that covers the entire width of the scanned area at once. The pixels on the CIS are roughly the same size as the scanned pixels on the page. In some CIS scanners the object actually touches the sensor. However, in some flatbed CIS scanners, the sensor is separated from the object by glass. Figure 11-2 on page 142 shows a CIS configuration. Notice that between the object and the original is a large number of special lenses, called "Selfoc lenses." These lenses help collimate the light shining on the sensor so that each sensor sees only a very small part of the original.

Advantages of CIS scanners.

- Size. With CIS scanners, the entire imaging system, including the light source (typically LEDs) can be contained in a very small bar. The bar may only be 1/2 inch on a side.
- Flexibility. The size and completeness of the imaging system make its application very easy.
- Cost. CIS sensors have been used in fax machines for years, and the costs are quite low.

Disadvantages of CIS scanners.

- One problem with this type of system is that the lenses are very inefficient—most of the light is lost. This limits the speed and quality of the scan.
- Poor depth of field. These sensors must be very close to the original or the image will be out of focus. In addition, scans of textured or wrinkled objects will be poor.
- Sensor alignment problems. Typically CIS sensors are created by taking several sensors and butting them up, end to end. Where the joints are made, image artifacts are often seen.
- Color accuracy. Color CIS sensors are just now being created, and the color quality is still quite limited. Most color CIS scanners use flashing

colored LEDs to separate the color. See "Light source separation scanners" on page 143.

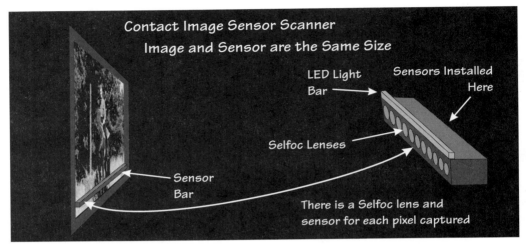

Contact Image Sensor Scanner
Image and Sensor are the Same Size

LED Light Bar

Sensors Installed Here

Selfoc Lenses

Sensor Bar

There is a Selfoc lens and sensor for each pixel captured

Figure 11-2   *Contact image sensor scanner*

■ Passes and Exposures

Exposures as opposed to passes is a subject of confusion in the industry. Some color desktop scanners use a three-pass, three-exposure system to capture color images: the object is scanned three times, once each with a red, green and blue filter placed between the object and the CCD. The three exposures are recombined in the computer to create a color image.

As technology advanced, color scanners that captured an image in one pass were developed. These one-pass scanners still capture the image in three exposures: one red, one green and one blue. The exposures are recombined, either in the scanner or in the computer, to create a color image. One-pass, three-exposure scanners are the most common technology used today.

A third class of scanners, beam-splitting scanners, capture the image in one pass and one exposure. This scanner can offer added flexibility and speed compared to multiple-exposure scanners (either one- or three-pass).

In the next sections we discuss the advantages and disadvantages of the different kinds of scanners in use today.

■ Three Primary Color Separation Technologies

The three primary technologies used are:

- Transmissive filter scanners.
- Light source separation scanners.
- Beam-splitting scanners.

Of the three, only the last is a single-exposure scanner. The others are three exposures and may be one- or three-pass scanners.

Transmissive filter scanners

In transmissive filter scanners, the original image or object is illuminated and the reflected light is passed through a red, a green and a blue filter. The red, green and blue exposures are recombined to create the RGB image of the object. Because three independent filters must filter the light, there are three independent exposures in this type of scanner. This is true even in one-pass on-chip filter scanners (discussed later). Transmissive filter scanners are the most common technology used today.

Light source separation scanners

In this type of scanner, three exposures of the original are captured under three (or more) colored light sources. Traditionally, these are red, green and blue lamps or white lamps with red, green and blue filters. Today, some film scanners are being built with LEDs as light sources. In this case, the LEDs may or may not be red, green and blue—in fact, there may be more than just three.

Beam-splitting scanners

The third technology involves using a beam splitter, such as diachronic filters or prisms, to split the reflected light from the original into red, green and blue (or other) components. Beam-splitting scanners capture all the information in one exposure and may have certain advantages as a result.

■ Transmissive Filter Scanners

The first class of scanners discussed is transmissive filter scanners.

Manual filter placement scanners

The first three-pass, three-exposure scanners relied on manual placement of the filters. For each of the three scans, a different colored, optical filter was put between the object and the copyboard. This worked, but there were practical problems:

- The exposures for each of the three colors had to be manually matched to preserve color balance.
- Aligning the three images was hard because the object had to be moved between each exposure.
- All three exposures had to be present in the computer at once, increasing processing time and requiring very large temporary disk files.

The energy and time needed for this kind of color scanning was beyond the tolerance of most people. Also, the image quality was poor and the technique had no practical application in industry. Figure 11-3 shows a diagram of a manual placement of the filters. Figure 11-4 on page 145 shows an example image from

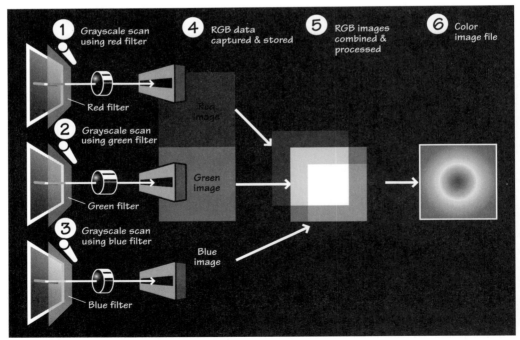

Figure 11-3   Manual filter placement scanner (color)

a manual filter placement scanner. Notice the difficulties in re-aligning the images

Figure 11-4   Example image from manual filter placement(color)

Automatic filter placement scanners

Many of the problems with the manual filter placement scanner were solved when the filters were included in the scanner's optical path and controlled automatically. This allows the manufacturer to control the filter design in terms of color accuracy and provide intensity control to balance the three exposures. It also eliminates removing the object to change the color filter. But alignment of the three passes can still be a problem in lower-quality scanners. Figure 11-5 on page 146 shows the optical path in this scanner. This type of scanner is becoming obsolete today.

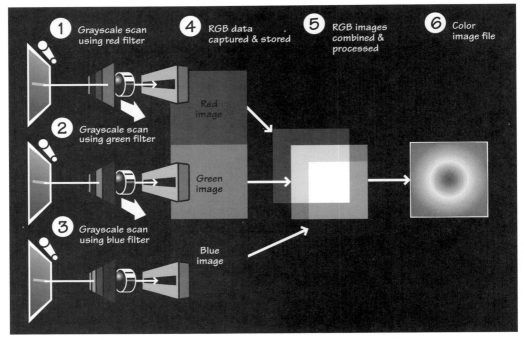

Figure 11-5   Three-pass scanner with filters in optical path (color)

Advantages.

- Three-pass, white-light-source scanners with automated filter placement have the advantage of simplicity. A grayscale scanner can easily be redesigned by the manufacturer to include a selectable color filter in the optical path while still using a standard, grayscale, single-line CCD. The cost is also minimized.

- Another advantage is for grayscale scans. If the scanner is designed so that the color filters used in color scanning can be removed from the optical path, the scanner can create grayscale scans using white light, preventing dropout colors in grayscale mode.

- These scanners can potentially increase speed by another factor of 3 or more in grayscale mode. With a white light and a clear filter, the CCD gets three times as much light as it does with one of the other filters in place, reducing the exposure time. We currently don't know of any scanners that take advantage of this fact.

- Finally, depending on the focal range of the optical system and the depth illumination, it may be possible to scan three-dimensional objects. Some of the color separation methods discussed later can't do this.

Disadvantages.

- Transmissive filters are typically not very efficient. You would expect a red filter to pass about 33% of the light (the red 1/3), but in fact, these filters pass only about 10%–12% of the light. The lack of efficiency means the scanner must operate slower or trade off signal-to-noise ratio for speed.
- In three-pass, white-light-source scanners, each color exposure must be captured completely and independently, then be reconstructed in the computer. Color images are large and need long processing times because the three exposures have to be stored independently before they are combined.
- Doing full-color preview scans is slow as three passes must be made for the preview scan. These scanners typically provide only grayscale preview images.
- Using this technology means that the maximum image size these scanners can capture is often limited by available temporary disk space. For example, an 8 x 10-inch color image scanned at 300 ppi needs buffer space of three 6.8-MB exposures for a total of over 20 MB of temporary storage plus 20 MB more for the final image.
- Any image processing that needs all three colors, such as 3 x 3 matrixing, has to be postponed until the image is reconstructed. Many of these processes are computer-intensive and better handled by dedicated image-processing hardware in the scanner. Since the three-color exposures in three-pass scanners are not available at any one time in the scanner, the scanner can't do any hardware processing.
- Registration of the three images is a problem. The scanner must move the carriage across the object three times to create three exposures. For a 300-ppi scan, this means that the position and motion of the carriage must be controlled absolutely and relatively to much less than 1/300th of an inch over the three passes. Any misalignment between passes causes color fringes in the reconstructed image. So registration for these scanners depends on manufacturing quality—some scanners are good and some are bad.

■ Illumination variations between the scans can cause color inaccuracies. It is hard to precisely control the illumination for three independent scans.

■ Finally, although I/O rates and computer optimization more often limit scanning speed, the time needed to buffer 20 MB does affect scanning time.

Three-exposure scanners with on-chip color filters

The most common single-pass color separation technology used is the on-chip transmissive filter scanner. This technology is used in most single-pass color scanners today. In this technology, the color separation is done with transmissive color filters put over the CCD elements themselves as part of the CCD manufacturing process. The process of putting color filters on a CCD was developed and made popular by CCD manufacturers for color CCD-based video cameras. The CCD used in these scanners has three rows of imaging elements. Each row has a color filter directly over the CCD elements, one row red, one green and one blue. The optical configuration of these scanners is simple, but you pay for that simplicity in a higher-cost, filtered CCD array and additional buffer memory.

These scanners capture the color image in one pass and three exposures (a red, green and blue exposure). Each line of the CCD array captures one of the three colors. As shown in Figure 11-6 on page 149, the three exposures captured by the CCD array at a given time during the scan are of three slightly different locations on the object. This means that the three exposures captured by the CCD can't be immediately combined. Two of the color exposures have to be stored or buffered for later processing. Figure 11-8 on page 150 shows an actual on-chip filter CCD. This image was captured by scanning the device directly on a high-resolution, single-exposure scanner—it is not a scan of a micrograph.

Figure 11-7 on page 149 shows how the red exposure, then the green exposure must be buffered until the blue exposure of the same location is created some number of raster lines later. The number of lines depends on the magnification of the optics and the spacing of the three CCD sensor lines.

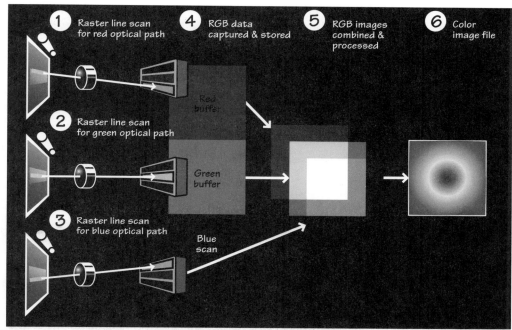

Figure 11-6 On-chip color filter scanner (color)

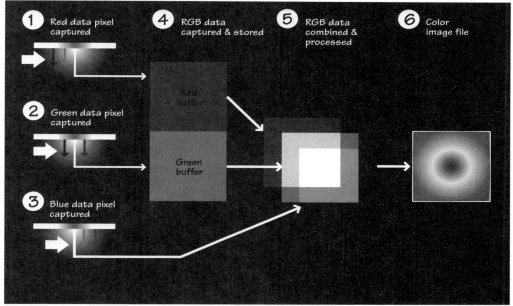

Figure 11-7 On-chip color filter scanning sequence (color)

Once all three colors have been captured for a given location on the object, the three colors are combined in the scanner software or hardware to create the color image. The difference between these scanners and the three-pass, white-light-source scanners is that only a small portion of each exposure has to be buffered instead of the whole exposure.

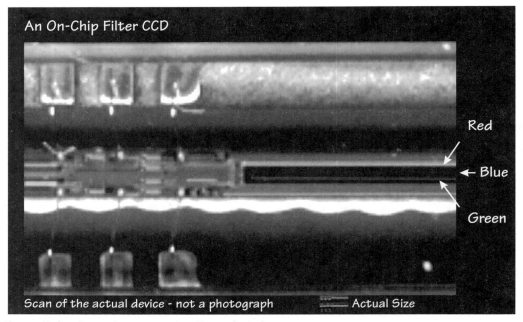

Figure 11-8   Scan showing on-chip filters (color)

Advantages.

These scanners have a number of advantages over three-pass or colored-light-source scanners:

- Although three exposures are still done, scans are completed in a single pass.
- The optical alignment of the scanner is simple since color registration is done by the CCD layout itself and doesn't depend on the optical alignment, assuming that the optics have no significant chromatic aberrations. Inaccurate carriage motion can cause color registration errors.
- All three colors are available in the scanner at the same time and it's efficient to use extra memory in the scanner for hardware-accelerated color processing.

- No lights have to be turned on and off so the scans are faster than with colored-light-source, one-pass scanners.

Disadvantages.

Disadvantages to this color separation technique are speed, cost, and image quality:

- Scanning of three-dimensional or textured objects may not work well because of the incident-light angle changes for each color. The result is colored shadows or fringes in the scans; these are like the effects in colored-light-source scanners but not as dramatic. The effect of incident-light angle changes and multiple-exposure scans is discussed in "Incident-Light Angle Changes and Multiple-Exposure Scans" on page 138.
- Grayscale scans may have dropout colors because only the green channel is typically used in grayscale modes. Grayscale scanning using multiple channels is possible with this architecture but is not often used.
- The choices of y-direction resolution available to the scanner hardware are limited. Because the separation between the red, green and blue focal points is fixed, the scanner must operate one of a few y-direction sampling rates to ensure that the color images are aligned. The effect on images is non-optimal y-direction scaling. (Some scanners use patented technology to eliminate this limitation.)
- To date, the filters on CCDs are relatively inefficient, which tends to decrease the signal-to-noise ratio in the image and limit the tonal resolution of the scanner. Tonal resolution is discussed in Chapter 15 • "Tonal Resolution, Density Range and Bit Depth" on page 213 and "What Do You Get for Your 10 (Or 12) Bits?" on page 126.

■ Light Source Separation Scanners

The next class of scanners achieves color separation by illuminating the original with colored light sources. While becoming rare in flatbed scanners, this technology is common for slide scanners (using LEDs) and may be used in very low-cost, low-quality, sheetfed color scanners, handheld scanners or flatbed scanners.

Three-pass, colored-light-source scanners

In this class of scanners, color filtering is done by illuminating the object with a colored light rather than filtering the reflected white light into three colors. This is illustrated in Figure 11-9 on page 153.

These scanners make three exposures in three passes, one each with a red, green and blue light source illuminating the object. The three images are again recombined in the computer to create the color image. The colored light sources can be either colored lamps or white lamps with colored filters between the lamp and the object.

Advantages.

- The advantages of these scanners are not as evident as those of the other technologies. Basically, the trade-off is elimination of the movable filters in the optical path at the cost of adding two additional lamps and a more complex light-control system.
- One possible advantage of this technology is efficiency. If colored lamps, such as noble gas lamps, are used (as opposed to white lamps with colored filters), there may be more light available for imaging, allowing faster scanning and possibly better signal-to-noise ratio. This advantage is not available if filtered white lamps create the colored light sources.
- A second advantage may be the fact that a one-pass mode may be available as described in the next section.

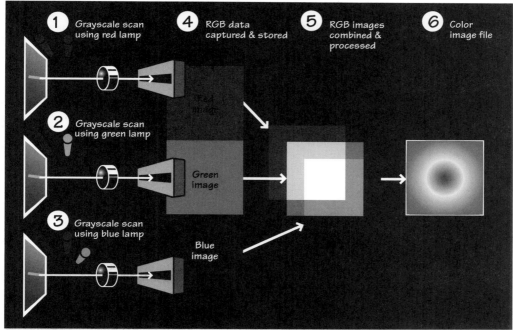

Figure 11-9 Three-pass scanner with colored light sources (color)

Disadvantages.

These scanners have the same disadvantages as the three-pass, white-light-source scanners, discussed earlier, with the following additional disadvantages:

- Because they no longer have the advantage of a white light source for grayscale scanning, there will be dropout colors in grayscale scanning. Although in theory all three light sources can be turned on during a grayscale scan to create a simulated white light source, it is not a very uniform white and may not give good results. In practice this is not often done.

- Even in color mode, these scanners may suffer from color errors because the three light sources, while they may cover the full spectrum of light, result in an illumination spectrum that is very peaked and not uniform. In particular, the colors that fall right between two of the primaries (red, green and blue) may be missed because there is not much light energy there.

- Many originals include fluorescent brighteners to make paper appear whiter. In a colored light source scanner, there may not be ultraviolet light available to excite paper brighteners, and the scanners will not see the white paper the same way you would.

■ Just like brighteners in paper, many inks have brighteners to increase colorfulness. Again, a colored light source scanner may not excite the brighteners. Even worse, it may record brighteners as the wrong colors. For instance, it may see red ink brighteners when the blue light is on and record the red brighteners as blue light.

■ Lighting systems are typically the most failure-prone part of scanners because they use high power and are fragile. Increasing the number of lights has the potential for increasing failures.

■ Scanning three-dimensional objects or objects with texture is a weak point in these scanners. Because the incident-light angle is very different for the three exposures, colored shadows are likely when you scan three-dimensional or textured objects, usually making the scan unacceptable. Refer to "Incident-Light Angle Changes and Multiple-Exposure Scans" on page 138 and Figure 11-12 on page 159 for an example.

One-pass scanners with colored light sources

One-pass scanners with a colored light source are much like three-pass, colored-light-source scanners and also use three colored light sources for color separation. But instead of scanning the whole object with each of the three colored light sources in turn, these scanners rapidly turn the three light sources on and off for each raster line of the image, as shown in Figure 11-10.

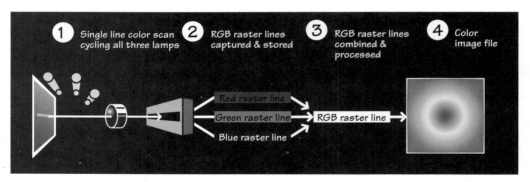

Figure 11-10   *One-pass scanner with colored light sources (color)*

Advantages.

- The biggest advantage of these scanners is that the image is captured in one pass, not three. Although there are still three exposures to combine into a color image, this is done one raster line at a time, eliminating the need for the computer to store and recombine three full color exposures. This makes capturing a full-color preview image much more reasonable. Combining the three exposures can be done either in a computer or in the scanner itself.
- Because all three exposures are available by raster line, complex color image processing, such as color correction, could potentially be done in the scanner on a line-by-line basis to off-load the host computer.

Disadvantages.

These scanners have most of the disadvantages of three-pass, colored-light-source scanners, along with some additional disadvantages, including:

- Scanning is typically slow because all three lights must be turned on and off for each raster line.
- Scanner lamps are often unstable and hard to control when they have just been turned on, so rapidly turning them on and off may cause more drift and color shifts as the scan progresses.
- Scanner lamps are often unstable and hard to control when they have just been turned on, causing more drift and color shifts as the scan progresses.
- Like the three-pass, colored-light-source scanners, these scanners have dropout colors, are more prone to failure of the lighting source and suffer from incident-light angle changes (discussed in "Incident-Light Angle Changes and Multiple-Exposure Scans" on page 138) when scanning three-dimensional or textured objects. Figure 11-12 on page 159 illustrates this effect for several technologies.
- Since some versions of these scanners can be used in a three-pass mode, users often avoid the disadvantages of the one-pass mode by using the scanner as a three-pass scanner.

LED-illuminated scanners

A new variation of colored-light-source scanners is LED-illuminated scanners. In this case, the colored lamps are replaced by color LEDs that are turned on and off. These scanners illuminate the object with colored light, much as do one and three-pass, colored-light-source scanners.

Advantages.

- One advantage these scanners may have over colored-light-source scanners is that the LEDs turn on and off much more rapidly and are much more stable than lamps. This means that a one-pass scanner using LEDs could be much faster than one using colored lamps. In addition, LED output is less likely to have light drift and color shift.
- Lamps are prone to variations in light intensity across the bulb. The center of a traditional lamp is brighter than the ends, and there is no way to independently control the intensity at various locations across the bulb. An LED array can be adjusted by turning single LEDs in the array up or down to change the lighting locally.
- For slide scanners, the scanner must only record the amount of cyan, magenta and yellow dye in the film. This is a much simpler problem than in general scanning because the LED needs to illuminate only a small band of frequencies that are absorbed by each dye to allow measurement of the dye concentration. It is not necessary to illuminate the entire spectrum, as is the case in a general-purpose scanner.

Disadvantages.

- LEDs emit light on a narrow band of light frequencies. Unless carefully compensated for, this peaked spectral emission of light causes serious color shifts and color errors. For optimal color accuracy, the lighting source should be a broadband white source whose spectral content is reliable and closely matched to D_{65} or some other standard (discussed in Chapter 19 • "Color Fidelity" on page 249). LEDs don't provide this kind of illumination source. (This does not apply for scanning slides.)
- LEDs are also dimmer than other light sources. The amount of light on the object affects CCD exposure times. Thus, less light means longer exposures and slower scans, and limits the signal-to-noise ratio of the

scan. Although high-intensity LEDs are becoming available, the colors are limited, and these LEDs are probably not appropriate for high-quality color scanning.

■ These scanners may not be suited to general-purpose, high-quality color scanning. They may be appropriate when the spectral response of the object is well characterized as in a 35-mm film scanner. In this case, it may be possible to tune the scanner to work well with this particular media.

■ Beam-splitting scanners

These scanners use some form of beam splitter to separate the light reflected or transmitted from the original into a red, green and blue component. Since all the information comes from a single white-light exposure, these are called "single-exposure" scanners.

HP Trichromatic beam splitter scanner

This type of scanner uses a patented technology called a "Trichromatic beam splitter" to capture all three primary colors in one exposure and one pass. The Trichromatic beam splitter achieves color separation in these scanners using dichroic filters to separate a full-spectrum, white-light, single exposure of the object into the red, green and blue (RGB) components. Conceptually, the beam splitter separates the light much the way a prism splits light (more expensive scanners often do use prisms). Figure 11-11 shows a conceptual drawing for the Trichromatic beam-splitter scanner.

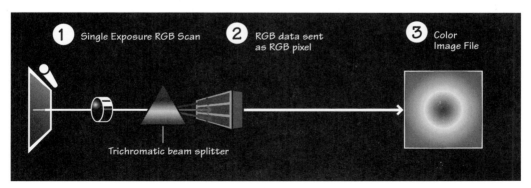

Figure 11-11 *One-pass, one-exposure scanner (color)*

Advantages.

Although it looks simple, this optical system is more complex than other systems, and its advantages and disadvantages are related to its complexity. The image is captured in one exposure, not three, and with one incident-light angle, offering these benefits:

- All color information (red, green and blue) is captured in a single exposure at the same time using one light source. Matching or realigning the red, green and blue exposures is not a problem because there is only one exposure.

- The single exposure means that the incident-light variations don't exist because all color information is captured using the same incident light. For example, scans for three-dimensional objects look natural with no color fringes. See Figure 11-12 on page 159 for an example of this.

- All the color information is captured for each pixel at the same time so sophisticated image processing such as 3 x 3 matrixing is done in the scanner at hardware-accelerated speeds. This kind of processing is desirable, but computer-intensive. Although you can do 3 x 3 matrixing in the computer, hardware acceleration in the scanner is preferable.

- Grayscale scans are done using full-spectrum data (full colors). The color information is mixed using hardware-accelerated 3 x 3 matrixing to create the grayscale information. This prevents dropout colors in grayscale scanning.

- The beam-splitter filters are two to three times more efficient than on-chip filters, providing a better signal-to-noise ratio for a cleaner final image and a faster exposure time (quicker scans).

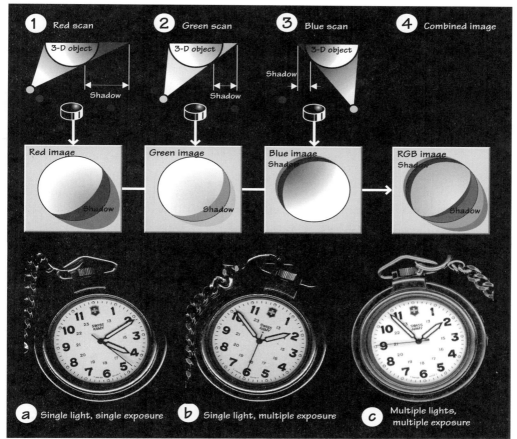

Figure 11-12 Incident-light angle changes on scans of three-dimensional or textured objects (color)

Disadvantages.

- This is a high-technology system needing a high-quality optical system that includes mirrors, lenses, and the dichroic filters. The manufacturing costs may be higher than for other scanners.
- Optical alignment is critical in this system. Since the color separation is a geometry-based physical process, the mirrors, lens, filters, and CCDs must be high quality, aligned to fine tolerances and held there.

■ Flying-Spot Drum Scanners

Flying-spot drum scanners, typically used for professional publishing, are expensive sensitive devices that can capture image information at a much higher resolution and much higher pixel depth than CCD-based desktop scanners. A professional drum scanner can capture shadow information in an image that is not visible to the human eye. It can transform that information into the visible region and improve the image. This is most often needed for scans of transparencies. Transparent media have a much greater tonal range than reflective media.

In a drum scanner, the object must be a transparent or a reflective print. It is mounted on a rotating drum and illuminated with a full-spectrum, white-light source. During a scan, the drum rotates and the focal point of the image sensor moves down the drum, capturing the full image. The transmitted or reflected light is focused on a series of dichroic mirrors that separate and reflect the red, green and blue components onto photo-multiplier (PM) tubes as shown in Figure 11-13. A PM tube is a light-sensing device with much higher sensitivity and lower noise than a CCD, giving the drum scanner much better tonal resolution than CCD scanners.

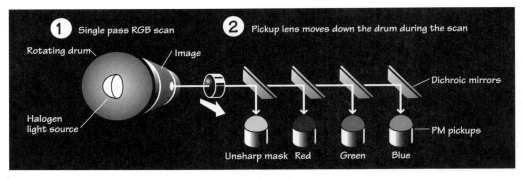

Figure 11-13 Typical flying-spot drum scanner (color)

Advantages.

- Variable sampling rate: The optical sampling rate depends on the drum rotation speed and the speed at which the pickup lens transverses. You can choose the perfect sampling rate for scanning and scaling.
- PM tubes have a high sensitivity to light, coupled with a high signal-to-noise ratio. A good PM-based scanner can capture detail in an image that

is not visible to the human eye, enabling a skilled operator to improve the image.

■ All color components are captured in one exposure.

Disadvantages.

Drum scanners have limitations in terms of ease of use, speed, versatility, and cost:

■ To use a drum scanner, you need expert knowledge of the scanner and the printing processes used for the final image.

■ Drum scanners are expensive, ranging from $10,000 to $100,000 and more.

■ Drum scanners are slow compared to CCD scanners. Exposing the image on a drum scanner is a serial process, one pixel at a time. (CCD based scanners expose a raster line at a time in a parallel process.) Mounting the object for scanning can also take time.

■ Drum scanners work only on flat objects such as transparencies and prints. You can't do three-dimensional scanning.

■ Drum scanners are inappropriate for OCR or document-management applications.

Drum scanners remain a tool of professional graphic artists and publishers, and are typically found in service bureaus. You need training and expertise to operate a drum scanner. Still, for all its cost and complexity, the drum scanner is much more capable than any existing desktop scanner and will probably continue to be the choice for commercial publishing.

■ Slide or Film Scanners

Slide or film scanners are those designed for the specific task of scanning 35-mm slides and, typically, 35-mm negative strips. Nearly any of the scanner technologies can be adapted to this format with the following changes.

■ Modification of the optical system to match the resolution requirements of 35-mm slide scanning (refer to "Resolution requirements for 35-mm slides" on page 125). Typically the entire CCD is imaged to the 35-mm slide resulting in 1200–2400 ppi sample rates and very high MTF.

- Increase in the amount of light available and the exposure time to allow the scanner to capture the higher densities in slides and negatives (see "Tonal requirements for transparent originals" on page 126)
- Tuning of the color separation and color matching for capture of slides. Negatives, in particular, pose a very difficult problem due to the orange film base.

■ Photo Scanners

This class of scanner is designed to scan photographs, such as 4x5 or 5x7 prints. Again, the fundamental technology is unchanged, just the application.

At least one scanner (the HP PhotoSmart scanner) is available that scans photos, 35-mm slides and negatives. This scanner has a unique dual optical path that can be modified to be optimized for each media type.

■ All-in-one Products

A new class of products has appeared called the 'all-in-one." Typically all-in-one products combine a printer, scanner and fax into one unit. From a scanner perspective, these are typically sheetfed scanners that use one of the technologies mentioned above.

Integrated with the scanner is a printer and, often, electronics for direct faxing. Be careful when considering an all-in-one to determine if the scanner is black and white or color. Often a black and white sheet feed is included with a color printer. It may not be obvious from literature. Earlier concerns about reliability and quality of components in an all-in-one are probably no longer important.

Advantages.

- One of the advantages of all-in-one products is that the printer and scanner can be optimized to work well together. Since both the printer and scanner are known to the designer, more robust optimization can be done.
- Cost sharing of common components, such as power supplies and circuit boards, can mean that the cost of an all-in-one is significantly less than the components alone.

- In addition, the all-in-one is much more efficient, in terms of desk space, than a separate scanner, fax and printer.

Disadvantages.

- The up-front cost is greater. You cannot purchase items piece by piece.
- Replacing one component with a newer or better one is not possible.
- There may be contention issues between the devices. Can you scan and print at the same time? Can you receive a fax when printing? The answers to these types of questions are not clear or the same for all devices.

■ Digital Cameras

Digital cameras fall into two categories, multi-sensor cameras and mosaic sensor cameras. Multi-sensor cameras typically have three separate CCD arrays and provide very high quality at a very high cost. In this book, we will limit ourselves to the cheaper mosaic type cameras being designed for consumers.

In a digital camera, the image is captured on a square or rectangular CCD array. This array acts like the film in a normal camera and records the image all at once. Figure 11-14 illustrates this. A scanner uses a linear (one-line) array that is moved over the original and captures the image a line at a time.

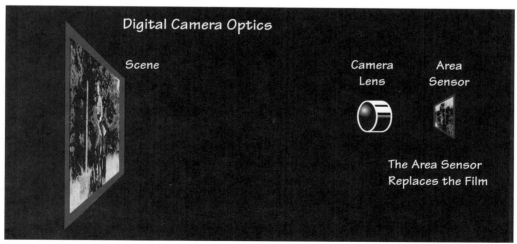

Figure 11-14   A digital camera's optical system (color)

Color separation in a digital camera

One major difference between digital cameras and scanners is in the way the color pixels are arranged. While digital cameras use on-chip filters to create the red, green and blue pixels, the filters are arranged in a pattern called a "mosaic" in which each pixel or group of pixels has a different colored filter over it. Figure 11-15 on page 164 illustrates this.

In a digital camera mosaic, red, green and blue pixels are physically separated. This means that no spot in the image is actually captured in full color. Instead, three images, one red, one green and one blue, are captured, but the pixels of the three images don't quite lie on top of each other. To create a color image from this a process called "demosaicing" is done. Demosaicing creates extra pixels of each color that line up with the other pixels.

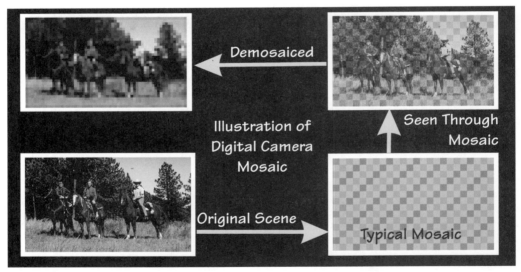

Figure 11-15   *A digital camera mosaic (color)*

Demosaicing is actually quite a complex process and prone to errors. If the image has a very fine pattern in it, such as a person wearing a striped shirt, demosaicing will fail, and color interference patterns will result. Mosaic patterns and demosaic algorithms are considered proprietary by many companies and are a significant difference between different digital cameras (and between cameras and scanners).

The light source for a digital camera

Unlike a scanner, a digital camera uses ambient light for image capture. One advantage of this is that the light used is, by definition, the light under which the original was viewed. A disadvantage is that the designer has no real information about what light to optimize.

Color accuracy in a digital camera

The factors impacting color accuracy in a scanner also apply to digital cameras. However, there is one distinct advantage that a digital camera has. Unlike the scanner user, the digital camera user does not have the original to which they can compare the result. The scene is transient—you cannot hold the original up to the computer screen and compare the color from the scan to the original scene. In fact, this is a characteristic of color photography that is often overlooked. Color photographs are, typically, not very accurate color matches. However, users expect scanners to be true to those, false, photographs! When evaluating color accuracy in a digital camera, be sure to photograph controlled subjects in controlled lighting conditions.

Resolution in digital cameras

The resolution of a digital camera is usually discussed in terms of pixels captured—as in a mega-pixel camera. As is the case with scanners, resolution specifications based upon the number of pixels may be misleading. The ability of a digital camera capture a sharp image is determined by:

- The focus mechanism.
- The quality of the optics.
- Vibration during exposure.
- The number of pixels captured.
- The mosaic and demosaic process.

Like a scanner, the pixel count is only one of the factors in determining the resolving power of a digital camera. Unlike scanners, pixel count is often a major limiter.

Confusing claims about the number of pixels captured in digital cameras

One word of caution. When looking at digital cameras, be wary of "mega-pixel" claims. Often the number specified is the total number of pixels captured, counting red, green and blue separately. The actual number of pixels of each color captured by a digital camera depends on the mosaic pattern. One popular mosaic pattern (Figure 11-15 on page 164) has two green pixels for each red or blue. A "million-pixel" camera with this pattern really captures only 500,000 green pixels and 250,000 each of red and blue. The color image is created by demosaicing where the color information from neighboring pixels is combined. While quality images can be captured, a demosaic process is not as effective as if each pixel was captured with all three colors. Thus, when comparing the sample rate of a scanner—which does capture each pixel in full color—to that of a digital camera, be sure to include possible demosaicing issues.

Chapter 12

Scanning Speed

Although scanning speed is often used as the basis for comparison between scanners, it is only one small part of the time it takes to get a scanned image into your document ready for use. Better reviews will focus on the time taken to achieve typical tasks, not just the raw scan time. The only time when raw scan speed is of great importance is during preview scans, or possibly multi-page OCR jobs.

■ Task Speed Versus Scan Speed

One of the more recent changes in scanners has to do with the way in which the speed of a scanner is measured, indeed, what the "speed" of a scanner is. Today, people use scanners as a tool to help them achieve a task required by their job. Less often is their job the use of the scanner itself (refer to "Scanner users of today" on page 44).

Some scanner manufacturers are now focusing on the task the user is trying to achieve, providing the tools and automation that will make that task easier and quicker. Examples include automatic recognition of columns and retaining page formats when performing OCR on complex pages. While the advanced processing may require longer and possibly even multiple scans, the total task time, from placing the page on the scanner to having a fully formatted and editable version in the computer, is much shorter.

Other interface changes, such as being able to drag and drop from the scanning application to a target application with no intermediate "insert/object," "acquire" or "import image" steps, dramatically improve and speed the process.

A scanner review that focuses on just raw scan time, or even the time to scan a standard image to a disk file, may be missing a large contribution of a particular scanner.

Be sure to consider:

- The time to achieve a complete task, not just the scan.
- Integration of the scanning application with other common applications, particularly innovative ways to eliminate steps and ease integration.
- Time needed to do the preview scan and set the exposures.
- Time needed to capture a well-exposed image; this can take more than one try.
- Time needed for retouching or adjusting the exposure controls after the scan to compensate for exposure problems.

As well as more traditional measures such as:

- Importing the image into the target application.
- Rate of data transmission from the scanner to the computer.
- Time needed to store the image on the disk; this may be an operation separate from the scan.

Ease of use can be more important than raw scanning speed

The best is a scanner that works quickly, is natural to use and gives you a quality scan the first time and every time. Ease of use may be the most important of a scanner's attributes when considering speed. The speed of a very fast scanner can be negated by cumbersome software. On the other hand, a slow scanner is hard to use because it forces people to limit scanning to only critical tasks, thus limiting creativity. For example, if a preview scan takes two minutes, not many people will do preview scans. A scanner that quickly and reliably provides quality images encourages use.

■ Typical Tests

The test for scanning speed is usually the time it takes to scan a set of typical images with default exposure settings at a given sampling rate on each scanner. Two examples are measuring the time it takes to scan a 4 x 5-inch photo at 150 ppi with 24-bit color, and the time needed to scan an 8 x 11-inch page as 1-bit black and white. The test is objective in that the user's familiarity with the scanner isn't a factor in the test results.

Limitations of the typical test

- The test does not represent how the user does a scan. The assumption is that, once the scan is done, all scanners are the same. That is not the case.
- Because of time limitations and with the goal of standardization, a scripted set of steps is always followed, even when that series of steps is not natural for a particular scanner or when a scanner provides a different but better method.
- No minimum level of quality is required for scans. Often the raw scanning speed is measured, but the resulting image is not examined to see if it is of acceptable or much lower quality. Tests that don't produce a usable image are not a measure of how the user does a scan unless they include time to rescan or touch up a poor image.
- Scanner speed is often limited by the computer and not by the scanner itself. A computer's performance can be affected by disk fragmentation, caching, and other factors not related to the scanner.
- The quality of the scanner for applications like OCR can dramatically affect processing speed. A low-quality scanner might do OCR slowly and need a lot of correction. Correction time should be included, as should reformat time.
- There are several ways to scan. For example, you may use a Photoshop plug-in, TWAIN image-transfer software, OLE or separate scanning software. The fastest method in terms of raw scanning speed may not be as fast (or may not even be usable) from the user's standpoint.

■ Recommended Test

The ideal test is to measure how long it takes equally capable users to perform a particular task or set of tasks on a scanner. For example, a test may include OCR of some text for inclusion in a document, scans of images and drawings into the document, preparation of the result for electronic communications and the time involved for any cleanup or manipulation of the document or images to correct for scanning artifacts. The steps would represent the steps the user follows, and the quality of the results would be acceptable to the user. The "speed" may be weighted by the quality of the result. Refer to "Steps to a Successful Review" on page 46.

Some things to consider:

- Spend sufficient time with each scanner to understand the methods provided by the scanner to achieve a task. Forcing all scanners into the same set of steps may overlook real improvements in speed and ease of use for a particular scanner.
- Set the minimum quality for scans from all speed tests. If rescans or image editing are needed to achieve that quality, include them in the scanning time.
- The resultant images should be evaluated and ranked for quality. A scanner that provides a better result in the same (or slightly longer) amount of time should be considered to be better than a fast scanner with poor or marginally acceptable results.
- Use a consistent start and stop point based on the user's start and stop point. For example, you might start using a desktop publishing package when you're ready to insert the image, and stop when an image is scanned and printed.
- The testing should include OCR and include the time to correct errors and reformat the document.
- If possible, use image-processing tools, such as sharpening, consistently on all the scanners.
- Use the scanner in all ways possible. For instance, if a scanner works with both TWAIN and direct-access software, test both. TWAIN may be faster if you want to use the image once and direct access may be faster if you want to store it for multiple uses.

Detailed test procedure

There is no step-by-step procedure provided; however, here are some suggested tests:

- Measure how long it takes a novice or trained user to scan a complex page, perform OCR, reformat, and correct the page. Include tables, figures, and images. Make the end point of the test an editable version of the original page with some changes incorporated.
- Don't stop with recreating the original—include in the test task adding a paragraph or moving items around. This is what users do.
- Measure how long it takes to create a page with OCRd text from one source and images and drawings from other sources.
- Time a color copy and rank by quality.
- Test with both novices and experienced users.
- Test a variety of problem pages and see if a slower scanner handles them better or worse.
- See Chapter 4 • "For the Technical Reviewer" on page 43 for more information on typical tasks you may want to consider.

Chapter 13

Resolution

The concept of resolution is probably the most misunderstood and misused specification applied to scanners today. The resolution of a scanner is most often discussed in terms of ppi or dpi (for example, a 600-ppi scanner). In fact, the relationship between the true resolution of a scanner and its ppi rating is tenuous at best—particularly for low-cost desktop scanners. This confusion is being further driven by unrealistic and inflated claims that provide no real information or benefit to the user. This chapter examines resolution and sampling rates, describes the limitations of typical tests for resolution, and offers a more accurate test that will measure the true optical performance of the scanner.

■ What is Resolution?

Resolution is the degree to which a scanner captures fine detail (high frequencies) in an original. Unfortunately, what is typically specified as the resolution of a scanner is really the optical sampling rate or ppi rating of the scanner. The optical sampling rate, the number of samples captured in the x-direction, is only one component of resolution but may not be the most critical. There are several other important factors:

- Optics quality (lens, mirrors, filters).

173

- Mechanical stability of the optical system.
- Motion of the carriage.
- Vibration of the object, the CCD, or the optical components.
- Focal range and stability of the optical system.
- Impact of temperature and humidity changes on the optical system.
- Frequency response of the electronic system.
- Image processing applied to the image.
- Manufacturing quality and process control—was the scanner well focused when built.

Resolution is not optical sampling rate

The confusion begins with the common misuse of the term 'resolution" to describe sampling rate. For example, someone might say that a scanner has a resolution of 600 ppi when what they mean is that a scanner has an optical sampling rate of 600 ppi. Sampling rate tells you what the maximum possible resolution of a scanner could be, but it doesn't tell you if the scanner actually performs to that level. In fact, almost no scanner can resolve detail to the limits that would be implied by the optical sampling rate.

When you measure the true ability of a scanner to resolve detail or the resolution of the scanner, you are measuring its optical frequency response. The frequency response of a system is how well it transmits high-frequency information. You can measure frequency response in mechanical systems (the suspension in your car), in electrical systems (your stereo amplifier), or in optical systems (a scanner). A system's capability to transmit frequencies is called the "transfer function." Given the transfer function and the input frequency, you can predict how well or how poorly a system transmits a frequency. Fine detail in an original represents high-frequency information to a scanner.

For example, a stereo amplifier might have a frequency response from 20 Hz to 20 kHz with less than 3 dB rolloff. Any frequency of between 20 Hz and 20 kHz fed into the stereo amplifier comes out the other side pretty much unchanged, just louder (amplified). At a higher frequency, such as 25 kHz, the sound comes out attenuated, distorted or not at all.

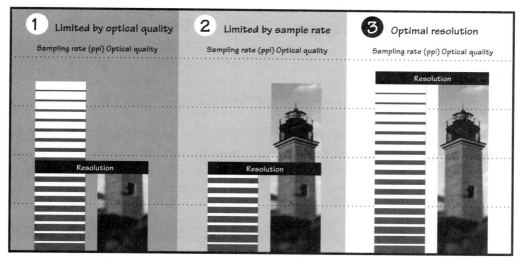

Figure 13-1 Resolution limitations: optical system and sampling rate

■ Resolution and Sampling Rate

To reiterate, the resolution of a scanner is the ability of the scanner to capture detail in the original. The optical sampling rate of a scanner is the number of samples (pixels) the scanner captures in the x-direction (across the page), and it is determined by the width of the scanned region and the number of elements on the CCD. For example, a scanner with 5100 CCD elements that scans an 8.5-inch wide area has an optical sampling rate of 5100/8.5, or 600 ppi. The optical sampling rate is determined by the sampling in the x-direction (across the page) only.

A scanner with a high optical sampling rate doesn't guarantee better resolution than a scanner with a lower optical sampling rate. For example, the resolution of a scanner with a high sampling rate of 600 ppi but a low-quality optical system may not be as good as a scanner with a 400-ppi sampling rate and a high-quality optical system. Figure 13-2 on page 176 shows scans from three different scanners, two high-resolution scanners and one lower-resolution scanner. Note that one of the high-resolution scanners is a 600-ppi scanner and the second is a 300-ppi scanner. Both can fully resolve the detail in the scan, includ-

Resolution of detail

Fine detail in dark and light areas
(300 ppi scanner)

Missing detail in dark and light areas
(400 ppi scanner)

Fine detail in dark and light areas
(600 ppi scanner)

A scanner should be able to resolve detail in both light and dark areas in the same image at the same exposure setting. In this example, the 400 ppi scanner is missing light and dark detail that both the 300 and 600 ppi scanners can see. PPI does NOT equal resolution!

Mt Sopris - Drawn by Wilma Gann

Figure 13-2   A higher ppi doesn't always produce better detail

ing light detail in dark areas and dark detail in light areas. A high-resolution scanner must be able to resolve both light and dark detail in the same image. Notice the image from the lower resolution scanner which has an optical sampling rate of 400 ppi. This scanner cannot fully resolve the details in either light or dark areas of the image, even though the ppi rating of the scanner is greater than the 300-ppi scanner. This illustrates that ppi does not define resolution.

Note: Two scanners with the same ppi may not have the same actual resolution.

You can't reliably evaluate the resolution of a scanner by looking at images

Evaluating the resolution of scanners by looking at images such as the one shown in this example is not a systematic or reliable process. The problem is a phenomenon called "aliasing." Aliasing is a digital sampling effect that occurs when sampling (scanning) frequencies that are above the Nyquist rate of a digital sampling device (a scanner). Aliasing pattern cannot be distinguished from real pattern, making evaluating resolution by looking at scans of high-frequency patterns unreliable, at best. You cannot tell if you are seeing the pattern or an aliasing effect. This is illustrated in Figure 13-3 on page 180 and is discussed more fully in "Nyquist Frequency, Aliasing and Moiré Patterns" on page 179.

X- and y-direction optical sampling rates

Scanner specifications typically include some optical or true ppi or dpi rating. Usually both the *x*-direction (across the page) and the *y*-direction (down the page) sampling rates are specified. In this case the *x*-direction ppi number is the optical sampling rate. In most cases the *y*-direction ppi number is not, although it may be labeled that way. The *y*-direction ppi specification is usually larger and results from moving the optical carriage in smaller steps down the page. For example, a scanner specified as 300x600 ppi probably has a 300-ppi *x*-direction optical sampling rate and a 600 ppi *y*-direction maximum sampling rate. Note that the higher sampling rate in the *y*-direction is not optical sampling rate because, while more samples are captured, optically they overlap. In fact, the overlapping samples in the *y*-direction are a form of interpolation. A higher *y*-direction optical sampling rate doesn't improve resolution (the ability to resolve detail) although it can help minimize aliasing artifacts. The one area where higher sampling rate in the *y*-direction can be important is scaling. See more about scaling in Chapter 14 • "Scaling and Interpolation" on page 197.

Three types of ppi specifications.

There are three types of ppi specifications provided for scanners. Ignoring, for the moment, the fact that none of these specifications really provide much value to the customer, it is useful to at least understand what the three specifications are really referring to. In the following list of specifications, we have included the typical but imprecise use of the term "resolution" for ppi. This is for consistency so you can understand what is being claimed.

- Optical resolution, for example, 300x600 ppi—usually the optical sampling rate in the x-direction and the maximum hardware sampling rate in the y-direction. Remember, when considering the optical sampling rate of a scanner, you should consider only the x-direction so the above specification is really the combination of two different ones.
- Hardware resolution, for example, 2400x2400 ppi—usually represents the maximum interpolation that the scanner hardware can achieve. Has no relationship to true ability to resolve detail.
- Maximum resolution, for example, 9600 ppi—usually represents the maximum interpolated ppi that can be created using a combination of scanning software and hardware. This specification is really meaningless because:
  - Essentially infinite (and useless) interpolation—limited only by disk space—can be achieved using the image editing software shipped with any scanner, so there is no real difference in the product.
  - Interpolation beyond four times the optical sampling rate is of questionable value.

Scanner specifications can be misleading.

In addition to the fact that the ppi rating of a scanner does not necessarily reflect the true resolution of the scanner, there are other problems with the manner in which the ppi specification is used that may mislead customers. For example, some manufacturers reverse the order of the x and y sampling rates to promote the purported resolution capability of their scanners. So instead of a specification like 300x600 ppi (x by y), you see the specification 600x300 ppi (y by x). Often the second number is dropped or missed. In this case not only are customers misled by the belief that two scanners with the same optical sampling rate have the same performance (true resolution), they are further misled by the reversed specification into believing they are buying a 600-ppi scanner when, in fact, they are buying a 300-ppi scanner.

■ Nyquist Frequency, Aliasing and Moiré Patterns

A scanner is a digital sampling device—it creates a digital image of a page. In this regard, detail in an original represents an "input frequency" to the scanner. According to digital sampling theory, any periodic function must be sampled at a rate of at least twice the maximum frequency of the signal to capture accurate information in that signal. (You need more than twice the frequency to capture all the information.) Inversely, the theoretical maximum frequency a sampling device can capture is the 1/2 sampling rate. This is called the "Nyquist frequency" or "Nyquist rate." Consider an original that has 200 line pairs per inch (lppi). This represents periodic function with a base frequency of 200 cycles per inch and would require a scanner of at least 400 ppi to resolve it. In practice, to accurately capture a frequency the scanner must sample at a rate significantly higher than the Nyquist rate.

Most scanners cannot resolve at their Nyquist rate. Thus do not expect a
   300-ppi scanner to resolve 150 lppi, or a 600-ppi scanner to resolve
   300 lppi

While few originals include patterns of black and white lines (line pairs), the detail in an original can be represented as a frequency of certain lppi.

Aliasing occurs in a digital sampling system, like a scanner, when a high frequency in the original is reflected around the Nyquist rate of the scanner to appear, in the image, as a lower frequency. In the image, you will see a pattern or image that results from aliasing. Unfortunately, it is impossible to tell if the pattern you see is in the original or is an alias pattern. The tests later in this chapter measure the true resolution of the scanner (not the ppi).

Figure 13-3 illustrates aliasing. On the left side is a scan, at 600 ppi on a 600-ppi optical sampling rate scanner, of a pattern of lines with a frequency of 180 lppi. The Nyquist rate of a 600-ppi optical sampling rate scanner is 300 lppi so the scanner can resolve the pattern—not well. There are 18 pairs of lines in the 1/10 inch image.

On the right is a scan of the same 180-lppi pattern using a scanner with a 300-ppi optical sampling rate. The scan was performed, using quality interpolation in the scanner, at 600 ppi (interpolated). However, Nyquist rate of a 300-ppi optical sampling rate scanner is 150, so the 180-lppi pattern is beyond the Nyquist rate and **cannot be resolved** by the scanner. Note that interpolation does not increase optical sampling rate.

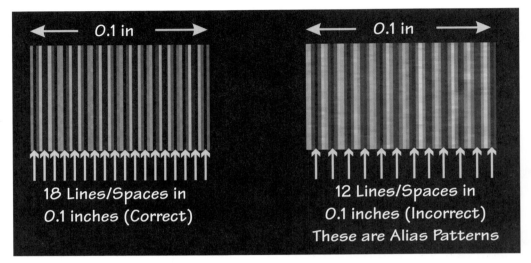

Figure 13-3   Aliasing limits evaluating resolution by looking at images

When you compare the two images carefully you will notice that the image on the right, even though it looks better, has only 12 pairs of lines in 1/10 inch—not the 18 that truly exist. The lines in the image on the right are aliasing artifacts. They are imaginary, introduced by the limitations of the scanner. Even though the image on the right appears sharper and has higher contrast, it is not real and, in a real scan, the image would be corrupted.

Aliasing.

If you scan objects with frequencies at or above the Nyquist frequency, the scanned image may show patterns that aren't in the object, a condition called "aliasing." These patterns aren't real, but rather a reflection of higher frequencies around the Nyquist frequency in frequency space.

Moiré patterns.

The most common form of aliasing in scanners is Moiré patterns that are often obvious in scans of printed images such as those in magazine articles. Moiré patterns result when the frequency of the printed halftone interacts with the sampling rate of the scanner.

Beat frequencies.

Another form of aliasing is the phenomenon of beat frequencies. These are periodic variations in the signal resulting when two signals of unequal frequencies interact. In a scanned image, the interaction is between the scanner sampling rate and frequencies in the scanned object. Where the beat is maximized, the signal and the samples line up perfectly, and the resolution is high. But where the beat is minimized, the signal and the samples don't line up, and the resolution is low. Beat frequencies are shown in Figure 13-4. When measuring the resolution of a scanner, it is important to account for beat frequencies by scanning a pattern that is not a harmonic of the scanner sample rate. (A harmonic is a signal whose frequency is an integral multiple of the scanner sample rate.)   If the frequency of the pattern being scanned is an exact harmonic of the scanner sample rate, it is not possible to tell if the resultant image represents the minimum or maximum of the beat, as shown in Figure 13-4. Consequently, the scan may not represent the true optical resolution of the scanner.

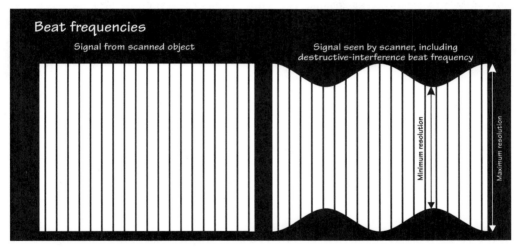

Figure 13-4 Beat frequencies

Limitations of typical tests

Wedge target.

One typical method of testing resolution is scanning a wedge target, a series of increasingly closer, wedge-shaped line pairs, and judging the point at which the line pairs are indistinguishable.

Microcopy test target.

Another common method uses high sampling rates to scan a microcopy test target, an industry standard target. This target has a series of line patterns in increasingly reduced size. When examined on a computer monitor or on hardcopy, the smallest line pattern fully resolved is considered representative of the scanner resolution. Wedge and microcopy targets are shown in Figure 13-5.

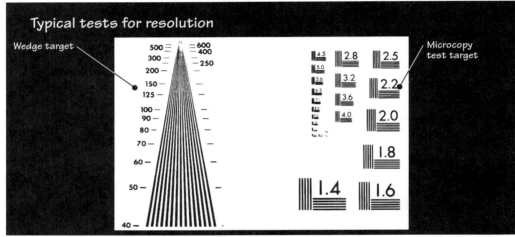

Figure 13-5   *A wedge target (left) and a microcopy target (right).*

Flaws in testing with these targets

The wedge target and microcopy test target are useful tools for a quick demonstration of what a scanner does but for the following reasons they aren't valid tests for resolution.

- The wedge test is invalid if the frequency of the line pairs exceeds the scanner's Nyquist rate. Aliasing at frequencies above the Nyquist frequency causes artifacts in the image that may look like fine detail and may be interpreted as resolved lines in the wedge target. Once the Nyquist frequency has been exceeded, it is not possible to tell if the signal is in the original or is an aliasing artifact.
- Both the microcopy and wedge tests are invalid because the signal isn't long enough to show the variations caused by beat frequencies. As a result, the pattern may be in the portion of the signal where the beat is maximum or it may be the portion of the signal where the beat is mini-

mum, and there is no way to tell from the image which it is. See "Nyquist Frequency, Aliasing and Moiré Patterns" on page 179.

■ For both the wedge and the microcopy targets, the exposure settings used for the scan can have a profound effect on the apparent "resolution" of the scanner. It is virtually impossible to assure consistent exposure across different scanners, even if an attempt is made to do so. Since the exposure can impact apparent resolution, objective comparisons are unlikely. Using "default settings" does not rectify this situation. The test in this chapter compensates for exposure differences.

■ Visually comparing the scanned images of the wedge target or the microcopy target is subjective because of the effects on perception of factors not related to resolution such as white point, black point, and jaggies.

■ Recommended Test

Modulation transfer function

The test we recommend is the modulation transfer function (MTF). MTF measures a scanner's optical frequency response when scanning line pairs whose frequency is within the limits of the scanner. The test measures the scanner's optical resolution and how well its optical system performs for a given frequency. MTF is expressed as a number between 0 and 1 at a given input frequency—for example, 0.5 MTF at 120 lppi.

The test compares the image of a high-frequency pattern captured by the scanner to the image of a low-frequency pattern captured by the same scanner. The scanner captures the low-frequency pattern accurately so we use this as the reference pattern. This eliminates exposure variations in the measurement. To calculate the MTF, we record the maximum-to-minimum excursion from the high-frequency test pattern and divide that by the maximum-to-minimum excursion from the low-frequency reference pattern. Because the pattern scanned is long compared to the beat frequency, the true optical resolution can be measured.

Advantages.

One advantage of the MTF test over visual inspection is that it is analytical. If a scanner's actual optical sampling rate is less than specified, the MTF test reveals it. For instance, if the scanner's specification for optical sampling rate is 600 ppi based on interpolation from 300-ppi samples, the MTF of the scanner is appropriately less. MTF tests can also be used to compare scanners at different optical sampling rates, in this way quantifying the benefit of the scanner with the higher optical sampling rate. The MTF test will reveal flaws in the optics, mechanics and processing of images. If a scanner with a high ppi specification has a lower quality optical system, the MTF will reveal that factor.

Another advantage is that the MTF test is independent of the scanner's exposure settings, enabling comparison of resolution even among scanners set for different exposures.

Finally, if you wish to compare scanners with different sampling rates (say, a 300- and a 600-ppi scanner), you calculate the MTF on both scanners using the MTF pattern for the 300-ppi scanner. The 600-ppi scanner should have a much higher MTF at this frequency.

To help you evaluate the results of the test, Table 5-4 on page 77 shows the importance of resolution for different applications.

■ Detailed Step-by-Step Procedure

The following procedure is a detailed discussion of the required steps. The test at first may seem overwhelming, but once understood, you can use a shorter simplified test procedure provided at the end of this chapter.

Step 1: assemble the equipment

You need the following equipment for this test:

- A scanner.
- An appropriate target (described below). The detailed test procedure assumes you are using the test target provided by Applied Image, Inc. and described in the appendix.
- Adobe Photoshop or similar image-editing software. Photoshop is recommended and is used for these examples. Step-by-step procedures may not be the same or achievable in other editing packages.

Step 2: pick a pattern frequency

- Scanners are digital sampling devices and the theoretical maximum frequency they can resolve is less than the Nyquist rate (1/2 the optical sampling rate). In fact, most scanners don't have good resolution at frequencies near this theoretical limit so use a pattern of lower frequency (typically 1/4 the optical sampling rate).

- Don't use a pattern frequency that is an exact harmonic of the scanner optical sampling rate. Scanning a harmonic may result in destructive interference between the pattern frequency and the optical sampling rate and doesn't represent the actual resolution of the scanner. Our recommendation is to use a pattern frequency of approximately 95% of 1/4 the optical sampling rate of the scanner, rounded up or down to the nearest multiple of 5.

- Scan at the optical sampling rate of the scanner even when you are comparing scanners of different optical sampling rates, such as 300-ppi and 600-ppi scanners. Thus the test shows how the lower optical sampling rate affects resolution so you can quantify the benefit of the scanner with the higher sampling rate. Scanning at other than the scanner's optical sampling rate introduces interpolation, which doesn't improve resolution and may reduce it.

- If you use the test target provided by Applied Image, you will scan patterns with frequencies appropriate for 300- to 600-ppi scanners. Then the MTF can be calculated using the appropriate pattern.
  - For a 300-ppi scanner, use the 70-lppi pattern.
  - For a 400-ppi scanner, use the 95-lppi pattern.
  - For a 600-ppi scanner, use the 140-lppi pattern.

Step 3: obtain a target

A pure MTF test needs a sinusoidally varying line pattern as a test pattern. These are expensive and hard to manufacture. Instead, use the more readily available bar pattern. The difference is that a sine pattern represents a fixed single-frequency image, whereas a bar pattern is a square wave with a broader frequency spectrum. The bar pattern's high frequencies make it a less pure pattern than the sine pattern. But since the scanner is probably limited in the higher frequencies, the bar pattern is suitable for our purposes.

Applied Image, Inc. has made available a test target for scanners with sampling rates of 300–600 ppi. The target is described in the appendix. Other sources include Stouffer and Sine Patterns. If you do not use the Applied Images target, use the following guidelines:

- Use the same physical target for testing all the scanners. If you can't use the same physical target, use the same kind of target in good condition from the same manufacturer and use the same test procedure.

■ Use reference and test patterns on the same physical target, if possible, for testing all the scanners. If you can't use the same physical target for both the reference and test patterns, use reference and test patterns from the same manufacturer, made with the same material using the same process. For example, the reference pattern could be a low-frequency (30-lppi) pattern (even just a black and white patch) from the same manufacturer, as long as it is made the same way as the test pattern. Using the same physical target is recommended because at the frequencies needed for the test, the MTF of the target itself is a factor. The target isn't a perfect image, and variation between targets can affect measured MTF results and give different results, even on the same scanner.

Step 4: set the controls

Setting the scanner controls precisely is very important for this test. The test procedure will compensate exposure differences only if appropriate settings are used. The following guidelines will help ensure a valid result. While they may seem complex, in practice it is quite simple.

■ Perform all scans at the optical sampling rate of the scanner. This is typically specified as the x-direction optical "resolution" of the scanner. Do not use the higher y-direction "optical resolution." For example, if a scanner is specified as a 300x600 (x by y) scanner, do the scans at 300 ppi (both directions).

■ If possible avoid automatic exposure and density controls. For scanners that always use automatic exposure, it is imperative that the reference and test pattern are scanned in one scan so that the same exposure is used.

■ Scan with a linear tone map. Set the controls for gamma correction at 1.0 or disable it and disable any shadow-enhancement tools or calibration. (Tone maps and gamma correction are explained in Chapter 9 • "Setting the Controls" on page 109; shadow-enhancement tools in Chapter 15 • "Tonal Resolution, Density Range and Bit Depth" on page 213 and calibration in Chapter 10 • "More on Image Quality" on page 121.)

■ If gamma compensation cannot be disabled, then it can be removed from the scanned image in an image editor after the scan.

■ If a scanner has the capability for **3 x 3** matrixing, disable it for this test. You may have to find out from the manufacturer if the scanner has this capability. The purpose of disabling 3 x 3 matrixing, which is desirable for color and grayscale scanning, is to use the scanner as though you were scanning line drawings; these are scans in which resolution is most important.

■ Scan in 24-bit color or 8-bit grayscale. Scans in 24-bit color allow comparison of the MTF for three color channels.

■ Consider the green channel the most important in MTF tests because scans of line drawings typically use only the green channel. Scanner manufacturers may correctly optimize green MTF at the cost of red or blue. Also, the eye is most focused for green light. Blue, in particular, is out of focus in the eye.

■ Use exposures that prevent clipping in the reference scan. This means that black should be more than 0 counts and white should be less than 255 counts. Default exposure settings will probably work, but you may need to do a test scan and look at the histogram with image-editing software to check. Adjust the exposures in the scanner if clipping occurs. Figure 13-6 shows histograms from a target with and without clipping. NOTE: If a scanner cannot be adjusted to prevent clipping in the reference pattern, refer to "What to do if clipping occurs" on page 191.

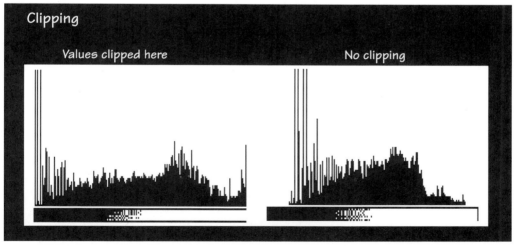

Figure 13-6   Clipping in the test pattern

■ Scan without sharpening unless it's the default for a given scanner. In this case, sharpening may be appropriate. If you use sharpening in the MTF test, use it for all other tests, such as image noise. Keep in mind that although sharpening may improve MTF, it's likely to degrade other test results such as noise.

■ Find out from the manufacturer if other settings should be adjusted for the MTF test.

Step 5: scan the patterns

Scan the following areas on the test target on each scanner.

■ Scan an area on the test target that includes all the MTF targets and the step grayscale located next to the MTF patterns. The step grayscale is included in case a scanner clips on the reference MTF pattern.

■ Perform one scan with the test target oriented such that the MTF patterns (lines) are vertical. This is for x MTF.

■ Perform a second scan with the test target oriented such that the MTF patterns (lines) are horizontal. This is for y MTF.

You can do additional scans if you want—for example, to measure the variation in MTF across the copyboard by scanning various locations on the copyboard. You can do scans to test sharpening and to test interpolation.

Step 6: extract the MTF data

In this test we use Adobe PhotoShop histograms, but you can use any image-editing software with histogram capability.

1. Open the scan for the x-direction MTF measurement.

2. Zoom in to 100%. If you do not, the histogram tool in Photoshop may provide inaccurate results.

3. If the gamma correction was not disabled for this scanner, remove the effect of gamma compensation using the procedure listed below under "Removing the effect of gamma correction" on page 191.

4. Select, using the selection tool, the reference portion (30 lppi) of the image. You must select the specific portion of the image so that Photo-Shop calculates the histogram based upon only the reference area.

5. Select "Image/Histogram."

6. Look at the histogram to make sure that there is no clipping.

7. If there is clipping on the reference pattern (the values extend to 0 or 255), see "What to do if clipping occurs" on page 191.

WARNING: If either the minimum or maximum level is 0 or 255 respectively, the reference image is clipping and cannot be used for MTF. A clipped reference image will cause an inaccurately high MTF calculation. In this case see "What to do if clipping occurs" on page 191.

8. If the scan is 24-bit color, use the histogram to independently identify the minimum and maximum gray levels for each color in the image Do not use the "gray" histogram—use independent red, green and blue histograms. Pick the minimum and maximum based on the bulk of the data but don't use an outlying value (a value at the extreme of either minimum or maximum).

9. Record the minimum and maximum levels. You may need to move the mouse cursor over the histogram to obtain the minimum and maximum levels. If possible use the center of the peaks for minimum and maximum rather than the furthest excursion, thus eliminating noise from the measurement.

10. Record the reference minimum (Ref min) and reference maximum (Ref max) for each color independently. Figure 13-7 shows you how to extract the reference maximum from the histogram of the reference image.

11. Using the selection tool, select the appropriate test pattern. Remember that the target has a pattern at 70-, 95- and 140-lppi intended for primary measurements on 300-, 400- and 600-ppi scanners, respectively. You can calculate MTF at any or all of the frequencies to allow comparison between scanners of different sampling rates. To compare a 600- to 300-ppi scanner for instance, calculate the MTF at 70 lppi for both. But be sure you always scan at the optical sampling rate of the scanner, even when comparing against a lower-ppi scanner.

12. Using the histogram tool, record the minimum and maximum levels for each color in each scan. These are Test min and Test max for each color.

13. Repeat steps 2 through 11 for the *y*-direction scan pattern (optional).

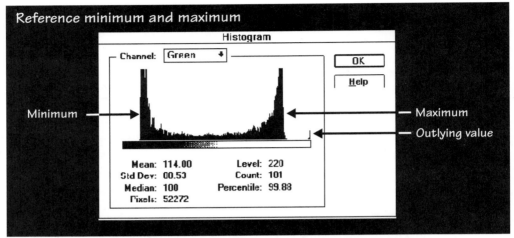

Figure 13-7 Extracting the minimum and maximum gray levels from the reference pattern

Step 7: Calculate the MTF

With the data you have just extracted, calculate the MTF for each scan using this formula:

$$MTF = \left(\frac{\text{Test max} - \text{Test min}}{\text{Ref max} - \text{Ref min}} \right)$$

The following table is sample data from an MTF test. The scanner tested has a green MTF of 0.47 at 105 lppi.

Table 13-1 Sample MTF Calculation

Parameter	Green reference data	Green test data
maximum level	220	172
minimum level	45	90
max - min	175	82
MTF at 105 lppi		0.47

Step 8: interpret the result

The result of an MTF test is a number between 0 and 1 and shows how well the scanner captures the frequency of the pattern. An MTF of 0.5 means that the resolution capability in a scanner is about 50% as good as the "perfect" scanner.

- The the higher the MTF at a given frequency, the better the resolution capability of the scanner.
- To compare different ppi scanners (say a 300 ppi and a 600 ppi), compare the calculated MTF at equal input lppis.
- To evaluate the effects of sharpening, interpolation and such, various scans can be performed.
- Sharpening will increase apparent MTF, but will also increase noise.
- MTF is only one performance parameter. Base scanner evaluations on a complete set of performance evaluations, not any one factor.

Removing the effect of gamma correction

If you were unable to disable gamma correction for a specific scanner, you can remove the effect of gamma correction by using the "Image/Adjust/Levels" function in Adobe PhotoShop. Do so before extracting the reference and test minimum and maximum levels. You must remove gamma correction from all scans—reference and test scans.

1. Open the image.

2. Select "Image/Adjust/Levels."

3. In the center box of the "Input levels:" line, enter a value that is 1/gamma where gamma is the gamma correction used in the scan. For example, if a gamma of 1.8 was used, enter $1/1.8 = 0.556$ in the box. If a gamma of 2.2 (sRGB) was used, enter 0.454 in the box (1/2.2).

4. Do the above for all scans in the calculation.

5. Continue the test as if gamma correction had been disabled in the scan.

What to do if clipping occurs

In some scanners the values in bright areas and dark areas may be clipped to 0 or 255. This clipping hides defects that some scanners suffer from and may enhance the apparent contrast of the image—at the cost of highlight and shadow detail and overall image fidelity. Typically, these scanners will clip the reference pattern in the MTF test as evidenced by a histogram (in Photoshop) in which all of the dark values are at 0, and/or all of the white values are at 255.

In scanners that clip the reference pattern, the test pattern contrast will likely be similarly enhanced and cannot be compared directly to other scanners. This would make the MTF of the clipping scanner appear higher than it is. A valid reference pattern is required for acceptable results.

If clipping occurs there are two choices to deal with the problem. The best method is to rescan the MTF test target on the scanner using different exposure settings to decrease the contrast in the image. The goal is to rescan until the reference pattern no longer clips at 0 or 255.

Note: You must redo all MTF scans with the new exposure settings so that both the reference and test targets are scanned with the same exposure.

The second method uses the gray step target as a reference instead of the low-frequency (30-lppi) MTF pattern. Then a correction factor is calculated to make up for the different references. This test is not as reliable as the normal MTF test so the above option is preferred.

- For the scanner that clips, recalculate the MTF using two of the gray steps in the step scale as the reference. Choose the gray patches that are as light and dark as possible without clipping (returning 0 or 255). Record which of the patches were used.
- Use the histogram tool to find the average value for the two gray patches. These average values represent the new Refmax and Refmin for this scanner.
- Calculate the MTF using the Testmin and Testmax from the high frequency pattern, the Refmax and Refmin from the gray patches.

Next, you must relate this measurement to the other scanners that did not clip. You can do this two ways:

- Recalculate the MTF of all of other scanners using the SAME two gray patches for the Refmax and Refmin. These new MTF numbers can be fairly compared. This is the preferred method but involves significant work.
- A second, less robust method is to calculate the MTF of one comparative scanner that did not clip using the SAME gray patches for the Refmax and Refmin. This new MTF number will likely be higher than one calcu-

lated using the reference pattern. The ratio of the two MTF numbers for the non-clipping scanner can be used as a correction factor for the scanner that did clip, allowing the MTF of the clipped scanner to be compared as shown in the example below.

Table 13-2   Compensating for clipping in MTF (less robust)

MTF of the clipping scanner using the gray patches as Refmax and Refmin	0.58
MTF of the non-clipping scanner using the normal calculation	0.52
MTF of the non-clipping scanner using the gray patch method calculation	0.64
Ratio of the normal and alternative calculation for the non-clipping scanner	0.64/0.52=1.23
Divide clipping scanner MTF by the ratio. This is an approximation of the MTF of the clipped scanner, compensating for the difference in method.	0.58/1.23=0.47

Signs of errors

Note that if you don't set the controls according to the recommendations under "Set the Controls," you may get incorrect results. For instance, if you get an MTF of more than 1.0, which is impossible, check your procedure and do the scans again.

These are signs to watch for that may indicate invalid results:

- An MTF of more than 1.0, probably the result of different exposures.
- An MTF that is much larger for one scanner than for comparable scanners. Use the "You get what you pay for" rule. If a scanner that is much less expensive is returning MTF much higher than the other scanners this is a warning flag.
- Outlying values or histograms with image noise, which artificially increase the MTF. You can use a filter that averages columns (x MTF) or rows (y MTF) to reduce image noise.

■ Comparison to Another Common MTF Measurement

Another common MTF measurement seen in the literature uses the formula

$$MTF = \left(\frac{Testmax - Testmin}{Testmax + Testmin}\right) \quad \text{Not Recommended}$$

Notice that in this measurement, a reference is not used, but instead the sum of the min and max are used as a reference. This method works well for a single system in which the "average" reflectance is known and controlled. However, when comparing different scanners, variations in the white point and black point of the different scanners make this measurement less reliable.

To illustrate this, consider two hypothetical scanners. One scanner tends to be too dark and returns Testmin and Testmax of 80 and 120, respectively and a Refmin and Refmax of 50 and 170. The second, which returns a more appropriate reflectance may return a Testmin and Testmax of 100 and 140, respectively and a Refmin and Refmax of 65 and 175. The second scanner can actually resolve the pattern better, and the recommend MTF equation reflects this, returning 0.33 for the first scanner and 0.37 for the second. However, using the above equation, the MTF of the first scanner is

$$MTF = \left(\frac{120 - 80}{120 + 80}\right) = 0.2.$$

The MTF of the second scanner is

$$MTF = \left(\frac{140 - 100}{140 + 100}\right) = 0.167,$$

making the second scanner appear to have lower resolving power. In addition, this method has limited physical significance, whereas the recommend method is easily understood physically.

■ Simplified Step-By-Step Procedure

This procedure describes the steps in a very simple manner with limited information. Make sure the detailed procedure is well understood before using this one!

Step 1: Obtain the test target.

Step 2: Scan the MTF patterns including the 30 lppi and the gray step scale. Use gamma 1.0 and scan at the optical sample rate of the scanner.

Step 3: If gamma 1.0 cannot be used, remove the effect of gamma as described in "Eliminating the Effect of Gamma Compensation."

Step 4: Extract the reference pattern min and max values from the histogram.

Step 5: If the reference pattern saturates, use two gray patches from the step scale.

Step 6: Extract the test pattern min and max values from the histogram.

Step 7: Calculate MTF as (Testmax-Testmin)/(Refmax-Refmin).

Chapter 14

Scaling and Interpolation

Most scanning is not done at the scanner's optical sampling rate, but instead includes interpolation or subsampling to a higher or lower ppi. Typically, this is done to optimize a scan for a particular output device (printer or display) or to scale an image to a particular output size. We will use the term "interpolation" to mean the creation of images with a ppi different than the scanner optical sampling rate and for both increasing ppi above the optical sample rate and decreasing ppi below the optical sample rate. This chapter describes how scanners achieve interpolation and how to test for high quality interpolation. Interpolation quality is a very important aspect of scanned image quality and is often overlooked in scanner testing.

■ Overview of Scaling and Interpolation

Whether for enlarging or reducing an image or matching an image to a particular output device, interpolation is done by increasing or decreasing the number of scanned pixels in the image. Interpolation is typically used both for converting to higher sampling rates (oversampling) and to lower sampling rates (subsampling). When evaluating the interpolation ability of a scanner, you must look at both the quality of the scan (jaggies) and the accuracy of the scaling (is the output image the correct size?)

The capability of a scanner for accurate interpolation is very important. It affects image quality, file size, and scanning and processing time. In addition, the quality of scanner interpolation routines and the quality of the resulting image vary widely from scanner to scanner. To evaluate scanners fairly, we recommend you test scaling at a variety of settings for each scanner.

Reviewing scanning systems for ppi settings

Some scanners determine appropriate sampling rates from user settings without making the user understand or deal with the tedium of selecting sample rates. While this chapter describes how a scanner operates, in a well-designed system, the users should never have to consider these factors. Unfortunately, this use model—not having to deal with ppi—is not always accepted well by reviewers and more experienced users because they are used to specifying items such as ppi. Consider that the scanner user today is much different than traditional DTP and graphic arts professionals, and do not need to know how to deal with detailed controls of scanners. Scanners have changed to address this new use, and reviews should reflect that change.

Formation of jaggies

The most common problem in interpolation is formation of jaggies. Jaggies often result from scaling up or down during or after a scan using poor image processing routines, either in the scanner itself or in scanning software, image-editing software or word processing software. Jaggies are usually associated with scans of drawings but can appear in scans of photos as well. Large image files, with the consequent increase in scanning and processing time, are another result of poor or missing scaling routines.

Scaling during scanning

To scale an image during scanning, you vary the number of saved ppi in the image file in relation to the number of samples needed by the output device. For example, if you are scanning a photo for printing at 100% on a 600-dpi printer, you would use a sampling rate of 150 ppi. To enlarge the photo 180% for the 600-dpi printer, you would scan the photo at 270 (150 times 1.8) ppi rather than at 150 ppi. So varying the scaling of an image is equivalent to varying the sampling rate at which you scan the image.

This process is usually done automatically: When you choose 150 ppi and 180% enlargement, a quality scanner will perform the scan at 270 ppi. The file created by the scan shows a 150-ppi sampling rate for this scan, although the scanner was operating at 270 ppi; the file may or may not show that the image was scaled at 180%. In fact, based on the information in the image file, you usually don't know the sampling rate the scanner used.

Scaling after scanning

Scaling or interpolation after a scan may be less successful than scaling during a scan. If the base scan doesn't have enough detail for interpolation, software cannot recreate the missing detail. Interpolating based on binary scans tends to give particularly poor results because the binary image data does not provide enough information for the scaling routines to use.

Scaling an image down (sub-sampling) after scanning slows processing and wastes resources because the computer must accept and process more data than necessary. Using a scanner to scale down quickly and accurately during the scan is better than using a scanner that relies on image editing software for scaling after the scan.

The majority of scans of images (pictures) are performed at something less than the scanner optical sampling rate. Thus, when interpolation occurs, the quality achieved is a very important aspect of scanning and can have profound impact on both image quality and, especially, scan speed.

■ Jaggies

Jaggies are a natural by-product of scanning. The jaggies produced by scanning an image at an appropriate sampling rate, by a high-quality scanner, are usually not visible on the output when viewed at a normal distance. They appear even and look natural, and important image detail is not lost. Jaggies produced by poor interpolation or scaling (either during or after the scan) may be uneven, look unnatural or be very obvious. How bad the jaggies look depends on the quality of the interpolation routine used. If the routine is good, the jaggies are minimized; if the scaling routine is poor, the jaggies are accentuated.

The best image is probably produced by interpolation during a scan, using a scanner that offers a good hardware scaling routine. Next best, though much slower, is image-editing or scanning software with good scaling routines operating on a full bit depth (8-bit or 24 bit) base image. Worse is a scanner with a poor or nonexistent scaling routine or scaling in the software based upon 1-bpp image data.

Figure 14-1 compares the jaggies produced by scaling during scanning with the jaggies produced by scaling after scanning. Both images were scanned at 300 ppi and scaled to 200%. The left image used high quality image-editing software after the scan. The right image used the capability of a high-quality scanner. In this case, it is apparent that even high-quality scaling done after the scan produces worse jaggies than high-quality scaling done during the scan. This is because the image-editing software is operating on a binary image, whereas the scanner had much more information to base scaling upon (8-bit or higher data and a wealth of sampling rates). The software scaling is also slower and requires a second step. Comparable scaling could be achieved in the software if high sampling rate, high bit depth data is sent to the image-editing software. However, that would be so much slower, at least eight times as much data would be required.

Figure 14-1   Jaggies from scaling after the scan and from scaling during the scan

■ *X-Direction Scaling*

Interpolation

X-direction scaling changes the number of samples (pixels) within each raster line. Scaling to above the optical sampling rate of the scanner (for example, scaling to 400 ppi on a 300-ppi scanner) is done with interpolation using pixel replication, bicubic interpolation, binary rate multipliers, nearest-neighbor interpolation, linear interpolation, convolution or some combination of these methods. Depending on the scanner, these kinds of interpolation are done with a scanner's software, hardware or a combination of both.

Typically, better interpolation is possible when the desired sample rate is an even multiple of the optical sampling rate. For instance, interpolating to 600 ppi probably works better on a 300-ppi scanner than a 400-ppi optical sampling rate scanner. However, some scanners (not necessarily the expensive ones) use very sophisticated interpolation methods and can scale arbitrarily.

Software versus hardware interpolation

Either software or hardware interpolation can produce quality results, but quality software scaling is usually much slower because all the image data must be sent to the computer. The higher the quality, the slower it is. Interpolation using hardware is much faster, but many scanners don't offer it or offer only very rudimentary hardware interpolation routines. If the scanner has good hardware interpolation, you have the best of both worlds (speed and quality).

Scaling down to less than the scanner optical sampling rate (for example from 300 ppi to 200 ppi on a 300-ppi scanner) can also be done with interpolation followed by subsampling. The image is interpolated to 600 ppi, then every third pixel is used to create the 200-ppi scan. If done in hardware, this method can be quite fast. If done in software, this method is likely quite slow, as it requires processing of 600-ppi data. A simpler method would be to reduce the sampling rate from 300 ppi to 200 ppi by dropping every third pixel (pixel dropping). The result is a 200-ppi scan, but of poor quality. Again, the quality of the image depends on the quality of the scaling routine, and the speed depends on whether the interpolation is done with software, hardware or a combination of both.

X-direction dynamic optical sampling rate

Some scanners have the capability to vary their *x*-direction optical sampling rate to match the demands of the scan. For instance, a 600-ppi scanner may be able to convert to 300 or 200 ppi in the *x*-direction. If done properly, this can improve the quality of the scan, as well as allow the scanner to operate two or three times faster. Figure 14-2 shows the results of two different kinds of interpolation to scale an image, one of low quality and one high.

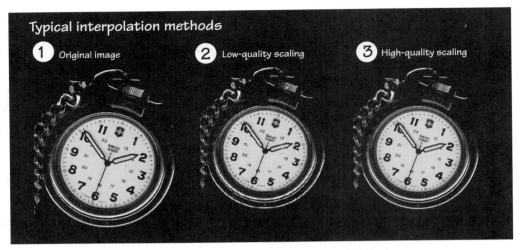

Figure 14-2   Comparison of two kinds of software interpolation (color)

■ Y-Direction Scaling

Y-direction scaling is typically done in one of the following ways:

- By scanning at the actual sampling rate desired, using a variable y-direction sample rate. For example, if 200 ppi is desired, the scanner will operate at 200 ppi in the y-direction. This method is best because it minimizes jaggies, maximizes speed and optically samples the image appropriately. Variable y-direction sampling rate is discussed later in this section.

- By scanning at a sampling rate above the desired rate, then doing line dropping. In this type of scanner a 200-ppi scan is achieved by scanning at 300 ppi and dropping (deleting) every third raster line. This method produces poor results. A better alternative, from an image quality standpoint, is a scanner that could operate at 600 ppi and use every third raster line. This method provides acceptable quality but is very slow because it requires exposing three lines for every one kept.

- By scanning at below the desired sampling rate and replicating (repeating) some lines. For example, a 300-ppi scan could be achieved by scanning at 200 ppi and replicating every third raster line in the image. The results of this method are poor.

- By scanning at below the desired sampling rate using interpolation to increase the effective sampling rate. This scanner would scan at 150 ppi and interpolate between every third and fourth raster line to create an extra line. This method can produce high quality but is typically very slow because it must be done in the software and also because most scanners cannot operate on image data in a vertical direction (raster line to raster line). In addition, important detail may be lost.

Figure 14-3 and Figure 14-4 illustrate interpolation from 300 to 400 ppi using raster line replication or linear interpolation.

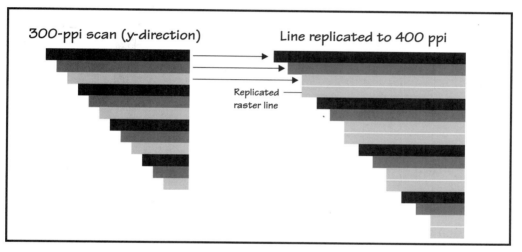

Figure 14-3 Y-direction scaling with line replication

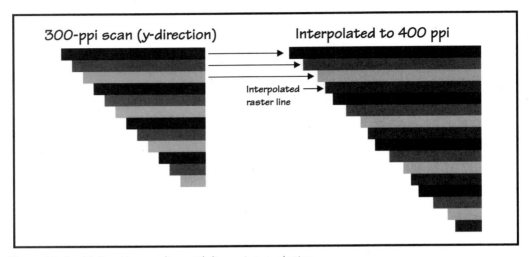

Figure 14-4   *Y-direction scaling with linear interpolation*

The best solution for these examples is to use a scanner capable of scanning at the 400-ppi rate you want.

Scaling using variable Y-direction sampling rate

The *y*-direction sampling rates available for a given scanner depend on both hardware and software. In many cases, the color separation technology used in the scanner may limit the variety of *y*-direction sampling rates available. In addition, generic software written for any scanner is the least likely to use a scanner's capabilities. In general, the more *y*-direction sampling rates a scanner offers, the better the scaling will be.

There is a difference between scanners that vary the actual *y*-direction sampling rate and scanners that offer various sampling rates using interpolation, line dropping, or line replication. Figure 14-5 shows true variable *y*-direction sampling rate scanning and scaling by line dropping.

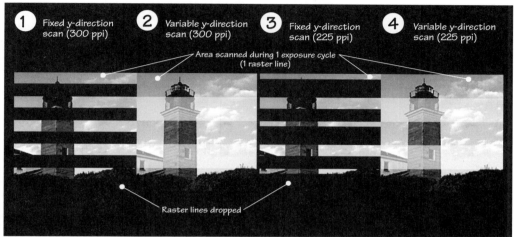

Figure 14-5 *Variable y-direction sampling rate and line dropping (color)*

Advantages of variable y-direction sampling[1].

As shown in the figure, for line dropping, the scanner must scan at a higher rate and then line drop, introducing more objectionable jaggies. Other benefits of variable *y*-direction scaling include:

- Only the data needed are captured, using fewer computer resources.
- Scan times are much shorter because only the lines needed are exposed. In the case on the right in Figure 14-5, the variable *y*-sampling rate scanner will operate up to four times faster.
- A lower sampling rate in the variable *y*-direction lessens aliasing artifacts such as Moiré patterns because the scanner is optically filtering the image before it is sampled (before the CCD turns it into "pixels"). Filtering after the scan may not be as successful because once aliasing has occurred (once the CCD turns the image into pixels), it is no longer possible to determine which frequencies were in the original and which are aliasing artifacts.

---

[1]. Hewlett-Packard patented.

■ Magnification or Scaling Accuracy

A scanner should capture an image of the correct size. If a 4-inch-wide object is scanned, the resulting image should be 4 inches wide. In addition, when enlarging or reducing an image, the image should be accurately and uniformly scaled in both the x and y direction. For instance, a scan of a circle should appear circular, not egg-shaped. A scanner that has anisotropic magnification or scaling will cause that circle to be stretched or squashed.

■ Positional or Stop-Start Errors

Often scanners will produce data faster than the computer can accept it. In this case, the scanner must pause and wait for the computer to catch up. The manner in which scanners do this varies; some simply stop in position and then restart. More sophisticated scanners will actually reverse, then proceed forward again to ensure the image is not distorted. Reposition algorithms may be quite sophisticated with carefully controlled acceleration and deceleration.

The image artifact caused by poor position accuracy, either during a stop-start, or just during normal scans, depends on the technology used. In single-exposure scanners (not just single-pass scanners), the artifact will look like a jaggy. In three-exposure scanners (such as single-pass, on-chip filter scanners), the error will likely appear as a colored stripe across the image or y-direction RGB misregistration.

■ Limitations of Typical Tests

Often the interpolation ability of scanners is not reviewed. When included, typical tests involve scanning detailed originals and examining the resulting image for jaggies by viewing it, greatly magnified, on a computer monitor. This tests for only one aspect of scaling capability, jaggies, but not for scaling accuracy or speed of scaling.

In addition, this test is usually only done at one sampling rate, often the optical sampling rate of the scanner. Certain sampling rates produce minimal jaggies in a given scanner, whereas others produce excessive jaggies in that same scanner. A given sampling rate may be good for one scanner and not for another. This can give the impression that one scanner is better at all sampling rates than another, which is not necessarily true. This is why we recommend testing each scanner at a variety of sampling rates.

■ Recommended Tests

The tests we recommend measure accuracy, quality of interpolation and creation of Moiré. In the first test, we scan at a given scale factor and examine the size of the resulting image using image-editing software. Evaluation using image-editing software is preferable to measuring printed output because printers can introduce scaling errors. Using this test, you can check the accuracy (size) of the image in both the x- and y-direction, and you can check for anisotropic scaling. Finally, if the scanner has bad skew (the x and y scan directions are not perpendicular) the image will reflect this. Perform this test at several scaling settings above and below 100%.

In the second test, scan a sharp, high-contrast, diagonal edge at a variety of sampling rates. A scanner with a good scaling capability produces an image in which the transition across the edge has the same number of pixels horizontally for each vertical transition, as shown in Figure 14-6. The Applied Images test target described in the appendix provides both these features.

The third test involves scanning halftoned images to evaluate how well a scanner deals with halftones.

Recommended test scans include a variety of sampling rates, including:

■ Sample rates above the optical sampling rate of the scanner to check for line or pixel replication.

■ Sampling rates that are not an even divisor of the scanner's optical sampling rate. If the scanner uses line or pixel dropping and then scans at odd sample rates, the results will be poor. For instance, in a 600-ppi scanner you might look at scans at 400 and 500 ppi.

■ Perform the test using both 1-bpp (line art) scans and higher bit depth (8 or 24) scans. Some scanners will do better or worse in each case.

■ See the table in the detailed test procedure for a comprehensive set of scans.

While testing be sure to:

■ Test the relationship between sample rate and scaling in the scanning software. For instance a 600-ppi, 100% scan should look identical to a 300-ppi, 200% scan.

- Record scan times to try to identify if the scaling is done in hardware, software or both. Typically, scanners will interpolate in hardware up to two times the optical sampling rate, then in software above that.
- Consider that jaggies are probably most important in line art scans.
- Compare the speed of scanning at various sample rates to see if the scanner is able to scan faster at low sample rates.

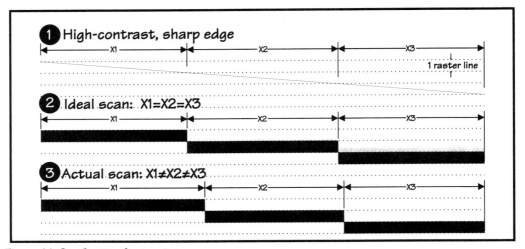

Figure 14-6   Testing for jaggies

Detailed test procedure

Step 1: identify an appropriate test target.

The target provided by Applied Images, described in the appendix, contains a square border with precise dimensions and can be used to evaluate scaling accuracy. In addition, the target provides a diagonal line set to be used for evaluating jaggies.

Step 2: identify a set of ppi and/or scaling settings to be used on each scanner.

Recall that the same ppi rate in a scanner can be achieved by either selecting that ppi or varying the scaling percentage. A good (comprehensive) set of ppi and scaling settings is given in the Table 14-1 on page 211.

Step 3: repeat one of the odd ppi (such as 133 ppi) scans in both grayscale mode (8 bpp) and in binary mode (1 bpp).

These two images will be compared to evaluate the difference in interpolation methods for the different image types. Also, record the time for these two scans.

Step 4: perform two scans that achieve the same effective sampling rate (as shown in the table) using two different settings.

For instance, scan once at 300-ppi at 200% and once at 600-ppi at 100%.

Step 5: perform the remaining scans and record the scan times.

Step 6: examine the scans in an image editor looking at the resultant image size.

In Adobe Photoshop, use the selection tool to select a dimension of interest. The Info box will provide the measured dimension in the image for comparison to the expected size.

Step 7: examine the two scans performed in step 4 to see if they appear identical.

The dimension in Photoshop should be twice as big for the 200% scaling image as the 100% image.

Step 8: scale the image using Photoshop.

Using "Image/Image Size" in Photoshop on one of the scans done in step 4, modify one image's ppi to match the other—be sure to deselect "Resample Image." For instance, change the 300-ppi, 200% image to a 600-ppi image by typing 600 ppi in the "resolution" box.

Step 9: compare the Photoshop-scaled image to the scanner-scaled one.

Using the "Image/Calculations" in Photoshop, subtract the image created in step 8 from the other one captured in step 4. If the scanner scaled precisely, the images should subtract to leave a black image. Non-black pixels in the resultant image show where the two scans differed because of positional errors in the scanner or differences in the scaling methods.

Step 10: compare the binary scans.

Convert the grayscale image from step 3 to binary using "Image/Mode—50% Threshold" in Photoshop. Using "Image/Calculations" subtract this converted image from the binary image captured in step 3. This will reveal differences in the scaling routines used for binary and grayscale (color) images. If significant errors are seen, examine a scan of a photograph scanned at the same pixel rate for artifacts from poor scaling.

Step 11: Look for uneven jaggies (poor scaling)

Examine the diagonal line patterns in the test images for apparent uneven jaggies. Look in particular for steps that are not the same "width," replicated lines and evidence of dropped lines. Quality scaling routines will result in even steps on the diagonal lines. Figure 14-6 illustrates this.

Step 12: Look for positional error (start-stop).

Perform a scan of the diagonals at very high sample rates and high bit depth (600-ppi or above and 24-bit). Select a large enough area to create a large image file. The goal is to force repositions or stop-starts during the scan to examine repositional errors. Errors may appear as a jaggy or as a colored streak or fringe.

Step 13: examine halftoned images.

Perform scans at 100 and 150 ppi of a halftoned image (such as an image from a magazine) and examine the result for Moiré. You must view these images on a screen at 1:1 scanned pixel per display pixel (100% in Photoshop) or the display may introduce Moiré that is not a result of the scan! You may choose to evaluate available anti-Moiré routines. Note, higher ppi scans will typically have worse Moiré.

Step 14: check for loss of detail due to anti-Moiré routines

Print the scans in step 13 on a 600-dpi printer and examine the images for loss of detail due to anti-Moiré routines.

The table on the next page lists ppi and scaling settings you might want to consider testing. The items marked with * are sample rates considered difficult to achieve.

Table 14-1   Comprehensive Set of ppi and Scaling Settings for Testing Scanner Scaling

ppi	Scaling	Effective scan ppi	Purpose of the scan
72*	100%	72	Typical for web pages (also 75)
72*	200%	144	200% scaled web pages
72*	178%	128	Results in 640-pixel-wide scan from 5x3 photo (for computer display)
72*	284%	204	Results in 1024-pixel-wide scan from 5x3 photo
100	100%	100	Typically used for photographs on 300-dpi printers.
100	200%	200	200% scaling for photos on 300-dpi printers
133*	100%	133	Often used for presswork (less common in desktop publishing). In addition, a hard number to achieve.
150	100%	150	Typical for photographs on 600-dpi printers
150	200	300	200% scaling for photographs on 600-dpi printers
200*	100%	200	Fax and document management
200*	100%	200	Typical for photos on 1200-dpi printers. (Note, consider using 150 for this type of scan. The benefit from 200 is minimal.)
300	100%	300	Typical for drawings on 300-dpi printers
300	200%	600	200% scaling for drawings on 300-dpi printers
600	100%	600	Typical for drawings on 600-dpi printers
600*	200%	1200	200% scaling for drawings on 600-dpi printer
1200	100%	1200	Typical for drawings on 1200-ppi printer. (Note, consider using 600 ppi for this type of scan. Benefit from 1200 ppi is very minimal)
The items marked with * are sample rates considered difficult to achieve.			

Chapter **15**

Tonal Resolution, Density Range and Bit Depth

Today, scanners are commonly specified with an increasing tonal resolution. Typically, this is specified as an increased "bit depth" as in a "30-bit color scanner." The bit depth or bpp specification is very similar to the specification of ppi in that it tells us something about the technology in the scanner, but nothing about the quality. In fact bpp, like ppi, is becoming meaningless. A better measure of tonal resolution is signal-to-noise ratio. A second specification often seen is density range (or dynamic range). Density range is a measure of how dark (dense) something is and is a specification more related to printing or prepress work than desktop scanning. This chapter examines what these specifications mean to users and how can they be measured.

■ Tonal Resolution

Compared to professional drum scanners and the human eye, desktop scanners have a limited capability to capture shadow detail, the small intensity changes in the darker portions of an image. Traditionally, scanners with higher bpp specifications (for example, 30- and 36-bpp scanners) were able to capture more information in the dark areas of images.

Bit Depth Claims

Today, many scanners claiming higher bit depth are simply increasing the number of levels converted by the analog-to-digital converter, with no consideration as to the quality of the signal being input to the A/D or to the use made of those extra "bits." In many cases these extra bits are just noise. It is unclear from either bpp or density range claims if a "30-bit" scanner:

- Provides real 30-bit data and not just 2 extra bits of noise.
- Actually captures 30 bits of calibrated image data.

In addition, many scanners may be using some of the bits captured for digital photo response non-uniformity (PRNU) compensation. See Chapter 10 • "More on Image Quality" on page 121. For instance, a scanner may capture 10 bits of uncompensated image data, then use digital compensation to correct for imperfections in the CCD response, light source uniformity and color calibration. These calculations effectively use some of the image bits of data compensating for the imperfections in the scanner itself, and those bits are not available as image data. Unfortunately, there is an inconsistency on how this is reported. More reputable manufacturers report the number of bits captured by the scanner after compensation. Manufacturers interested in presenting bigger numbers likely do not.

Note: When reviewing a scanner, ask the manufacturer if the bit depth claim is for image data after PRNU and DSNU compensation, or if the claimed bit depth data is not yet calibrated.

Tonal transformations

In addition to tonal resolution, a very important factor for scanned images is the ability of a scanner to perform tonal transformations such as gamma compensation and auto-exposure. The quality of these tonal transformations depends on both the number of bits captured and the quality of the image-processing routines.

Improved tonal transformations are also a major benefit for scanners that capture higher bit depth, such as 30- and 36-bpp scanners. In fact, a 30-bit scanner may provide a slight improvement in image quality over a 24-bit scanner, even if the signal-to-noise ratio does not provide more image detail. Of course, a 30-bit scanner with a corresponding four times improvement in signal-to-noise ratio will provide better image quality yet.

Density range

Density range (sometimes called "dynamic range") specifications are intended to communicate the ability of a scanner to capture shadow detail and should be closely related to image noise and tonal resolution. However, the manner in which density range is reported for scanners is often misleading or incomplete. In addition, density range is not a particularly useful specification for reflective scans on desktop scanners.

Density relates to how dark a portion of an image is and is related to reflectance or transmittance. Density specification should also include spectral information used in the measurement, as in status-T density. (status-T is more like a scanner, but status-A is often used in the printing industry). To calculate the density of the portion of an image, you would measure the reflectance or transmittance of the image, using a spectral response curve, then apply the following calculation:

$$\text{density} = \log\left(\frac{1}{\text{reflectance factor}}\right),$$

where

$$\text{reflectance factor} = \frac{\text{reflectance (in \%)}}{100}.$$

The transmittance factor can also be used.

Thus, an image with a reflectance of 20% would have a density of:

$$\text{density} = \log\left(\frac{1}{0.2}\right) = 0.69.$$

Density range applied to scanners.

Density is more commonly related to printing, either photographic or digital, and is used to control the intensity of colors and inks on a printed photo or page. Most often, when discussing scanning, density is used to calibrate a particular drum scanner to a particular press to achieve a desired color. This use is common in professional scanning for pre-press and press work. When applied to a desktop scanner, this use of density is not common because most users have no control or understanding over the printing density for their printer.

Thus, for typical desktop scanners, density should relate to how well the scanner can capture very subtle changes in dark areas of an image. Unfortunately, there are three problems with how density range is applied to scanners today:

- Density range is not a particularly useful specification for scanning reflective originals.
- Often the density range specification is based upon bit depth, not actual capability, and thus does not represent the capability of the scanner.
- Typically, the specified density range ignores spectral content.

The last problem is simple to understand because a density range specification should always include spectral information. Typically it does not and, thus, the specification is incomplete.

Why density range is not a useful specification for desktop scanners.

For scanners, a density range should reflect the range of densities the scanner can capture faithfully. Let's consider what density is required for a typical desktop scanner. To understand this, consider the density that exists in reflective originals.

Reflective originals, whether they are photographs or printed pages, typically have a maximum density below 2.0. More typical densities for printed photographs range from 1.4 to 1.6. Again, for printed material, the maximum printed density is usually on the order of 1.5. The limiting factor is often the surface reflection of the material the image is printed on or the gloss of the inks used. Note: creating a reflective original with a density greater than 2.0 is quite difficult.

Thus, for scans of reflective material, regardless of the scanner used, the ability of a scanner to capture densities greater than 2.0 is of little importance as those densities do not exist in the original.

For transmissive originals such as slides and negatives, a much greater range of density, to 3.0 and above, is possible in the original. Thus, we see that for the special case of scanning quality transmissive originals, higher densities may be useful. However, most users of desktop scanners do not perform transmissive scans, and the originals they scan are not of high enough quality to require high-density scanning.

Density range specifications—real or not?

In addition to the lack of usefulness of density range specifications, there is often a problem with how density range is calculated for desktop scanners. In particular, some scanners manufacturers appear to be basing density range specifications solely on the number of bits per pixel captured by the scanner—a number that has little or nothing to do with the actual capability of the scanner or density in a strict sense.

For instance, consider a 24 bpp scanner. This scanner converts the image using 8 bits of data per pixel per color, so the smallest change the A/D converter could report is 1 8-bit count or $\frac{1}{256}$. A change of $\frac{1}{256}$ corresponds to a reflectance factor of

$$\frac{1}{256} = 0.0039.$$

If we assume that the scanner could actually "see" a 1-bit image, the corresponding density (ignoring the spectral part of density) would be:

$$Dmax = \log\left(\frac{1}{0.0039}\right) = 2.4.$$

This, of course, ignores the fact that:

■ A reflective original will probably not have a density of 2.4.
■ The signal-to-noise ratio of the scanner will probably not support a 1-bit image.

Performing the same calculation on a 30-bpp scanner:

$$Dmax = \log\left(\frac{1}{(1/1024)}\right) = \log(1024) = 3.0.$$

And for a 36-bpp scanner:

$$Dmax = \log(4096) = 3.6.$$

None of these specifications are real, because the ability of a scanner to capture very dark originals is not limited by the bit depth. The limit is more often stray light, image noise, and the original. Furthermore, you cannot measure a density of 3.0 on a reflective print because you cannot get a reflective print with a density of 3.0, so this specification goes unchallenged and untested.

Density range—summary.

To summarize:

■ Density ranges above 2 are not useful for scans of reflective originals.
■ Density range specifications are typically incomplete (no spectral information).

- Density ranges above 2.0 cannot be measured on reflective test targets because the target is difficult or impossible to create. Consequently, these specifications are not tested or verified.
- Scanner density range specifications based upon bit depth are not useful and not realistic in most cases.

Measuring density range—don't.

Since densities above 2.0 cannot be measured on reflective originals and are not important there, we suggest a more appropriate measurement of image quality and the ability of a scanner to capture dark detail. This is signal-to-noise ratio (S/N ratio).

■ Limits and Needs

The tonal resolution of a scanner can be limited either by the number of bits per pixel captured or, more often, by the signal-to-noise ratio of the scanner. Signal-to-noise ratio is the ratio of the usable signal, in this case the image, to noise in a scan. A high degree of noise can mask the shadow detail in an image, regardless of the number of bits captured. An analogy is a very high-quality stereo system installed in a convertible car driving with the top down. The stereo reproduces all the subtleties in the music but the traffic noises drown them out.

When is tonal resolution important?

Tonal resolution is most important in scans of the following:

- Dark or underexposed images.
- Photo transparencies such as slides.
- Images in which the important detail is in a dark area.

While it may appear that tonal resolution is most important in professional scanning, in fact, high tonal resolution is also important for the business or home user.

- The business user, unlike a professional photographer, often has imperfect images such as underexposed photos.
- The subject of a photo may not be what the business user wants; in a group portrait the user may want just one person in the group.

■ Tonal Transformations

Scanned images undergo a number of tonal transformations during the scan process. Examples include gamma compensation, shadow enhancement and exposure correction (brightness and contrast) or auto-exposure. The quality of the tonal transformations plays a very important role in determining the final image quality, particularly for scans of photographs.

Quantization in tonal transformations

Limited tonal resolution or poor tonal transformations cause quantization in the image. Quantization is the artificial forcing of adjacent gray levels into the same gray level in an image, creating contours or bands in the image. Quantization in a scan can be intensified by many of the tools used during or after the scan, such as gamma correction and sharpening. (Gamma correction is covered in Chapter 10 • "More on Image Quality" on page 121, and sharpening is covered in Chapter 9 • "Setting the Controls" on page 109.) Figure 15-1 shows two scans, one with quantization resulting from 8-bit tonal resolution, the second with improved tonal resolution from a 10-bit scanner.

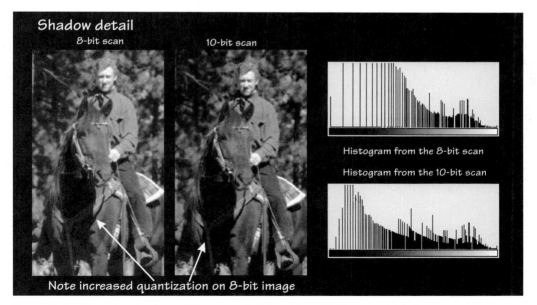

Figure 15-1 Quantization in an 8-bit scan (left) and in a 10-bit scan (right)

In Figure 15-1, the quantization is due to poor tonal transformations. Notice how the gray tones in the image on the left do not change smoothly from dark to light. The scanner on the right exhibits much better tonal resolution and tonal transformations.

When are tonal transformations important?

Tonal transformations are important in:

- Almost all images—because gamma compensation is almost always applied.
- Dark or underexposed images.
- Photo transparencies such as slides.
- Images in which the important detail is in a dark area.

■ Limitations of the Typical Test

The typical test for shadow detail is scanning the dark end of a grayscale reflectance target to see how many grayscale steps (areas of increasingly darker gray) the scanner can distinguish. The test is often done with default exposure settings, which is the primary limitation:

- Some scanners, particularly scanners with more than 8 bits of tonal resolution, have capabilities that aren't evident when scanning with default exposure settings for dark images.
- The quantization introduced by the scanner can be mistaken for resolution of additional gray levels. Using a tone map to enhance shadows makes it easier to distinguish between true tonal changes and the effects of quantization.
- Signal-to-noise ratio is not typically measured.

■ Recommended Tests

There are three recommended tests related to the tonal resolution of the scanner. First is a test to measure the ability of a scanner to resolve a grayscale step target. Second is a test of signal-to-noise ratio. Third, a test for quantization or the quality of tonal transformations.

Test one: tonal resolution test

The test we recommend is very similar to the typical test described above except that the exposure is set to enhance shadow detail. Scans of a very dark grayscale target are examined with image-editing software to see how many grayscale steps are distinguishable. All quality 24-bit scanners should be able to fully resolve the grayscale steps for a reflective test target.

For this test, a high-quality, continuous tone step grayscale target is required. Targets such as these are available from numerous sources, or the gray step target on the Applied Images test target can be used.

Step 1: scan the grayscale step target with the following settings:

- 150-ppi sampling rate
- Sharpening should be applied consistently across all scanners.
- Grayscale image type (an optional color scan test is described in step 5).
- Gamma correction of 2.2.
- Auto-exposure should be used if available.
- Optionally, a shadow-enhancing tone map can be applied to the scan to bring out fullest ability of a scanner, or the brightness and contrast settings can be modified. The goal is to lighten the darkest patches on the test target.

Note: If gamma correction or shadow enhancement is not done, the results will be misleading because the darkest patches on the gray patch will likely not be distinguishable. This is a failure of the test procedure, not the scanner.

Step 2: open the image in an image editor such as Adobe Photoshop. (The following procedure assumes Photoshop 4.0).

Step 3: in Photoshop, select the "Image/Adjust Levels" function (Ctrl-L).

Step 4: in the "Levels" dialog box:

- Make sure the "Preview" checkbox is selected.
- Make sure the image is visible behind the "Levels" dialog box.
- Below the input levels "Histogram," grab the right most slider—the highlight slider (it looks like a small triangle) and drag it left.

- Periodically release the highlight slider and examine the image. You will see the darkest steps in the gray step target are lightened as you move the slider left.
- As you move the slider left, you will be able to see if the scanner could distinguish all the gray step targets or if some were indistinguishable. This is an indication of the tonal resolution of the scanner.

Figure 15-2 shows two images from two scanners after the "Levels" tool has been used, as described in step 4. Note the difference in the number of gray levels visible.

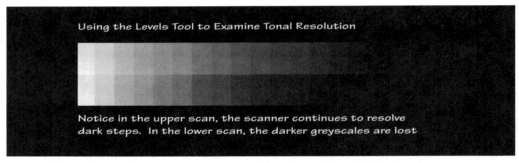

Figure 15-2   Enhanced tonal resolution using 8-bit (bottom) and 10-bit (top) scanners

Step 5: (optional) If desired, you can repeat this test using a color scan of the grayscale target. This allows measurement of the tonal resolution for each color channel. Unbalanced signal-to-noise ratio on various channels can lead to color shifts in the image.

If this is done:

- Before you open the "Levels" dialog, make sure you select one channel
- To select a channel:
    - Use the Ctrl-1, Ctrl-2, Ctrl-3 shortcut keys to select red, green or blue or use the "Channels Info" box to select a channel ("Windows/ Show Channels").

Test two: tonal transformation test (quantization)

In this test we scan a continuously varying grayscale (not a step scale) and look for quantization in the image.

Step 1: obtain or create an appropriate test target.

- The easiest way to create this target is to simply prop the lid of the scanner up and scan the lid. Because the lid surface becomes farther and farther away from the scanner, the light reflected will decrease continuously. **Note:** This assumes the scanner has a white document cover. If this is not the case, attach white paper to it.
- Note, scanners with more light available will require the lid to be lifted further.
- Stray light around the scanner may impact this test, and it may be necessary to cover the scanner with a black cloth cover.
- The goal is to have the darkest part of the scan be very dark (ideally 0 counts).

Step 2: scan a narrow vertical strip that includes a light to a very dark part of the image with the following settings.

- 150-ppi scan.
- Grayscale scan (an optional color test is discussed in step 5 of the previous test).
- Gamma compensation of 2.2.
- Auto-exposure should be used if available.
- Sharpening should be applied consistently across scanners. Note: Sharpening may either hide or exaggerate quantization.

Step 3: examine the image in an image-editor for visible step or contours in the image.

- In addition to visually examining the image, the "Image/Histogram" tool may reveal steps or gaps in the tonal response of the scanner.
- A quality tonal transformation should result in few or no steps in the image.

Step 4: (optional) repeat the test using a color image type.

- Most scanners, because they are three-exposure scanners, will have color fringes in this type of a scan. Those color fringes reveal limitations in the color separation technology, but are not necessarily the result of poor tonal resolution or transformations.

■ When examining the color image, examine each color plane independently (use the "Channels" dialog to view only red, green or blue).

Test three: signal-to-noise ratio test

This test examines the effect of random noise on the scan quality. Typically, random noise, rather than bit depth, is the primary limiting factor of the tonal resolution of the scanner. Measuring the signal-to-noise ratio of a scanner can be quite difficult, and special care is required. This test consists of scanning a grayscale target twice, subtracting the two images and examining the standard deviation of the results. Subtraction should remove all non-noise components, and the standard deviation is a good measure of random noise.

Special concerns:

■ The test target must be a high-quality, continuous tone target.
■ Gamma correction must be disabled or compensated for in this test.
■ Dirt, dust, scratches, fingerprints, etc. can have a significant impact on the results of this test. Although the test attempts to eliminate the effects of noise, cleanliness is key.

Step 1: obtain a target. This test uses a step grayscale target such as the one on the Applied Images target.

■ Assure the target is clean and in good condition.
■ Assure the scanner is clean!

Step 2: perform several practice scans to allow the scanner lamp to warm up and reach a stable temperature.

■ Alternatively, you may wish to test with a cold lamp to see what the "first scan of the day" is like.

Step 3: perform two independent scans of the grayscale step target with the following settings:

■ Color image type (24 bit).
■ 150 ppi.

- Sharpening should be applied consistently across all scanners. Using the default amount of sharpening is probably appropriate. However, you can optionally test with various sharpening levels.
- Since sharpening can dramatically increase noise, it is probably appropriate to scan with a normal or default level of sharpening.
- Perform the two scans of exactly the same area of the test target.
- If possible, scan twice without exiting the scanning software.
- In some scanners, the software will exit after each final scan, requiring you reselect the grayscale for the second scan. In this case, scan an area slightly larger than the grayscale. The images will be cropped in the image editor to match.

For this test gamma correction must be:

- Turned off or gamma of 1.0 (recommended).
- Or consistent across all scanners (use 2.2).
- Or compensated for after the scan (see below).

Warning: If different gamma compensations are used for different scanners, the results cannot be compared across scanners and may be misleading!

Step 4: open the two images in Photoshop.

Step 5: if the two scans were not of the exactly the same location, crop the images to exactly the same size and location in Photoshop by carefully selecting the images and cropping them.

Step 6: adjust for different gamma compensation.

- If all the scans were done with gamma of 1.0 (or no calibration), this step is not necessary.
- If some scans were done with gamma compensation other than 1.0, the effect of that gamma compensation must be removed before the test can proceed.

To remove gamma compensation, use the procedure described in "Removing the Effect of Gamma Correction" in Chapter 13 • "Resolution" on page 173.

Warning: Failure to remove the effect of having a gamma compensation value not equal to 1.0 during the scan will invalidate the test. Applying gamma during the scan amplifies the noise in the image. Comparing a scan with gamma compensation turned on to one with gamma set to 1.0 is invalid and misleading.

Step 7: subtract the two images from each other:

- Select "Image/Calculations."
- Select image one as source 1.
- Select the second image a source 2.
- Select "Subtract" as the blending method (not "Difference").
- Enter 128 into the "Offset."
- Select "New" for the result to create a new image.
- Press "OK."

Step 8: verify that the subtraction eliminated dust and scratches:

- Examine the resulting image for dust that remains after the subtraction. If the two scans were well aligned, dust should essentially disappear. Check this by locating a dust speck in one of the original scans, then examining the same location in the subtracted scan
- If dust is not eliminated because the two scans did not align, re-crop and re-subtract the images.
- **Note:** Some scanners may not be able to repeat exactly the same scans due to inaccuracy in the scanning mechanism. In this case, the elimination of dust may not be possible, and noise results will suffer (as is appropriate for lower-quality scanners).

Step 9: in the resulting subtracted image, any structure visible represents random noise. To analytically calculate the noise:

- For each (or a selected few) gray step in the resultant images use the selection tool to select the patch.
- Open the histogram tool ("Image/Histogram") and record the median and standard deviation for each patch. Note the median is typically close to 128 because that was the offset used in the calculation.

Step 10:calculate the signal-to-noise ratio.

- Signal-to-noise is calculated by dividing the median of each gray step (or selected ones) in one of the original scans to the standard deviation of that patch in the new subtracted image—as follows:
- Open one of the original scans.
- Select a patch in Photoshop using the selection tool.
- Use the "/Image/Histogram" tool to measure the median of the patch. Examine each color independently.
- Open the subtracted image in Photoshop.
- Select the same patch in the subtracted image.
- Use the "/Image/Histogram" tool to measure the standard deviation of the patch. Examine each color independently.
- Calculate S/N as (median from original scan)/(standard deviation from subtracted scan).

Chapter 16

Image Noise

Image noise is a distortion or unwanted signal introduced into the captured image by a scanner. Image noise can take the form of random distortions (snow) or correlated distortions (streaks or patterns). Typically, noise is injected into the analog voltage signal captured by a CCD before it is converted to a digital number. That signal is quite small and susceptible to interference. Once digitized by the scanner analog-to-digital converter, an image is immune to the addition of noise. However, further processing such as sharpening can extenuate the impact of noise in an image.

■ Impact of Noise on Bit Depth and Density Range

Image noise will typically limit the effective bit depth of a scanner. Today, more and more scanner manufacturers are claiming 30 or more bits of image data per pixel. That claim is usually based upon the number of bits in the analog-to-digital converter without regard to the noise in the system. While it may be true that a scanner is converting data with 30 bpp of precision, if the data being converted is noisy, many of the benefits of the higher bit depth are lost. See Chapter 15 • "Tonal Resolution, Density Range and Bit Depth" on page 213, for more information on image noise and bit depth.

229

■ Correlated Noise

Correlated image noise is noise that appears in a regular pattern, such as a streak, diagonal or horizontal line. Correlated noise is much more objectionable because people see streaks and patterns more easily.

Streak noise

Correlated noise is a recognizable pattern of change in the image file. The change is an increase or a decrease in the brightness of the pixels compared to what they should be. The pattern can be horizontally across a raster line, vertically down through the raster lines, or diagonally down and across the raster lines. Vertical correlated noise is often called "streak noise" and is a common problem with CCD technology. The most common source of streak noise is poor PRNU or DSNU compensation, explained in Chapter 10 • "More on Image Quality" on page 121.

A noise that is correlated with the exposure of a raster line causes horizontal streaks across the image. It can result from a fluctuation in the intensity of the light, causing a change in the exposure for that raster line, or by a change in the DC ground for the CCD. All the elements in the CCD array use the same DC ground, and a momentary change in this reference affects the whole array.

Crosstalk

Diagonal correlated noise can be the result of crosstalk from the digital electronics to the analog electronics. The diagonal streak caused by correlated noise represents an interaction between the digital-clock frequency and the mechanical movement of the carriage. Digital signals are usually between 3 V and 5 V, large when compared to the CCD signals, which are usually less than 1.0 V.

Transitions

The intervals at which the digital signals change, called "transitions," are indicated by the digital clock. At every clock pulse, significant voltage may surge through the scanner. If the digital and analog grounds are not adequately shielded, the surge can cause a "bump" in the analog signal.

Correlated noise can be reduced by improving the isolation of the digital electronics.

■ Non-Correlated Noise

Random Distortions

Non-correlated noise is a random distortion in the analog signal causing snow, speckles or random spots throughout the image. The distortion can be the result of electronic noise in the amplifiers or the CCD array, electrical spikes somewhere in the system (the scanner, printer, or monitor) or random fluctuations in the scanner light.

The primary impact of excessive non-correlated noise is to reduce the quality of scan in the darker parts of the image, and to limit the tonal resolution of the scanner. While non-correlated noise is discussed here, **the test for this is covered in** Chapter 15 • "Tonal Resolution, Density Range and Bit Depth" on page 213.

Causes of random noise

An electronic system always has noise. But the signal-to-noise ratio of the analog electronics can be increased so that the effects of the noise are less noticeable. In addition, a better optical system, a brighter light source, or a longer exposure are ways to increase the signal-to-noise ratio. Effective use of the dynamic range of the scanner can also impact the signal-to-noise ratio of the scanner. When scanning a light object in a well-designed scanner, the CCD will be operating near its saturation level and produce the highest possible voltage for that pixel. (Saturation level is light intensity that exceeds the maximum level designed for a CCD.) This maximizes the signal-to-noise ratio in the scanner.

Random electronic noise can also cause correlated noise. If there is random noise in the PRNU compensation, it is memorized, causing a CCD element to be incorrectly calibrated. This in turn causes vertical correlated noise. If random noise momentarily changes the DC reference voltage or changes the light intensity, a horizontal streak results in noise.

■ Comparison of Correlated and Non-correlated Noise

Correlated noise is worse than non-correlated noise because it's more noticeable. For example, if the signal in a television set is weak, the screen has snow or speckles on it (non-correlated noise), but the noise is fairly uniform throughout the picture. The quality is lower but it's not that bad.

If the signal is strong and another periodic signal causes interference (correlated noise), the image is sharp but there may be lines or other regular patterns throughout the image. The lines or patterns are worse than the snow because they are in such sharp contrast with the rest of the image. Typically, non-correlated noise can be 5–10 times larger than a corresponding correlated noise before it becomes noticeable.

When considering noise in CIELAB space, noise that causes a streak with a ΔL of 0.5 or greater when compared to the surrounding area is probably noticeable because it is correlated. For random noise, a level ΔL of 1.0 is probably not noticeable.

■ Typical Tests

Image noise is generally not tested.

■ Recommended Test

The test for random image noise is described in the signal-to-noise ratio test in Chapter 15 • "Tonal Resolution, Density Range and Bit Depth" on page 213. The following test is for correlated noise. This test involves scanning a wide gray patch located on the Applied Images test target. Two scans are done, one with the patch oriented across the page and one oriented down the page. The images are filtered in Photoshop with a custom filter that will emphasize streaks and de-emphasize random noise and the signal-to-noise ratio is calculated.

Step 1: Locate an appropriate test target.
The full-width gray strip located on the Applied Images test target is designed for this test.

Step 2: perform a scan of the gray strip with the target oriented horizontally across the page.
For the scans, use the following settings:

■ Scan the image as a color image.

- Scan with gamma compensation set to a gamma of 1.0. If you cannot set the gamma compensation to 1.0, you will need to remove the effect of gamma compensation after the scan. Note: If gamma compensation is not disabled (set to 1.0) or adjusted for the image, noise will be overestimated when compared to other scanners.
- Scan at the optical sampling rate of the scanner. Recall that the optical sampling rate, often called the "optical resolution," is defined by the CCD direction, not down the page. Use this for both scans. For instance, for a scanner claiming 600x1200 (*x* by *y*) optical "resolution," scan at 600x600 for both scans.

Step 3: open the image file in Photoshop.

If the image was scanned with a gamma other than 1.0, you must adjust the image to remove the effect of gamma compensation. See "Removing the Effects of Gamma Compensation" in Chapter 13 • "Resolution" on page 173.

Step 4: create a custom filter with the kernel.

- Select "Filter/Other/Custom."
- Enter the following values into the kernel. (The 0 entries can be either 0 or blank.)

0	0	1	0	0
0	0	1	0	0
0	0	1	0	0
0	0	1	0	0
0	0	1	0	0

- Enter a "Scale Factor" of 5.
- Apply the filter to the image several times. (Apply the filter the same number of times for each scanner.)

Step 5: in the filtered image, vertical streaks will have been emphasized and random noise will have been minimized.

To calculate the signal to noise ratio:

- Select several regions in the image using the selection tool. It is not recommended you calculate the noise based upon the entire scan, but rather on small (1 inch or less) portions of the scan.

- Open the histogram ("Images/Histogram").
- Record the median and standard deviation.
- Calculate the signal-to-noise ratio as median/(standard deviation). Bigger is better.

Step 6: measure row-correlated noise

To measure row-correlated noise, repeat the test from step 2 with the following modifications:

- Orient the test target vertically (up and down the page) instead of horizontally.
- Before applying the filter in Photoshop, rotate the image 90 degrees using "Image/Rotate Canvas/ 90 CW."

<big>**17**</big>   Chapter

Uniform Illumination

To produce consistent, high-quality scans, a scanner needs to have a light source that uniformly lights the original object during the scan. When illumination isn't uniform, lightness varies within a scan or between several scans. If the spectral output of the lamp changes, color in the scan can vary. For a discussion of the various light sources used in scanners, see Chapter 11 • "Some Scanner Technologies" on page 139. The lamp in a scanner is a critical part of achieving accurate color in the scanner. Refer to Chapter 19 • "Color Fidelity" on page 249 for a discussion of how lamps impact the color accuracy of the scanner.

■ Types of Lamps

Most scanners use fluorescent lamps, which are well suited for scanning. They are efficient and cool and give a wide illumination spectrum. But they can also vary both in the color of the light and intensity over time and across the lamp. They are particularly sensitive to variations in temperature so they may change as the lamp warms up.

Other kinds of lamps are becoming more common. Xenon gas discharge and cold-cathode fluorescent are two relative new light sources in scanners. Cold-cathode fluorescent lamps, in particular, have been receiving a large amount of emphasis—probably more properly termed "hype." The type of light source used in a scanner represents an engineering trade-off, and each of the three common light sources has advantages and disadvantages. This is illustrated by the fact that one major scanner manufacturer uses all three types of lamps in different scanning applications.

Warning: Most scanner lamps are not customer replaceable and the scanners are not UL listed for customer replacement of bulbs. However, some manufacturers supply lamps and replacement instructions to customers anyway, on request. This is a violation of UL product safety regulations and a safety concern for customers.

■ Intensity and Temperature

Lamp intensity often changes dramatically with lamp temperature. (Increasing temperature does not always mean increasing intensity!) Some scanners control the intensity of lighting with a feedback loop that monitors intensity and lamp color during scans and compensates to maintain uniformity. In addition, lighting variations across the copyboard are usually measured and adjusted automatically during photo response nonuniformity (PRNU) compensation. PRNU is the pixel-to-pixel variation in a CCD array's response to a fixed intensity light. See Chapter 10 • "More on Image Quality" on page 121 for an explanation of PRNU compensation.

Other, typically lower-cost scanners, may assume the lamp is stable and not compensate. This assumption may be valid for some lamps or after the lamp has been on for a long time (hours). Typically, a scanner that assumes the lamp is stable will show some non-uniformity during long scans or during scans that occur shortly after the lamp has been turned on.

In some scanners, the lamp is on all the time to keep a steady temperature. (A steady temperature produces stable light.) These scanners often have the most stable lighting, but their operating cost is higher and they may need more warm-up time. In addition, most scanners that leave the lamp on all the time cannot compensate for CCD dark voltage before each scan; however, some may monitor dark voltage and turn the lamp off to re-calibrate when needed. See Chapter 10 • "More on Image Quality" on page 121 for an explanation of dark-voltage compensation.

■ Blowout and Clipping

Uneven lighting during a scan has the most effect on the highlights in an image (brightest portions). Increases in light after the exposure is set can overexpose (called a blowout) a highlight during the scan. A less dramatic, but still important effect is clipping of the shadows caused by a decrease in lighting. In the scan, a clipped shadow appears as pure black; a blown-out light area appears as pure white.

Clipping or blowout can happen on one channel (red, green or blue) of a color scanner and appear as sudden color shifts in shadows or light areas. Since the intensity of most lamps increases as the lamp warms up, clipping is less likely than blowout.

In Figure 17-1 the image on the left is exposed correctly and the image on the right has blown-out highlights. The overexposure is exaggerated in this image, but even a small change in lighting can cause blowouts.

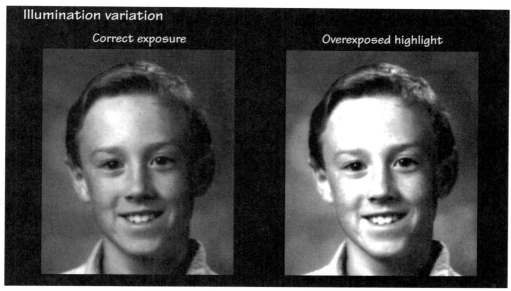

Figure 17-1 A blowout caused by varying light

Although it is hard to quantify an acceptable amount, some degree of light variation in desktop scanners is common. Variation usually shows up near the edges of the page or at the top and bottom. Slight variation at the edges is less important than variation in the center of the image, which is typically the subject of the image.

■ Design Trade-off

Achieving uniform lighting is a design trade-off. Some scanners keep the lamp on all the time, which means long warm-up times, higher power consumption, and burned out bulbs. Others have stable lamps with more limited spectral content (Xenon and noble gas discharge lamps). These methods improve uniformity at the cost of durability, operating expense or color fidelity. Best is a scanner that offers an acceptable degree of uniformity without leaving the lamp on all the time or sacrificing spectral content in the light.

Scanning software can help

Scanner software can also reduce the effects of lighting variations by setting the exposure to leave an appropriate margin for light intensity changes during the scan. For example, software can leave a margin between the highlight value of the image and the maximum value the scanner can return. If the exposure is set to return 255 for the image highlight, a very small increase in the brightness of the light can cause blowout. This situation needs software that is tuned to the scanner hardware and scanner lighting that is well characterized.

Some software provides an excessive margin, with two resulting problems:

- Less contrast, causing muddy images.
- More quantization as a result of tonal compensation by image-editing software to correct the low contrast.

Another solution, used by some scanners, is setting the exposure so those white parts of the image always clip to pure white (return a value of 255). If highlights are always clipped, (always blown-out) lighting variations are hidden. Some scanner hardware and software are designed so that anything above 85% reflectance is treated as 100% reflectance. The disadvantage is that detail in the bright part of the image is lost, exposure is not optimal, and images may have too much contrast.

■ Light Sources

The following sections review the three major types of lamps used in scanners:

- Xenon gas discharge.
- Hot cathode fluorescent.
- Cold cathode fluorescent.

Xenon gas discharge

Green xenon bulbs have been used in many scanners. White xenon bulbs are less common but are starting to appear in scanners. Here are some of the advantages and disadvantages of Xenon gas discharge lamps:

Table 17-1   Advantages and Disadvantages of Xenon Gas Discharge Lamps

Advantages	Disadvantages
Very fast turn on (less than one second)	Low efficiency (light out, versus power in)
Very stable light source (virtually no variation in output intensity or color)	Non-ideal spectrum (peaks and valleys in the spectrum can cause color errors)
Physically small (can install in small devices)	Physically small (limits area illuminated)
Long life	Very high voltage drive (typically greater than 2000 volts)

Hot cathode fluorescent

The hot cathode fluorescent lamp is the most common fluorescent lamp made and is widely used in many applications. In scanners, there have been some concerns about the lifetime and the temperature of this type of lamp. However, these concerns are only valid for scanners that do not turn off the lamp between scans.

Table 17-2   *Advantages and Disadvantages of Hot Cathode Fluorescent Lamps*

Advantages	Disadvantages
Very efficient (one of the best)	Less stable output (requires closed loop control of light output and color balance; a more complex system)
Very readily available (this is what is used in light fixtures)	Large
Broad spectrum good for color accuracy	
Spectrum can be adjusted (widely available phosphors for tuning of the output spectrum)	
Relatively fast turn on (3-5 seconds if properly controlled)	Not "instant" on
Moderate life of 1000 hours (sufficient for a scanner that does not leave the lamp on all the time)	Burns out if always left on
Cool (if not left on continually)	

Cold cathode fluorescent

Cold cathode fluorescent lamps are relatively new light sources with claims of better lamp lifetime, lower operating temperature, and improved color accuracy. These claims may be true, depending on what other type of lamp is used for the comparison. The lifetime and temperature claims are only relevant when compared to hot cathode lamps in scanners which leave their lamps on continually. Claims of improved color are unfounded over hot cathode lamps because the spectral outputs of cold and hot cathode lamps can be made similar. In fact, most colt cathode lamps are optimized for intensity, not spectral quality, so they may not work well for color scanning.

Table 17-3   *Cold Cathode Fluorescent Compared to Hot Cathode Fluorescent Lamps*

Advantages of cold cathode	Disadvantages of cold cathode
Long life of 5000–10,000 hours—only an advantage if the scanner lamp is always left on.	Very slow turn on. The lamp must be left on continually or the user must endure a long turn on time. Typical turn on time is 30 seconds to several minutes.
Cooler—only when compared to a scanner in which the lamp is left on continuously.	Not environmentally friendly—continuous power consumption because the lamp is on all the time.
Cheaper—This is the primary advantage.	Potentially poor color—most are optimized for use as back light in computer flat panel displays and provide poor spectral quality for scanning.

In summary, cold cathode lamps are an advantage only for those scanners designed to leave the lamp on continuously, because they address lamp life limits for continuously "on" lamps. Indeed, the primary driving factor for cold cathode lamps is cost. Cold cathode lamps are a disadvantage for those scanners designed to turn on the lamp only when needed because they impose turn on time limitations or increase the standby power used.

■ Limitations of Typical Test

Since uniform lighting is not often included in reviews, there is no typical test.

■ Recommended Test

The test we recommend is scanning a uniform midtone target such as a gray card or gray paper. We calculate the average intensity in small blocks and compare the variation in those averages across and down the page. Scans of high-reflectance targets can also be used to look for clipping.

Consider testing lamps both cold (just turned on) and warm (after several scans). One case represents a typical case, the other the best the scanner can achieve. For scanners with lighting-stability controls, the test should be done with the controls set to maximize lighting stability. Using contrast controls or automatic exposure to exaggerate lighting variations is likely to over emphasize the variation. For this reason, we use default exposure settings and no automatic exposures.

We test variations during a scan and between one scan and another. Scans of midtone targets illustrate the variation and scans of high-reflectance targets show clipping.

Detailed test procedure for uniform lighting

Step 1: obtain an appropriate target

This test uses the full width gray strip on the Applied Images test target or (optionally) a full page gray target (not a printed dither!)

Step 2: scan the entire Applied Images test target twice.

Once oriented across the scanner bed, once oriented down the scanner bed. One scan of a full page grey target can be used. Use the following settings:

- Gamma correction 1.0 or disabled.
- 150-ppi, 24-bit color.
- Default exposure or automatic-exposure based upon the full target.
- Consider performing several scans to allow the lamp to stabilize if this is the first scan of the day. Allowing the scanner to stabilize demonstrated the best the scanner can do.
- On the other hand, testing the "first" scan after a period of inactivity is more typically what users do.

Step 3: open the images in Photoshop and measure the variation in the gray stripe.

- If gamma compensation other than 1.0 was used, remove the effect of the gamma compensation as described in "Removing the effect of gamma correction" on page 191.
- Select the small portions of the gray strip across the target, usually one at each end and one in the middle is enough. Avoid dust specks or streaks, but note them as an image quality defect.
- For each portion, use the "Image/Histogram" tool to record the median red, green and blue counts.

Step 4: calculate L* for each measured portion.

- For each area measured above, calculate L* from the RGB counts.
- Calculate ΔL* for the scan. Refer to Appendix A • "CIELAB to RGB Calculations and NTSC Equations" on page 273 for more information.

Step 5: compare ΔL* to an ΔL* of 1.0 (just noticeable difference) or 5.0 (pretty obvious).

- In the above, consider that a gentle change of even 5.0 may not be very visible. An abrupt change of 1.0 to 3.0 counts may be quite visible.

Step 6: optional—calculate C* and ΔC* to see if the color changed noticeably.

Chapter 18

Color Registration

Color registration error is misalignment in the scanner red, green and blue (RGB) channels. Color registration error will vary with the color separation technology used and may be quite different in the *x* and *y* directions.

■ Overview

Color scanners capture a color image as red, green, and blue (RGB) components. Depending on the color separation technology used in the scanner, the colors may be captured in three passes or one pass and in three exposures or one exposure, (see "Passes and Exposures" on page 142). Regardless of the number of passes or exposures, there is typically some misalignment in the RGB components. The misalignment appears like a colored fringe on the edges of sharp lines in the image. The degree of misalignment depends on the quality of the optics and, in the case of *y*-misregistration in 3-exposure scanners, the uniformity and consistency of the scanner optical carriage motion. Color separation is discussed in Chapter 11 • "Some Scanner Technologies" on page 139.

In earlier scanners, color registration error was a major problem. Edition 2 of this *Reviewing and Testing Desktop Scanners* reported, "Reputable scanners today rarely have enough color registration error to be a problem." Unfortunately, for two reasons, color misregistration is again a problem:

■ The drive for cost savings, design shortcuts, and smaller size has again

243

resulted in scanners with objectionable color misregistration.

■ At the same time, a change in the nature of scanning has resulted in tighter requirements for color misregistration. The use of scanners is changing, and quality requirements must keep pace.

In the past, images in which registration error would be evident, such as scans of line drawings, were typically not scanned in color but in black and white. In this type of image, color misregistration causes slightly lower resolution (MTF) because the misaligned colors will blur the edges but is not typically objectionable unless extreme. Today use of color in scans of drawings or mixed images and text has increased dramatically. This is driven mostly by color copying needs, but also by document capture, color fax and a general desire to preserve color when scanning complex originals.

■ Typical Test

A typical test for color registration error is scanning black and white line drawings in 24-bit color mode and very high sample rates (600 ppi), then viewing the image, greatly enlarged, on a computer display. One drawback is that this is not representative of how scanners are used, even today with an increased emphasis on color scanning. Another drawback is that it is hard to relate misalignment measured this way to real-world scanning. Some misregistration is usually evident, yet the question is how important is the error.

Scanning drawings at 600 ppi in 24-bit mode is cumbersome and not realistic. For example, to scan an 8.5 x 11 inch page at 600 ppi and 24 bits would result in a 93.6 Mbyte file with much more data than is useful, even on 600-dpi color laser printers. In fact, most color printers (claims not withstanding) provide, at best, 300 dpi dot placement. A more reasonable test would be to send a 300-ppi, 24-bit scan of text to a high-quality color printer and see if the misregistration is evident in the printout—except that many printers have as much or more misregistration error than a quality scanner! In addition, dithers or halftones may introduce what appears to be misregistration in a printed output.

■ Recommended Test

There are two recommended tests:

1. Measurement of misregistration due to optical misalignment.

2. *Y*-direction misalignment due to inconsistent carriage motion.

The first test is similar to the typical test but is done in a way that enables you to make repeatable and reasonably quantitative measurements. Remember, only gross errors are important for most users. For a 600-ppi scanner, errors on the order of one pixel are common and not very important. Errors of on the order of one pixel on 300-ppi scanners are probably excessive.

A second test looks for *y*-direction registration errors as a result of poor control of the optical carriage motion down the page in three-exposure scanners using, such as those using on-chip filters.

Test 1: measurement of misregistration due to optical misalignment

Step 1: obtain a Target.

To test color misregistration you need a target with very sharp lines. Most printed targets aren't suitable. The coarsest (30-lppi) MTF pattern on the Applied Images test target is quite suitable for this test.

Step 2: scan the target twice.

Do two scans of the test target, one with the target test pattern lines oriented in the x direction and one with the lines oriented in the y-direction. Scan only a small area (1/4 inch square). The scan is enlarged 10 times during the test so even a 1/4 inch square scan will result in a 6.75-megabyte image file. Scan in 24-bit color, near the center of the scanner bed, and use the scanner's optical sampling rate. Set the controls as follows.

- Scan at the optical sampling rate of the scanner (e.g., 600 ppi).
- Scan 24-bit color.
- Don't use sharpening or use similar sharpening on all scanners.
- Use default exposure or automatic exposure and use the same settings for both scans. Exposure differences between scanners are minimized by the test procedure.
- Scan with a gamma correction of 1.0 if possible. If not, remove the effects of gamma correction from the scan.
- Avoid clipping: the brightest area in the image should be less than 255 counts and the darkest more than 0 counts.

Step 3: measure the color registration error.

Measure the color registration error by following these steps:

1. Enlarge the image 10 times using linear interpolation.

2. Separate the image into the red, green and blue channels.

3. Subtract the red channels from the green, the blue channels from the green, and the red channels from the blue.

4. Use a threshold to convert the subtracted channel images to binary (1-bit) images.

5. Examine the subtracted images to find red-to-green, blue-to-green and red-to-blue registration error.

6. (Optional) Repeat the test for several locations across the page and down the page. RGB misregistration may vary significantly around the scan bed.

Here is a step-by-step procedure for achieving this in Photoshop:

1. Open the image file you have just created.

2. If gamma other than 1.0 was used, remove the effect of gamma as described in "Eliminating the Effect of Gamma Compensation" in Chapter 13 • "Resolution" on page 173.

3. Select "Image/Image Size."

4. Make sure the "Resample Image" checkbox is checked.

5. Select "Bilinear" interpolation method.

6. Set the width units to "Percent" and enter "1000%."

7. Select "Image/Calculations" and use the following settings:

   - For source 1 channel, select "Red."
   - For source 2 channel, select "Green."
   - For "Blending," select "Subtract."
   - For "Offset," enter "128."
   - For "Result," select channel "New."
   - Click "OK." This procedure will create a new channel, called "Channel #4" which shows the registration error between the red and green channels, magnified by 10.

8. Make sure the new channel (#4) is the only channel selected for editing. Press Ctrl-4 to select Channel 4.

9. Adjust the new channel to show sharp edges as follows:

   ■ Select "Image/Adjust Levels."
   ■ In the "Levels" dialog, move the left slider to just below 128 and the right slider to just above 128. Click "OK.'

10. The image in Channel #4 now shows gray with white and black stripes. The width of the black and white stripes indicates the registration error between red and green. Measure the width of the stripes as follows:

    ■ Make sure the "Information" window is open ("Windows/Show Info")
    ■ Using the selection tool, select a box the same width as one of the black or white stripes. Be sure to select just the black area, or just the white area, do not include any of the gray area.
    ■ Note the width of the selection in the info box beside "W." Make sure the units are pixels ("File/Preferences/Units and Rulers").
    ■ The width, in pixels, is 10 times the registration error.

11. Calculate the registration error.

    ■ Divide the width in pixels, measured above, by 10. For instance, if the width of a stripe was 8 pixels, the registration error is 0.8 pixels.
    ■ Remember, this registration error is in pixels. A 0.8-pixel error on a 600-ppi scanner is 1/2 the error of a 0.8-pixel error on a 300-ppi scanner.

12. Repeat steps 7 through 12 using channels red and blue, and blue and green in step 7.

13. Repeat for *y*-direction.

14. (Optional) Repeat at various sample rates and various locations to see how uniform the optics are and how well scaling routines operate.

Test 2: y-direction misalignment due to inconsistent carriage motion

This test examines for misregistration due to optical carriage motion problems. This test uses a set of slanted lines like those found on the Applied Images test target, and the following procedures assume you are using that target. As an alternative, a target with a set of slightly slanted black and white lines is useful.

Step 1: do full-width scans.

Perform full-width scans of the test target including the heavy black slanted lines. Perform the scans at various sample rates such as 72, 100, 133, 150, 200, 300, 400 and 600 ppi. Note: the misregistration may only be apparent at certain sample rates!

Step 2: examine for streaks or fringes.

Examine the image in an image editor for horizontal colored streaks or for colored fringes on the slanted test lines.

Step 3 (optional):perform the calculations used in the RGB registration test previously described.

Step 4: Redo the test at several locations on scanner bed.

Perform the test at several locations down the scan bed to see if the error is progressively worse as the scan proceeds.

Step 5: test at a high sample rate.

Perform the test once at very high sample rates (600 ppi or above), which forces the scanner to pause during scanning. This tests the reposition capability of the scanner and exposes misregistration.

19

Color Fidelity

The color accuracy of a scanner depends on many factors, including the scanner, but also including the original and the light source under which the original is usually viewed. Often more of a limit in color fidelity, when using a scanner, is the output device and how well the scanner and output device were matched.

■ What Determines the Color of an Object

When you look at an object, three elements determine its color: the object's spectral reflectance characteristics, the spectral content of the light source, and the human vision system. A scanner is very similar. The color a scanner sees depends on the object, the light source in the scanner, and the characteristics of the detector. Because there are major differences in the light source and detector used by your eyes and those in a scanner, a scanner will not see the color of an object exactly the same way you do.

At best, a scanner will capture a metameric match

At best, the scanner captures a metameric match to what you see. A "Metameric match" means that the colors will appear the same under certain lighting conditions. However, they may look completely different under other lighting conditions. We've all experienced this. For example, consider how different the color of a car may appear when the car is viewed under a mercury street lamp at night. One design goal of a general-purpose scanner will be to "see" colors as closely as possible to the way a person sees in typical lighting conditions. This chapter discusses one way to measure how well a scanner achieves this.

■ The Object

The most important determiner of the color appearance of an object is its spectral reflectance or transmission. Specifically, how does the object transmit or reflect various wavelengths of light? In addition, the surface treatment of the object can have a significant impact on the color appearance. A glossy treatment will reflect more of the surrounding light and may impart an apparent color to the object. For example, shiny objects in red rooms tend to look red.

Figure 19-1 on page 250 shows the spectral response function of the green paint and a visually similar green that is made with photographic dyes (basically a photograph of the green paint). Notice how the spectrum of the paint has one, relatively main peak. The spectrum from the photographic dyes has a broader peak and a second peak at long wavelengths.

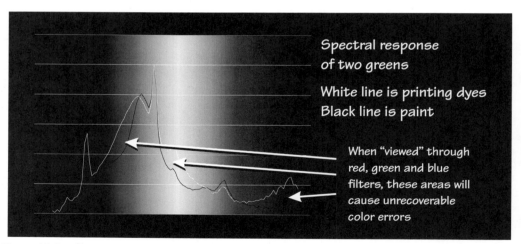

Spectral response
of two greens

White line is printing dyes
Black line is paint

When "viewed" through
red, green and blue
filters, these areas will
cause unrecoverable
color errors

Figure 19-1   *The spectral response function of green paint*

The differences in the spectra will cause the red, green and blue response from a scanner to be different for these two colors. The scanner will see different greens. The fact that these two greens appear the same to a person under daylight means they are a metameric match.

Given the spectral information shown, you could correct for the color error in a scan, making scans of the two greens appear similar. But the scanner user does **not** have this spectral information—so they cannot make this kind of correction (except by guessing). Even if you applied the proper correction to this pair of colors, that same correction would cause errors in other colors (blues, for instance). Since you typically scan something with more than one color, fixing one color, such as the greens, will cause other colors to be corrupted. Typically scanners are optimized so that important colors, such as skin tones and the sky, will be correct. Other colors will suffer.

■ The Detector

When an object is illuminated, it reflects or transmits light with a power distribution of wavelengths from one end of the spectrum to the other. In our eyes, there are three color photoreceptors (called "cones"), each sensitive to light in a range of wavelengths. These three types of cones, which we will call "rho," "gamma" and "beta," send signals to the brain in proportion to the intensity of light being received in each of their sensitivity ranges. The brain interprets the rho, gamma and beta signals as color. There is an additional photoreceptor in the eyes, the rods that are used for monochrome and low-light vision.

In a scanner, the red, green and blue sensors replace rho, gamma and beta cone responses. But the spectral response of the red, green and blue sensors in a scanner are not at all similar to the response of the rho, beta and gamma cones in the eye. This means the scanner, by definition, will not see color as the human does and that the errors are unrecoverable.

Given all the above considerations, it may seem amazing that a scanner can capture a recognizable color image at all! In fact, the primary light source in the world is pretty stable (the sun), and most artificial light attempts to mimic that light to some extent, so a well-designed scanner can actually do quite well.

Furthermore, most objects scanned tend to have similar spectral response functions. Photographs, for instance, use cyan, magenta and yellow dyes, as do color printers and printing presses. Thus, if a scanner is optimized for typical spectral responses of these dyes, it can do quite well. If you scan other objects, however, such as some fabrics or natural objects, the results from scanner to scanner may vary significantly.

Not all scanners are created equal.

Because a scanner can be optimized for typical dyes, not all have been. In addition, some scanners will do a much better job with natural object, or non-printed colors, than others.

■ Light Source

The most common light source is sunlight. Our eyes and our whole vision system work best in natural daylight. One common standard that describes daylight is the Daylight 6500K or D_{65}. The D_{65} standard is a statistical average of many measurements of actual daylight around the world, and no artificial light source matches it exactly (this is one of the limits of D_{65}). However, many artificial light sources (such as fluorescent lights) are similar. D_{65} is a good model for approximating the light spectrum an object will be viewed under because it is based upon the natural world we live in and is thus often used as a standard to which scanners are optimized. For a scanner to best match D_{65}, the spectrum of the light source should be close to D_{65}. Some scanner light sources do a good job of this, some do not.

If the light source in a scanner is missing a significant portion of the visible spectrum or has too high an intensity for some wavelengths, the colors represented by that portion of the spectrum will be corrupted because they aren't illuminated by the appropriate light intensity. A real-world analogy that many of us have experienced is the riddle game in which the question and answer are printed on a card and viewed through a red filter. The answer, printed in red, is not visible until the card is removed from behind the filter because the red filter will not allow red reflected light to pass. A scanner with no red light in its light source would also not be able to see the red words on the game card.

Figure 19-2 shows D_{65} as well as the spectrum from several typical light sources in scanners. Note that all the artificial light sources have some significant differences as compared to D_{65}. This means that all scanners will have some color errors. The more profound the differences, the more colors will be misinterpreted in relation to how they would be seen under natural light. The light source may not include a portion of the spectrum, thus missing colors. Or it may have a peak that causes a wavelength to be overemphasized and changes a color.

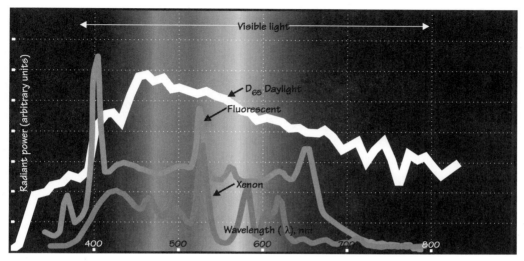

Figure 19-2 Spectra of various light sources

In addition, a scanner with a non-ideal light source can be optimized for a particular original, if the spectral response of the original is known. For instance, if you were designing a scanner to scan slides, all you need is an accurate measurement of the amount of cyan, magenta and yellow dye in each part of the image. You don't need to measure the entire spectrum of each dye, because you know the spectral response of the dyes and can infer how much is there from measuring just a small portion of the spectrum.

Figure 19-3 shows two images photographed under two different scanner lamps. Notice the pronounced green tint in the image on the bottom. Both lamps are cold cathode fluorescent lamps, both have the same phosphors, but the relative mix of the two phosphors is slightly different. Either lamp can be used successfully in a scanner, but the rest of the scanner must be optimized for the specific lamp. Clearly, if a these two lamps were interchanged in a given scanner, the color returned by the scanner would be different.

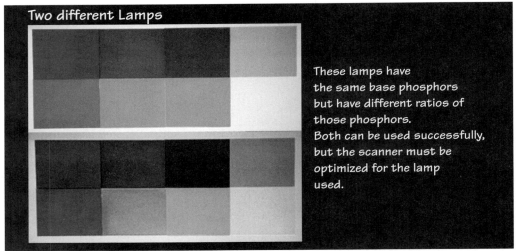

Figure 19-3   A tale of two lamps (color)

Color errors may be non-recoverable.

Color errors due to a deficient light source can never be recovered because the spectral information is not there—the red words on the game card cannot be seen, and no amount of image processing will retrieve them. Similarly, a scanner can't accurately predict the colors of an object when that object is viewed under a light source that is different from the scanner's.

Ultraviolet light.

The light source in a scanner has to include more than visible light. Many papers and colored inks have fluorescent brighteners to make them look brighter. For the scanner to capture this brightness, it has to supply ultraviolet (UV) radiation like the UV in our daily lives. The brighteners then convert this UV into radiation that falls within our range of visible light.

A three-light-bulb scanner may be particularly poor in this case. Consider a scan of an image with fluorescent brighteners that absorb blue light and re-radiate it as red light. In a three-lamp scanner, the red image is captured with only a red lamp on, no blue light is present to excite the red brighteners and the scanner will not "see" the effect. In addition, when the blue light is on, the red brighteners will radiate red light, but the scanner will interpret this as blue light and the color will be wrong.

Infrared light.

Infrared light in the source presents a different problem. Most CCDs are very sensitive to infrared light, and most transmissive filters (such as those in an on-chip filter) do not filter it out. That means that any infrared light reflected from the object will be equally seen by all three channels. This infrared light will be converted to a voltage by the CCD as if it was visible light and will be interpreted as reflected light on all three channels—a low-level flood effect. Scanners with light sources strong in infrared light must include an infrared cut filter or sacrifice image quality. In beam-splitting scanners the infrared light is removed by the filter system, and this is not an issue. Low-cost scanners may not include the infrared cut filter since the effect of infrared light is subtle and may be overlooked by casual users.

■ CIELAB Color Model

If one goal of a scanner is to capture color information in the same way a human would see it, we must have a way to evaluate how well a scanner does this. The first step is to define a color space (or color system) in which errors in scanned colors can be related to how obvious the error will be to the typical person. While not perfect, one model that is useful for this is the CIELAB color system. CIELAB was designed by the Commission Internationale de l'Eclairage (CIE) in 1931 and is designed to closely match the human visual system.

The model consists of three variables: L* for lightness, a* for red-greenness, and b* for yellow-blueness. Figure 19-4 shows the relationship between the variables and their relationship to color.

A key characteristic of CIELAB is that for any of the variables (L*, a* or b*) or any geometric combinations of the variables, a fixed change in those variables is equally apparent to a human observer, no matter what the actual color or lightness of the object. In other words, a change of 10 units of L* is the same apparent change in lightness, no matter the color of the object.

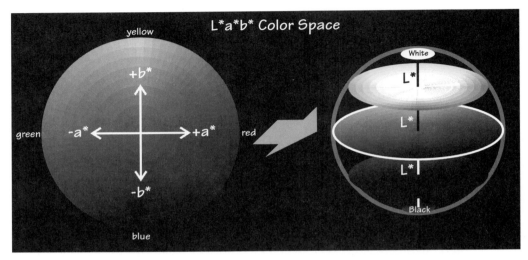

Figure 19-4 *CIELAB color model (color)*

The CIELAB model was tested against the Munsell color order system and shown to be a good model of human vision. The Munsell system was based on over 3 million observations of what people perceived to be like differences in hue, chroma, and intensity. The participants chose the samples they perceived to have like (similar) differences.

Advantages of CIELAB

Here are some reasons why the CIELAB model is useful in tests for color fidelity.

- Changes in intensity and color are separable:
  - A change in variable L* with no change in variables a* or b* means that the lightness has changed but the color has not.
  - If a* and b* change, but L* does not, the color has changed but the lightness has not.
- Differences can be related to human perception. This is the key factor for scanner evaluation.
- A fixed change in L* represents the same change in lightness, no matter what the hue and chroma are or whether the scene is light or dark. Differences in color or lightness can be related to how likely it is that a person will notice the difference.

- A change in L* of 1.0 is called a "just noticeable difference" and is just noticeable to a trained observer under ideal viewing conditions.
- A change in L* of 5.0 is apparent to most observers most of the time.
- A change of between 1.0 and 5.0 may or may not be apparent to the average user.
- The relationships described above between error and perception are the same for a* and b* and for changes in chroma (ΔC), hue (ΔH), and total color error (ΔE).
- Detail in an image is seen in the lightness channel (L*). The color information, a* and b*, can have much lower sharpness with no apparent impact in the sharpness of the image.
- A given magnitude (size of the value) of color error according to the CIELAB model is the same perceptible error to a person, regardless of the color or intensity of the scene. In other words, a change from L*=10 to L*=15 will appear to be of the same magnitude as a change from L*=80 to L*=85.

Disadvantages

Some disadvantages of the CIELAB model for testing color fidelity are as follows.

- It doesn't account for context. For example, a greenish tint in the sky is more obvious to people than the model predicts because people have strong expectations about the proper color of the sky.
- It doesn't include any scene effects. If an error such as a streak or a line occurs abruptly in an image, the error is much more perceptible than a gentle or diffuse error of the same magnitude. For instance, a streak that is an ΔL^* of 0.5 is typically visible in uniform parts of the image.
- ΔE is often used as a global color error. Using one number to represent a complex system can be misleading.
- An error value tells you nothing about the source of the error (particularly for ΔE).
- CIELAB requires assumptions about light source and white points.
- Concepts such as a just-noticeable difference aren't precise and vary from person to person.

■ Color Errors: Recoverable and Non-recoverable

Color errors can be either recoverable or non-recoverable. Well-designed color-separation systems and closed-loop calibration systems, available in some scanners, can eliminate most recoverable errors. An example might be compensating a scanned image for viewing on a bluish monitor. A 3 x 3 matrix multiplication of the RGB color values easily eliminates this error. Other kinds of recoverable errors are eliminated with a three-dimensional, color-correction table.

A non-recoverable error can be caused by a deviation from the spectral sensitivity of the human eye, a deficiency or spectral peak in the light source and other design limitations in a scanner. non-recoverable errors can't be fixed by image-editing software because the information is simply not in the image. non-recoverable errors are most commonly instrument metamerism.

■ Gray Balance

Another important factor in color accuracy is the gray balance of the scanner. A well-balanced scanner should preserve the neutrality of an image. An easy way to see this is to scan a black and white photograph in color mode on a color scanner. If properly balanced, the resultant image should have no color and the black and white photo should look black and white, with no color shifts or hue. By definition, the black and white original has no color information and no color dyes so a scanner should not record any color. Figure 19-5 shows a black and white photo and gray step target scanned in color on two scanners. The image on the right shows no color—the scanner has maintained the neutrality of the image. The image on the left shows color and hue shifts throughout the tonal range—this scanner has poor color balance. One should realize that these color shifts, so obvious in this black and white photo, also exist in color scans on this scanner and degrade the quality of the color image, even if the shifts are not so obvious.

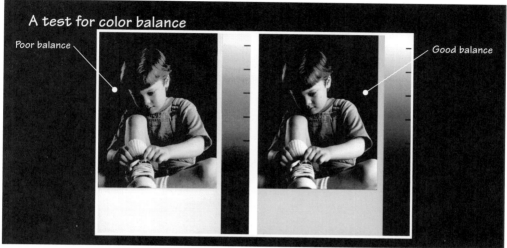

Figure 19-5   Black and white photo and gray target scanned in color on two scanners (color)

■ Limitations of Typical Tests

Typical tests for color fidelity are:

- Scanning a calibrated color test target with an RGB color and comparing the scan to the known color in terms of RGB.
- Scanning a calibrated color test target with a known CMYK density and comparing it to the results of converting RGB to CMYK from a scan.
- Scanning a color image and allowing a jury of viewers to pick the most accurate or pleasing (or both) when the image is displayed on a computer or printed on a color printer.

Each method has limitations:

- Comparing a scan to a known color in terms of RGB or CMYK counts doesn't indicate how apparent the color error is to a person. An error that may seem large in RGB or CMYK counts could be unnoticeable or very apparent, depending on the lightness or color of the object. For example, a 10-count difference in a very dark region represents a large error while the same 10-count difference in a very light region of a scan is imperceptible.

■ Conversion from RGB to CMYK is more a function of printing than of scanning. Thus, evaluating errors in CMYK percentages is not relevant to a scanner's color error except in trying to match a certain scanner to a certain press and process. Historically, in commercial presswork, this type of comparison was relevant and important. In the evaluation of typical flatbed scanners for desktop publishing work, it is not. CMYK density testing is not recommended.

■ The calibrated colors used as test targets assume the light in which the target was measured. But that light, and the light used for viewing, may or may not match the light source in the scanner.

Limitations of the second (jury) method include the following:

■ Printers (in particular) and computer monitors have a more limited gamut (range of colors) than good scanners, and errors may be exaggerated.

■ Printers and monitors often introduce more color errors than the scanner. Thus, evaluations based upon prints or monitors may be more related to the capabilities of the printer or monitor than the scanner.

■ Individual perception of color varies; what looks good to one person may look bad to another.

■ Juries react to the content of the scan as well as to the color: errors that emphasize or de-emphasize portions of the scan may affect that reaction.

■ Juries often choose a pleasing image, such as one with enhanced colorfulness, over an accurate one. An image captured accurately can always be enhanced, whereas the reverse may not be true.

■ Default exposure settings are rarely the right choice for color comparisons, but test scans are often done this way. The test scans may have errors that could be prevented by different settings.

■ Jury tests are very useful but must be controlled very carefully.

■ Recommended Tests

There are two recommended tests. In the first test, a calibrated color target is scanned and the resulting RGB color values are converted to CIELAB values and compared to the correct CIELAB color values. For the second test, a neutral gray step target is scanned, and again the results are compared to the actual values in CIELAB. The scans are done with no gamma correction but can include different exposure settings or use of automatic exposure.

It is important that gamma correction not be used for this test. Not using gamma correction will result in images that appear much too dark on a computer screen or printer but are appropriate for calculations. If gamma correction is used, apparent errors will be magnified. If it is not possible to turn off gamma correction, then it is possible to undo gamma correction in image editors.

Test one: calibrated color target

For the first test you will need a calibrated color target for which you know the actual color in CIELAB and for an assumed light source (D_{65} is recommended). The Applied Images test target described in the appendix provides eight well-controlled colors and can be used for this test. CIELAB values are provided with the target. Other targets that could be used include a MacBeth Color Checker or an IT8. However, CIELAB values for these targets must be measured or calculated. The IT8 poses a problem in that the color patches are quite small. The color calculations in the appendix show how to convert from various color spaces to others, and the CDROM provided with this book includes a spreadsheet to achieve CIELAB calculations.

One factor that may be of concern in using either the Applied Images Target or the MacBeth is that both of these targets are manufactured using dyes that are different from photographic dyes. This means that a scanner that is optimized just for photographs may not do as well on these targets. One alternative is to photograph the targets then scan the photographic target. Again, however, the colors on the photograph will have to be measured independently.

For all these targets an illumination must be assumed. We recommend D_{65}, which is also the source used in the new sRGB standard.

Note: Although Adobe Photoshop reports CIELAB values (L^*, a^* and b^*) and reportedly uses CIELAB as an internal color space, we have not been able to determine what color model is used by Photoshop. Nor do the CIELAB values returned match any of the standard color spaces discussed in this book. For these reasons we cannot recommend using Photoshop CIELAB values for the calculations in this test.

Step 1: scan the color region of the test target:

- Use gamma correction of 1.0 (preferably) or a known gamma correction. It is important to use a known gamma so that its effect can be removed. The sRGB uses a gamma of 2.2. Note, gamma correction is often applied automatically, and disabling it may require special calibrations or special effort.
- A sample rate of 150 ppi is sufficient.
- Use default settings or automatic exposure.

Step 2: remove the effect of gamma correction.

If a gamma other than 1.0 was used, remove its effect using the procedure in "Removing the effect of gamma correction" on page 191.

Step 3: record the RGB values.

Using Photoshop or a similar editor:

1. Open the image at 100%.

2. Select each color.

3. Use the "Image/Histogram" tool to record the red, green and blue counts. Note, you must record red, green and blue separately, not the "Luminosity" or gray value. Make sure you are viewing the image at 100% and do not use the Adobe Photoshop-reported CIELAB values.

Step 4: convert the RGB to CIELAB.

Convert the RGB values to CIELAB using the equations in the appendix or the spreadsheet on the CDROM.

Step 5: evaluate the error in terms of ΔL, ΔE, ΔC and ΔH.

Recall that an error of less than 5.0 is typically not visible to most people most of the time. Errors of less than 1.0 are typically not noticeable even in ideal conditions. Note that most scanners will have errors greater than 5.0 for some colors. Also, a test based on only eight colors is limited.

Step 6: augment the above by scanning and viewing scenes (the jury method).

Be sure to use calibrated monitors, controlled viewing conditions, and specific instructions. We recommend the analytical method in steps 1–4 be weighted higher than the jury method.

Test two: gray balance

This test uses the gray step target in the center of the Applied Images test target. Any similar step target for which actual CIELAB values are known can be substituted.

Step 1: scan the gray step target:

- Use gamma correction of 1.0 (preferably) or a known gamma correction. It is important to use a known gamma so that its effect can be removed. The sRGB uses a gamma of 2.2. Note, gamma correction is often applied automatically, and disabling it may require special calibrations or special effort.
- A sample rate of 150 ppi is sufficient.
- Use default settings or automatic exposure.

Step 2: remove the effect of gamma compensation.

If a gamma other than 1.0 was used, remove its effect using the procedure in "Removing the effect of gamma correction" on page 191.

Step 3: record the RGB values.

Using Photoshop or a similar editor:

1. Select each grayscale step.

2. Use the "Image/Histogram" tool to record the red, green and blue counts. Note, you must record red, green and blue separately, not the "Luminosity" or gray value.

3. To reduce the number of steps, use every other gray step on the target. Just be sure to use the same steps on all scanners.

Step 4: calculate the CIELAB values.

Using the equations in the appendix, or the CDROM spreadsheet, calculate the CIELAB L*, a* and b* values for the target.

Step 5: calculate the CIELAB error.

Compare the actual CIELAB values against the grayscale target. Calculate the lightness error ΔL and the chromaticity for each patch. Since the gray step target has very little color component, ideally the a* and b* values as well as the C* value should be near 0.0. In addition, a scan of a grayscale in color mode will reveal if the three channels do not track in reflectance or have quantization errors that do not match. These effects will cause color bands in the image.

Step 6 (optional):obtain and scan, in color mode, a high-quality black and white photograph.

Visually inspect the scans for color shifts and non-neutral hues. Note that many color printers introduce hue shifts when printing neutral images, so printing and viewing the scans from this test may be misleading.

20 Chapter

Scanning for Black and White Output

While great growth has occurred in color scanning, the ability of a scanner to create black and white output is still quite important. Although high-quality color printers are quite affordable today, most of these printers are relatively slow. Many documents are destined for copiers for wide distribution, so many scans are created in grayscale (black and white). In addition, color image files are typically at least three times larger than a grayscale image file—further limiting the use of color scans. However, while most hardcopy output is still black and white, most originals being scanned are color. This chapter discusses evaluating the ability of a scanner to scan a color original for grayscale output. The related subjects, tonal accuracy, tonal resolution and ability to record shadow detail are discussed in Chapter 15 • "Tonal Resolution, Density Range and Bit Depth" on page 213 and Chapter 16 • "Image Noise" on page 229. Color balance of the scanner is covered in Chapter 19 • "Color Fidelity" on page 249.

■ Scans of Black and White Photos

Scans of black and white photos are relatively rare today. For black and white photos, the most important factors relate to tonal resolution and image noise and are addressed in Chapter 15 • "Tonal Resolution, Density Range and Bit Depth" on page 213 and Chapter 16 • "Image Noise" on page 229.

■ Colored Objects in Grayscale Mode

More common are scans of colored originals in grayscale mode. In this case, the key is how well a scanner can convert colors in the original to appropriate gray levels in the output. Ideally, we would like the scanner to do this the same way as our vision system does. Scanners vary in this capability. The ideal would be a scanner that has the same bell-shaped spectral sensitivity as do the rods in our eyes—however, this is not usually the case. A more common method is to use the NTSC grayscale conversion, developed to display color TV signals on black and white television.

Some of the things that impact how well a scanner can scan a color original for grayscale output include:

- ■ Dropout colors—colors that the scanner can't see at all in grayscale mode.
- ■ Two colors the scanner sees as different lightnesses that you see as the same lightness.
- ■ Two colors the scanner sees as the same lightness that you see as different lightnesses.

Figure 20-1 shows grayscale scans of a color original from two different scanners. In the image in the center, only the green channel was used for the scan. Notice how the different colors in the flower were converted to the same grayscale. The image on the right uses a scanner with full spectrum color to create the grayscale rendition and the two colors are transformed to two different gray levels—preserving the detail in the image. The image on the right is more representative of how the human vision system would work in low light conditions.

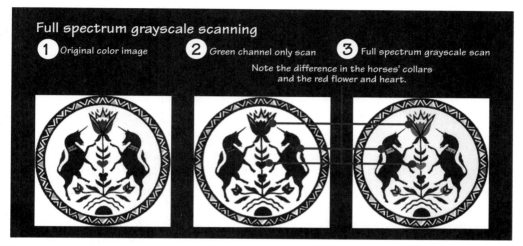

Figure 20-1   Full-spectrum, white light (right) and green channel only (left) (color)

■ Grayscale Objects in Color Mode

A color scanner should show tonal neutrality when scanning grayscale objects in color mode. This is related to the color balance of a scanner and is discussed in Chapter 19 • "Color Fidelity" on page 249.

■ Limitations of Typical Tests

Typically, this area is not tested in reviews, although it should be.

■ Recommended Tests

Three different tests are presented, in order of preference, each with the same goal but with different limitations. The choice of test(s) used is left up to the tester. Additional testing for tonal range, accuracy and signal-to-noise ratio are discussed in Chapter 15 • "Tonal Resolution, Density Range and Bit Depth" on page 213. The three recommended tests are:

- **L* Comparison Test:** Scan a calibrated color test target in grayscale mode. Calculate the equivalent L* value from the grayscale scan and compare to the L* value of the calibrated color target.
- **NTSC Conversion:** Scan a calibrated color target in grayscale and compare the grayscale levels recorded by the scanner to that achieved by an NTSC conversion. The NTSC-converted values for the color targets on the Applied Images test target are provided in the appendix. This method compares the scanner to the well-accepted NTSC convention.
- **Photoshop Comparison Test:** Scan a color photograph or drawing both in color mode and grayscale mode. Then, using a quality image editor such as Adobe Photoshop, convert the color image to grayscale and compare the image converted in Photoshop to the one captured by the scanner.

■ Detailed Test Procedures

L* comparison test

This test measures how well a scanner in grayscale mode represents the CIELAB L* (lightness) of a color. Since CIELAB L* represents the non-chromatic portion of an image, it could be argued that a scanner should create a non-chromatic (grayscale) image in the same way. One strength of this test is that the CIELAB ΔL^* (delta L* or change in L*) value can be calculated and related to human perception of the error (a just noticeable difference). However, this is not a common application, and it is unclear if this is an area in which scanners have been optimized—results may vary widely.

Step 1: scan the color test target in grayscale mode.

For all scans, use a gamma of 1.0 or compensate for gamma correction (see "Removing the Effect of Gamma Compensation" in Chapter 13 • "Resolution" on page 173). Use default settings or auto-exposure for this test.

Step 2: record the grayscale counts in Photoshop.

Select each color patch in Photoshop and, using the "/Image/Histogram" tool, record the average reflectance (in counts). Remember that the scan was done in grayscale so only a grayscale value is available in Photoshop.

Note: Although Adobe Photoshop reports CIELAB values (L*, a* and b*) and reportedly uses CIELAB as an internal color space, we have not been able to determine what color model is used by Photoshop. Nor do the CIELAB values returned match any of the standard color spaces discussed in this book. For these reasons we cannot recommend using Photoshop CIELAB values for the calculations in this test.

Step 3: calculate an equivalent L* for the color patch using the formulas in the appendix.

To calculate L* in this special case, use the grayscale reflectance measured in step 2 for the green counts in the equation. Use zero for the red and blue counts.

Step 4: calculate ΔL for the scanner compared to the actual L* of the target.

NTSC Conversion

For this test, you will need a color test target and the NTSC grayscale equivalents for the target. Given the RGB values from the target, the NTSC grayscale values can be calculated as described in the appendix. This test compares a scanner to the well-accepted NTSC standard—more likely the standard for which a scanner has been optimized. A big limitation to this test is that, like any test based on reflectance or density, the perceived visual impact of the error is not easily related to human perception, i.e., is 10 counts of error a large or small error? Also, the spectral response of the scanner is likely to be quite different from NTSC.

Step 1: scan the color test target in grayscale mode.

For all scans, use a gamma of 1.0 or compensate for gamma correction (see "Removing the Effect of Gamma Compensation" in Chapter 13 • "Resolution" on page 173). Use default settings or auto-exposure for this test.

Step 2: record the grayscale counts in Photoshop.

Select each color patch in Photoshop and, using the "Image/Histogram" tool, record the average reflectance (in counts). Recall that the scan was done in grayscale so only a grayscale value is available in Photoshop.

Step 3: compare the grayscale value recorded in step 2 to the NTSC grayscale value for the patch.

For the Applied Images test target, the NTSC values are supplied with the target. Otherwise, the NTSC value can be calculated as discussed in the appendix.

Step 4: when evaluating the error between the scanned value and the NTSC value recall that a fixed number of counts of error is much more apparent (visible) in dark areas than in light areas.

Photoshop comparison test

This test procedure presumes that the conversion routines in Photoshop represent a high-quality conversion from color to grayscale and compares the ability of the scanner to do this conversion to Photoshop's. The obvious limitation to this test is that a scanner may actually be better than Photoshop and may be misrepresented. To repeat—this test presumes the color-to-grayscale conversion in Photoshop is an "ideal" that should be matched.

Step 1: scan a color photograph or color drawing in color mode.

The best image for this test would be a drawing such as the image shown in Figure 20-1. The more subtle color differences in the image, the better. However, the image should have a full range of colors—reds, greens, blues plus combinations.

Step 2: repeat the same scan, but as a grayscale image.

Step 3: open both images in Photoshop.

Step 4: convert the color image to grayscale mode using "Image/Mode/ Grayscale."

Photoshop uses a robust conversion algorithm that can be considered high quality.

Step 5: visually compare the two grayscale images for loss of detail due to poor conversion.

As an example, refer to the images shown in Figure 20-1.

Step 6: as an alternative to visual comparison, you can use "Image/Calculate/Subtract" to subtract the two images.

Use an offset of 128 in the calculation so that the resultant image is "centered" around 128 counts and not clipped.

Step 7: examine the histogram of the subtracted image.

The extent (min–max) and standard deviation of the histogram will give some measure of the difference in the two images. Two identical images would have and extent and standard deviation of zero. The larger the number, the greater the difference.

Back to Choppin' Wood

CIELAB to RGB Calculations and NTSC Equations

This appendix contains a set of formulas to transform RGB to CIELAB (and XYZ) and back. Only a brief description and an equation set for RGB to CIELAB transformations are included. Thus, no discussion of the theory behind CIELAB or these transformations is included. The equation for the NTSC (National Television System Committee) system of color TV transmission signals is also included. A spreadsheet is provided on the CDROM which achieves many of these calculations.

Note: This information is provided without warranty or guarantee and is simply a compilation of published information.

■ RGB-to-LAB Conversion Overview

The conversion from RGB to LAB is performed in two steps:

1. Convert RGB to XYZ using coefficients normalized for an illuminant.

2. Convert the XYZ to CIELAB assuming an ideal or scene white.

Assumptions

The above steps require assumptions about (1) the illuminant used and (2) ideal or scene white. Included are typical values for illuminant D_{65} and sRGB from the literature, but be aware that published values vary slightly. The variation in the literature is slight and probably not of concern for most applications, provided the same values are used for all calculations and comparisons.

■ RGB-to-LAB Conversion: Detailed Steps and Equations

1. Choose an illuminant. The coefficients used to calculate XYZ from RGB depend upon illuminant. The key factor is that you use the same illuminant for all measurements that you are comparing. The coefficients provided here are typical values from the literature for illuminant D_{65} and sRGB.

2. Convert the RGB counts from the scanner to normalized RGB values. This process removes the 'bit depth' dependence from the scanner by normalizing the RGB counts to a maximum of 100. For example, for a 24-bpp color scanner (8 bits per color per pixel), R, G and B are:

$$R = \frac{RedCounts}{255} \times 100 \qquad \text{(EQ 1)}$$

$$G = \frac{GreenCounts}{255} \times 100$$

$$B = \frac{BlueCounts}{255} \times 100,$$

where the constant 255 is

$$255 = 2^{bits} - 1 \quad \text{with bits} = 8. \qquad \text{(EQ 2)}$$

Note: It is important to use, for bits, the number of bits per pixel stored in the scanned image file. Thus, for a 10-bpp per color scanner that transforms the image to 8-bpp per color before the file is stored, the correct value for bits is 8, not 10. Very few (if any) image files are stored with more than 8-bpp per color.

3. Convert the normalized RGB to XYZ using the appropriate conversion coefficients. The equations for this conversion are of the form:

$$X = A_{11} \times R + A_{12} \times G + A_{13} \times B \qquad \text{(EQ 3)}$$
$$Y = A_{21} \times R + A_{22} \times G + A_{23} \times B$$
$$Z = A_{31} \times R + A_{32} \times G + A_{33} \times B$$

in matrix notation

$$\begin{bmatrix} X \\ Y \\ Z \end{bmatrix} = \begin{bmatrix} A_{11} & A_{12} & A_{13} \\ A_{21} & A_{22} & A_{23} \\ A_{31} & A_{32} & A_{33} \end{bmatrix} \times \begin{bmatrix} R \\ G \\ B \end{bmatrix} \qquad \text{(EQ 4)}$$

where R, G and B are the normalized red, green and blue values calculated in equation (EQ 1), and A_{nm} are the conversion coefficients.

For sRGB the equations become:

$$\begin{bmatrix} X \\ Y \\ Z \end{bmatrix} = \begin{bmatrix} 0.4124 & 0.3576 & 0.1805 \\ 0.2126 & 0.7152 & 0.0722 \\ 0.0193 & 0.1192 & 0.9505 \end{bmatrix} \times \begin{bmatrix} R \\ G \\ B \end{bmatrix} \qquad \text{(EQ 5)}$$

4. Convert the X, Y, Z values to CIELAB values.

$$L^* = 116 \times \left(\frac{Y}{Y_n}\right)^{\frac{1}{3}} - 16 \qquad \text{for} \qquad \frac{Y}{Y_n} > 0.008856 \text{ (typical)} \qquad \text{(EQ 6)}$$

$$L^* = 903.3 \times \left(\frac{Y}{Y_n}\right) \qquad \text{for} \qquad \frac{Y}{Y_n} \leq 0.008856$$

$$a^* = 500\left[\left(\frac{X}{X_n}\right)^{\frac{1}{3}} - \left(\frac{Y}{Y_n}\right)^{\frac{1}{3}}\right] \qquad \text{valid for} \qquad \frac{X}{X_n}, \frac{Y}{Y_n} \geq 0.01 \qquad \text{(EQ 7)}$$

$$b^* = 200\left[\left(\frac{Y}{Y_n}\right)^{\frac{1}{3}} - \left(\frac{Z}{Z_n}\right)^{\frac{1}{3}}\right] \qquad \text{valid for} \qquad \frac{Z}{Z_n}, \frac{Y}{Y_n} \geq 0.01 \qquad \text{(EQ 8)}$$

where the ideal white is defined by X_n, Y_n, and Z_n. For D_{65} and sRGB,

$$X_n = 95,\ Y_n = 100,\ Z_n = 109, \qquad \text{(EQ 9)}$$

and the equations become:

$$L^* = 116 \times \left(\frac{Y}{100}\right)^{\frac{1}{3}} - 16 \qquad \text{for} \qquad Y > 0.8856 \text{ (typical)} \qquad \text{(EQ 10)}$$

$$L^* = 903.3 \times \left(\frac{Y}{100}\right) \qquad \text{for} \qquad Y \leq 0.8856$$

$$a^* = 500\left[\left(\frac{X}{95}\right)^{\frac{1}{3}} - \left(\frac{Y}{100}\right)^{\frac{1}{3}}\right] \qquad \text{valid for} \qquad X \geq 0.95,\ Y \geq 1 \qquad \text{(EQ 11)}$$

$$b^* = 200\left[\left(\frac{Y}{100}\right)^{\frac{1}{3}} - \left(\frac{Z}{109}\right)^{\frac{1}{3}}\right] \qquad \text{valid for} \qquad Y \geq 1,\ Z \geq 1.09. \qquad \text{(EQ 12)}$$

Coefficients for illuminant D$_{65}$

For illuminant D$_{65}$, the coefficients in matrix in equation (EQ 4) are:

(EQ 13)

$$\begin{bmatrix} X \\ Y \\ Z \end{bmatrix} = \begin{bmatrix} 0.5879 & 0.1792 & 0.1831 \\ 0.2896 & 0.6058 & 0.1046 \\ 0.0 & 0.06826 & 1.02 \end{bmatrix} \times \begin{bmatrix} R \\ G \\ B \end{bmatrix}$$

Calculating color differences (CIELAB)

Once CIELAB values are calculated from scanned data, color difference calculations can be made between the scan data and the nominal CIELAB values for the target or between different scans. Several CIELAB difference values are of interest. The following equations list some CIELAB color difference parameters.

Symbol	Meaning	Equation	
$C*$	Chroma, colorfulness. Large values mean highly colorful.	$C* = \sqrt{(a*)^2 + (b*)^2}$	**(EQ 14)**
h	Hue angle	$h = \mathrm{atan}\left(\dfrac{b*}{a*}\right)$	**(EQ 15)**
$\Delta E*$	Color difference	$\Delta E* = \sqrt{(\Delta a*)^2 + (\Delta b*)^2 + (\Delta L*)^2}$ or $\Delta E* = \sqrt{(\Delta L*)^2 + (\Delta C*)^2 + (\Delta H*)^2}$	**(EQ 16)**
$\Delta L*$	Lightness difference Negative means sample is lighter.	$\Delta L* = L*_{ref} - L*_{sample}$	**(EQ 17)**
$\Delta C*$	Color difference Negative means sample is more colorful.	$\Delta C* = C*_{ref} - C*_{sample}$	**(EQ 18)**
$\Delta H*$	Hue difference	$\Delta H* = \sqrt{(\Delta E*)^2 - (\Delta C*)^2 - (\Delta L*)^2}$	**(EQ 19)**
$\Delta a*$	Red-green difference Positive means sample is greener.	$\Delta a* = a*_{ref} - a*_{sample}$	**(EQ 20)**
$\Delta b*$	Yellow-blue difference Positive means sample is bluer.	$\Delta b* = b*_{ref} - b*_{sample}$	**(EQ 21)**

Perception of color or lightness difference

For these parameters, a difference of 5.0 is considered visible to most people. A difference of 1.0 is considered a just noticeable difference visible only to trained observers in ideal conditions. Generally global color error (ΔE) is viewed as too global and not very indicative of perceived errors.

Inverse calculations (LAB to RGB)

The equations given above can be inverted to calculate RGB from LAB.

1. Calculate XYZ from LAB:

$$X = X_n \times \left[\frac{a^*}{500} + \frac{(L^* + 16)}{116} \right]^3 \qquad \text{(EQ 22)}$$

$$Y = Y_n \times \left[\frac{(L^* + 16)}{116} \right]^3 \qquad \text{(EQ 23)}$$

$$Z = Z_n \times \left[\frac{(L^* + 16)}{116} - \frac{b^*}{200} \right]^3 \qquad \text{(EQ 24)}$$

2. Calculate normalized RGB from XYZ:

$$\begin{bmatrix} R \\ G \\ B \end{bmatrix} = \begin{bmatrix} B_{11} & B_{12} & B_{13} \\ B_{21} & B_{22} & B_{23} \\ B_{31} & B_{32} & B_{33} \end{bmatrix} \times \begin{bmatrix} X \\ Y \\ Z \end{bmatrix} \qquad \text{(EQ 25)}$$

3. Calculate RGB counts from normalized RGB:

$$RedCounts = \frac{R}{100} \times 255 \qquad \text{(EQ 26)}$$

$$GreenCounts = \frac{G}{100} \times 255$$

$$BlueCounts = \frac{B}{100} \times 255$$

In generalized form:

$$counts = \left(\frac{NormalizedValue}{100} \right)(2^{bits} - 1) \qquad \text{(EQ 27)}$$

Again, the coefficients of the *B* matrix depend on the illuminant. They can be calculated from inverting matrix *A* in equation (EQ 4). For sRGB and D$_{65}$ typical values are:

sRGB

$$
\begin{bmatrix} B_{11} & B_{12} & B_{13} \\ B_{21} & B_{22} & B_{23} \\ B_{31} & B_{32} & B_{33} \end{bmatrix} = \begin{bmatrix} 3.241 & -1.5374 & -0.4986 \\ -0.9692 & 1.876 & 0.0416 \\ 0.0556 & -0.204 & 1.057 \end{bmatrix}
$$

(EQ 28)

Illuminant D$_{65}$

$$
\begin{bmatrix} B_{11} & B_{12} & B_{13} \\ B_{21} & B_{22} & B_{23} \\ B_{31} & B_{32} & B_{33} \end{bmatrix} = \begin{bmatrix} 1.972 & -0.5497 & -0.2975 \\ -0.9534 & 1.936 & -0.02741 \\ 0.0638 & -0.1295 & 0.9821 \end{bmatrix}
$$

(EQ 29)

For more information on colorimetry and color conversions, recommended books include:

Anni Berger-Schunn, *Practical Color Measurement*, Wiley, New York, 1994, ISBN 0-471-00417-0.

R. G. W. Hunt, *Measuring Colour,* 2nd ed., Hemel Hempsted, Herts Simon and Schuster International Group 1991, ISBN 0-13-567686-X.

R. G. Wyszecki and W. S. Stiles, *Color Science,* 2nd ed., Adam Hilger, Bristol, 1986.

■ NTSC Equations

The National Television Systems Committee (NTSC) of the USA recommended a system of color TV transmission signals in 1953. The NTSC system is intended to be used with a color receiver with the following chromaticities:

	x	y	z	u'	v'
Red (R)	0.67	0.33	0.0	0.477	0.528
Green (G)	0.21	0.71	0.08	0.76	0.576

Table A–1 NTSC Calculations

Blue (B)	0.14	0.08	0.78	0.152	0.195
White (Sc)	0.310	0.316	0.374	0.201	0.416

Table A–1   NTSC Calculations

Assuming these RGB chromaticities, an NTSC grayscale or luminance version of an image is calculated as:

$$L = 0.299 \times R + 0.587 \times G + 0.114 \times B$$

When calculating NTSC grayscale from a scanner using these equations, there is an inherent error in that you probably don't know the chromaticities of the scanner, and they probably are not the same as above. However, by assuming these chromaticities and using the grayscale (luminance) equation above you can evaluate how close a scanner grayscale is to NTSC grayscale. Note, NTSC is not inherently better or worse than others, just well recognized and accepted.

■ Applied Image Test Target

A custom scanner test target has been created that can be used for all of the tests described this book. The target also includes some other features that can be used for other tests or experiments. The test target is available from Applied Image, Inc. at the address given below.

A scan of the target is shown in Figure A-1. This figure is not a target itself and cannot be used for testing. Supplied with the target is a detailed specification providing color and grayscale values for the target as well as a description of the various areas on the target and their uses.

Applied Image
1653 East Main Street
Rochester, NY 14609
(716) 482-0300
Target # QA-69

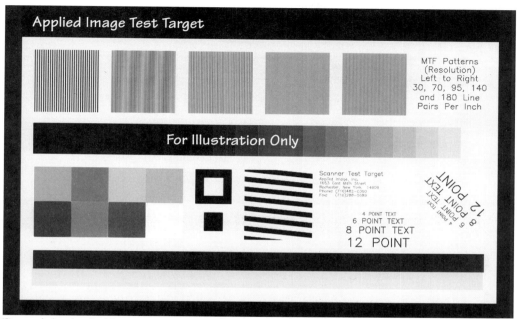

Figure A-1 Applied Images test target (color). For illustration only—this printed image is not appropriate for testing

Table A-2 on page 282 gives nominal CIELAB values for the eight color patches and the grayscale on the target. Note these are nominal values—actual targets will vary slightly. In addition, if target processes change, these values may change. If a target is supplied with a new set of data, then use that data instead. On the CDROM are spreadsheets with these values already entered as nominal values and which can be used for calculations. Note that the color patches on the target are made with various inks and may represent spectral responses unlike those seen in traditional CMYK printing. They should reflect a more general case, but many scanners optimized specifically for CMYK or CMY (photographic) dyes may do poorly on some of the colors. In fact, the colors can be considered "difficult" for many scanners. As with all testing, failure on a given color patch may not indicate general failure of the product on all colors. A second target that may be useful is a MacBeth Color Checker, available at photographic supply stores. Other targets, such as an IT-8 target, may provide a more robust and more focused set of colors, but they will have to be measured independently.

Color Patches	sRGB Values			D$_{65}$ Values		
	L*	a*	b*	L*	a*	b*
White	96.1	0.1	0.4	96.1	0.1	0.4
Blue	26.8	32.3	-63.0	29.0	18.2	-62.2
Green	50.3	-41.0	24.2	47.5	-62.2	21.8
Red	33.4	55.8	32.7	38.6	66.2	47.6
Amber	82.1	11.1	23.9	83.1	19.6	28
Yellow	92.7	-18.1	82.0	91.6	-12.8	95.2
Magenta	61.1	49.3	-15.2	65.2	58.0	-9.0
Cyan	50.4	8.5	-53.1	50.6	-7.5	-55.7
Grayscale						
Target White	93.3	0.5	-1.1	93.3	0.3	-1.1
Gray Patch 1	85.0	0.5	-0.9	85.0	0.4	-0.9
Gray Patch 2	78.2	0.4	-0.8	78.2	0.3	-0.8
Gray Patch 3	71.9	0.4	-0.5	71.9	0.3	-0.5
Gray Patch 4	65.7	0.3	-0.3	65.7	0.3	-0.3
Gray Patch 5	60.0	0.2	-0.2	60.0	0.2	-0.2
Gray Patch 6	54.9	0.2	0.0	54.9	0.2	0.0
Gray Patch 7	50.8	0.0	0.0	50.8	0.0	0.0
Gray Patch 8	44.1	0.0	0.1	44.1	-0.1	0.1
Gray Patch 9	41.6	-0.1	0.2	41.6	-0.1	0.2
Gray Patch 10	38.6	0.0	0.1	38.6	0.0	0.1
Gray Patch 11	36.3	-0.1	0.2	36.3	-0.1	0.2
Gray Patch 12	32.6	0.0	0.3	32.6	0.0	0.3
Gray Patch 13	30.9	0.0	0.4	30.9	0.0	0.4
Gray Patch 14	29.0	0.0	0.5	29.0	0.1	0.5
Gray Patch 15	27.4	-0.1	0.5	27.4	0.0	0.5
Gray Patch 16	25.6	0.1	0.4	25.6	0.2	0.5
Gray Patch 17	24.1	0.0	0.6	24.1	0.1	0.7
Gray Patch 18	22.7	-0.1	0.7	22.7	0.0	0.7
Darkest	21.6	0.2	0.7	21.6	0.4	0.8

Table A-2   Nominal CIELAB Values for the Applied Images Target

Glossary

3 x 3 matrixing: A mathematical operation that takes the RGB components of a color separation and creates a new RGB output based on the relative values for the input components. Also called "color matrixing, color mixing."

aliasing: Reflections of higher frequencies at about the sampling rate of a scanner that cause unwanted effects such as Moiré patterns in an image. These patterns can appear to be a "real" image. Aliasing artifacts cannot be out without degrading the image because they are mixed in with the real image. See also artifacts, Moiré pattern.

array: A grouping of like elements. See also CCD.

artifact: A reflection of higher frequencies at about the sampling rate of a scanner that appears as an unwanted pattern in an image. See also aliasing, Moiré pattern.

beat frequency: A periodic variation in a signal resulting when two signals of unequal frequencies are combined. Where the beat is maximum the signal and the samples line up perfectly, and the resolution is high. But where the beat is minimum the signal and the samples don't line up, and the resolution is low.

bit: Computers store numbers in binary format, as a group of ones and zeros. Each one or zero is called a "bit." If a number is an 8-bit number, then inside the computer (or scanner), it is described by a collection of 8 ones and zeros. An 8-bit number can range from 0 to 255 or 0 to 2^8 -1.

bit depth: The number of bits per pixel per color captured by a scanner. See also tonal resolution.

black point: The color that when scanned produces values of 0, 0, 0 in an 8-bit scanner. Ideally, the black point is 0% neutral reflectance or transmittance. See also white point.

calibrate: To standardize by determining the deviation from a standard so as to find the right correction factors.

carriage: A scanner's imaging head that moves down a page to capture an image. Also "called optical imaging element, optical imaging head."

CCD (charge-coupled device): A miniature photometer that detects light intensity and represents the intensity with an analog voltage. A CCD array is made up of CCD elements, the smallest discrete CCD.

chroma: A quality of color combining hue and saturation. See also hue, saturation.

CIELAB (L*a*b*): A color model to approximate human vision. The model consists of three variables: L* for luminosity, a* for one color axis, and b* for the other color axis. CIELAB is a good model of the Munsell color system and human vision.

clipping: The assignment to a cutoff value of all the samples that are above or below that cutoff in the input. The result is that any input detail in that portion of the intensity spectrum is lost in the output.

closed loop: A signal path that includes a forward path, a feedback path and a summing point, and that forms a closed circuit.

color matrixing: See 3 x 3 matrixing.

color-matching functions: The mathematical relationships that assign a weight to red, green and blue color separations to reproduce the original color. 3 x 3 matrixing is the use of a color-matching function available on some scanners. See also 3 x 3 matrixing.

color mixing: See matrixing.

continuous tone: An image such as a photo or a painting that has a range of tones or a gradation of tones.

copyboard: The flat glass plate on which originals are placed for scanning.

correlated noise: A recognizable pattern of change in an image file. The change is an increase or a decrease in the brightness of the pixels compared to what they should be. The pattern can be horizontally across a raster line, vertically down through the raster lines, or diagonally down and across the raster lines. Vertical correlated noise is often called "streak noise" and is a common problem with CCD technology. Also called "periodic noise." See also noncorrelated noise.

count: An increment or decrement of 1 in the analog-to-digital converter connected to a CCD element in a scanner. A count represents the difference of 1 gray level as perceived by a scanner.

dark voltage: The voltage from a CCD when no light is incident on the CCD. Also called "dark current."

density: A measure of reflectance or transmittance equal to $\log_{10}(1/\text{reflectance})$ of $\log_{10}(1/\text{transmittance})$. Also should include a spectral specification such as "status-T."

density range: See dynamic range.

depth of field: See focal range.

destructive interference: The condition that results when two signals combine and cancel each other out.

diffuse dither: A method for printing continuous-tone images on laser printers in which the grayscale information is represented by randomly located printer dots. Diffuse dithers don't photocopy well because of the small, random dot location in the image.

dithering: Creating halftone dots by combining the printer dots in a halftone cell. A printer's halftone cell is the equivalent of the halftone dots produced by traditional halftone screening. See also halftone cell, halftone dot.

dot: See halftone dot, printer dot.

dpi (dots per inch): The number of dots that can be printed per inch by a laser or InkJet printer. Each dot is either on or off, printed or not printed. In this document, dpi is used for devices that use bilevel data. See also ppi.

driver: A low-level program that controls a piece of computer hardware. Also an electronic circuit that supplies input to another electronic circuit.

dropout color: A color that is invisible when you scan a color object in grayscale mode, causing any detail in this color to disappear.

dynamic range: The range of the lightest to the darkest object that a scanner can distinguish. Also called "density range."

flashpix: A new file form designed to allow progressive display of images at higher and higher resolution.

focal range: The portion of an object that is in focus. Also called "depth of field.'

frequency response: See optical frequency response.

gamma correction: A form of tone mapping in which the shape of the tone map is a gamma. See also gamma curve, tone map.

gamma curve: The mathematical function $y = x^g$ that describes the nonlinear tonal response of many printers and monitors. The compensating function is $y = x^{1/g}$. A tone map that has the shape of this inverse function cancels the nonlinearities in printers and monitors.

gamut: The range of colors that can be captured or represented by a device. When a color is outside a device's gamut, the device represents that color as some other color.

halftone: A representation of grayscale information in a printed image in which black dots create the appearance of different gray levels.

halftone cell: A square area in a halftone grid that holds an array of printer dots. A halftone cell can represent a discrete number of gray levels equal to the maximum number of printer dots that the halftone cell can hold, plus 1.

halftone dots: Differently-sized black dots produced by turning particular dots on and off during printing on a laser printer, an image setter or a printing press. The dots repeat in a regular pattern, creating the illusion of continuous tone. Halftone dots are not the same as printer dots. See also printer dot.

harmonic: A component of a signal whose frequency is an integral multiple of the signal's frequency.

highlight: The brightest part of an image.

histogram: A bar graph for variables measured at the interval and ratio levels. A histogram has one axis showing the number of samples for each specific intensity level. A histogram shows the portions of the intensity spectrum where the image information is concentrated.

hue: The color mixed from red, green and blue. See also chroma, saturation.

identity tone map: A 1-to-1 mapping of the input values to identical output values without changes in contrast or brightness. See also non-identity tone map.

image type: The different representations of an original that can be captured by a scanner. For instance: 24-bit color, 8-bit grayscale, or 1-bit drawings.

imaging element: See carriage.

instrument metamerism: A phenomenon in a scanner in which two colors that look the same to an observer look different to the scanner, or two colors that look different to an observer look the same to a scanner. Instrument metamerism is a non-recoverable error because based on the output there is no way to determine what the input was. See also non-recoverable error.

intensity: The amount of light reflected or transmitted by an object with black as the lowest intensity and white as the highest intensity.

interpolated sample: A sample that is created by interpolation as opposed to real samples that are created during the scan.

interpolation: The process of creating estimated values between known values. In scanning, interpolation can be used to increase the number of samples by adding the estimated samples to the real samples. It can also be used to decrease the number of samples by creating an estimated sample from two or more real samples and discarding the real samples.

irreversible transformation: A change in an image during scanning and postscan image editing in which information about the image is irretrievably lost.

jaggies: The stairstep effect in diagonal lines or curves that are reproduced digitally.

just noticeable difference: In the CIELAB color model, a difference in hue, chroma, or intensity or some combination of all three that is apparent to a trained observer under ideal lighting conditions. A just noticeable difference is a change of 1; a change of 5 is apparent to most people most of the time. See also CIELAB.

like differences: Differences in color or lightness that are of similar magnitude to the average observer.

line drawing: A drawing that consists only of black and white with no intermediate gray-scale information.

line dropping: Sub-sampling to reduce the number of raster lines in an image by dropping every *n*th raster line from the scan. See also pixel dropping.

line pairs per inch: The frequency of a pattern of black and white lines. A line pair is one black and one white line. Thus, a pattern with 100 lppi will have 50 black lines and 50 white lines in one inch.

line replication: Creating more raster lines than are actually scanned by replicating every *n*th raster line from the scan. See also pixel replication.

linearity: The degree to which the input of a signal is proportional to the output.

lpi: Lines per inch. This measurement is related to screen frequency in printing and is not to be confused with lppi.

lppi: See line pairs per inch.

metamerism: See instrument metamerism.

midtones: Tones in an image that are in the middle of the tonal range, halfway between the lightest and the darkest tones.

Moiré pattern: An unwanted effect that appears in scans of printed images or other high-frequency scans. Moiré patterns are reflections of the high-frequency components of an image that are at about the sampling rate of the of the scanner. Moiré patterns are a kind of aliasing and are also called "artifacts." See also aliasing, artifacts.

MTF (modulated transfer function): The frequency response of an optical system. Also a test that measures the optical frequency response of a scanner or other optical system. See also transfer function.

Munsell color system: A system consisting of over 3 million observations of what people perceive to be like differences in hue, chroma, and intensity. The participants chose the samples they perceived to have like differences. See also CIELAB, chroma, hue, saturation.

noise: A distortion of an image's analog signal. This distortion can be correlated or non-correlated. Noise is an analog problem that is confined to the analog electronics in a scanner. Once a signal is digitized it is relatively immune to noise. See also correlated noise, non-correlated noise.

non-correlated noise: A random distortion in an analog signal causing snow or speckles—random spots throughout the image. The distortion can be the result of electronic noise in the amplifiers, electrical spikes somewhere in the system (the scanner, printer or monitor) or random fluctuations in the scanner lights. Also called "random noise." See also correlated noise.

non-identity tone map: The mapping of the input data from the scanner to the output data with tonal transformation. Non-identity tone maps are used for exposure manipulation, gamma correction and mapping 10-bit data to 8-bit data.

non-recoverable error: A deviation from the original color in an image that can't be corrected by a mathematical operation using a color-matching function. See also color-matching function, recoverable error.

NTSC: National Television Systems Committee.

Nyquist frequency: The theoretical maximum frequency that can be sampled by a digital sampling device such as a scanner. The Nyquist frequency of any digital sampling device is 1/2 the sampling rate of the device. To capture full information about a signal, the frequency content of the signal must be significantly below the Nyquist frequency of the device.

offset voltage: DC potential remaining at the input terminals in the amplifier when no output voltage is present.

optical frequency response: A scanner's capability for capturing a given frequency or range of frequencies.

optical filtering: Selectively transmitting or blocking a range of wavelengths.

optical sampling rate: The number of samples, in ppi, that are taken by a scanner per linear distance as determined by the CCD array, the optical system and the motion of the carriage. Optical sampling rate can be changed by interpolation or sub-sampling and no longer be the scanner's true optical sampling rate. Optical sampling rate is not the same as resolution. Also called "ppi rate."

outlier: A unit of analysis that has extreme values on a variable.

oversampling: Scanning at more than an optimum sampling rate. See also sub-sampling.

periodic noise: See correlated noise.

photometer: An instrument for measuring luminous intensity, luminous flux, illumination or intensity.

pixel: (PICture ELement) The smallest individual element in an image. For scanners, a pixel is the same as a sample.

pixel depth: See bit depth.

pixel dropping: Sub-sampling to reduce the number of pixels in an image by dropping every *n*th pixel from the scan.

pixel replication: Creating more pixels than are actually scanned by replicating every *n*th pixel to create the *n*+1 pixel.

pixelization: Graininess in an image that results when the pixels are too big.

ppi: (pixels per inch) Often used interchangeably with dpi, although a dot is a bilevel entity, either on or off, and a pixel can hold multiple levels of information. For instance, for an 8-bit scanner, 1 pixel has 256 possible values (0 to 255). In this book, "ppi" is used for devices that use multilevel samples such as scanners. See also dpi.

ppi rate: See sampling rate.

printer dot: The individual pixel in a halftone image. The size of a printer dot is variable, ranging from zero (all white) to the size of the halftone screen (all black). See also halftone cell, halftone dot.

PRNU: (photo response nonuniformity) Pixel-to-pixel variation in the response of a CCD array to a fixed-intensity light. Ideally, the response to each CCD element in the array is identical; deviations from that response are caused by PRNU.

process control: The stability of a manufacturing process that assures the products produced are stable and consistent.

quantization: The artificial forcing of like gray levels to the same gray level as a result of limited tonal resolution in a scanner. Quantization is most often seen in the shadow portion of scanned images. See also tonal resolution.

raster line: A thin horizontal strip across an image. Raster lines are captured one at a time by the CCD elements in a scanner. When displayed or printed in sequence, raster lines make up the image. Raster lines in a TV or monitor work the same way.

recoverable error: A deviation from the original color in an image that can be corrected by a mathematical operation using a color-matching function. See also 3 x 3 matrixing, color-matching function, non-recoverable error.

reflectance: The fraction of the light incident on a surface that is reflected and varies according to the wavelength distribution of the light. Also called "reflectivity."

reflectance linearity: The degree to which a plot of scanned reflectance or transmittance vs. absolute reflectance or transmittance is a straight line. Deviations in this plot either above or below a straight line represent tones that are recorded by the scanner as too light or too dark, respectively.

resolution. The degree of detail captured in an image. The resolution of a scanner is the ability of that scanner to resolve fine detail in the original. Resolution is affected by sampling rate but also by other aspects of a scanner such as lens quality, filter quality and the motion of the carriage. See also carriage.

sampling rate: The number of samples, in ppi, that are created by a scanner per linear distance. In this book, "sampling rate" means the optical sample rate changed by interpolation (mathematical estimation of more pixels) or subsampling (throwing away some pixels). Also called "ppi rate." Optical sampling rate is determined in the x-direction by the CCD array and magnification of the optical system.

saturation: The amount of color in a specific hue. See also chroma, hue.

saturation level: Light intensity that exceeds the maximum level designed for a CCD.

scale: To enlarge or reduce an image by increasing or decreasing the number of scanned pixels, or the sampling rate, relative to the number of samples per inch needed by the printer or other output device. See also interpolation.

shadow detail: Subtle features in the darker part of an image.

sharpening: An option on some scanners that emphasizes detail by increasing the contrast of the boundaries between light and dark areas of an image.

signal-to-noise ratio: The ratio of the usable signal to unusable noise in a scan. A high degree of noise can mask the shadow detail in an image regardless of tonal resolution. See also noise, shadow detail, tonal resolution.

sinusoidal: Relating to a sine wave.

spectral sensitivity: The relationship between the radiant sensitivity and the wavelength of incident light.

standard colorimetric observer: An entity described by the CIELAB color model consisting of three spectral-sensitivity curves called "color-matching functions." See also CIELAB, color-matching function, spectral sensitivity.

standard deviation: A measure of dispersion of a frequency distribution.

streak noise: Vertically correlated noise in a scanner. See also correlated noise.

sub-sampling: Scanning at a less than optimum sampling rate. See also oversampling.

target: In the context of testing, the portion of the original to be scanned.

threshold: A value to which a signal is compared when transforming from a multilevel value to a binary value. In binary scan, parts of the image below the threshold will be recorded as black and parts above the threshold will be recorded as white.

tonal resolution: The number of bits per pixel used in the digital representation of an image. The intensity and color of each pixel in the image are represented by an integer value or set of integer values. Tonal resolution is a measure of a scanner's resolution capability for small changes in intensity. Also called "pixel depth" or "bit depth."

transfer function: The capability of a device to transmit frequencies. See also MTF.

transmittance: The fraction of the light that passes through an object.

transition: The portion of a signal between a first nominal state and a second nominal state.

tri-stimulus value: The amount of each of the three primaries red, green and blue (R, G and B) needed to match the color of the light on an object.

value: The color or intensity of a pixel. How dark it is.

visible light: The portion of the electromagnetic spectrum that the human eye can see.

white balance: The balancing of color components to create pure white when you scan a white object.

white point: The color that, when scanned, produces values of 255, 255, 255 in an 8-bit scanner. Ideally the white point is 100% neutral reflectance or transmittance. See also reflectance, transmittance.

x-direction optical sampling rate: A scanner's sampling rate in the horizontal direction (across the page). The x-direction sampling rate is determined by the number of CCD elements in the CCD array. See also y-direction sampling rate, optical sampling rate and sampling rate.

y-direction sampling rate: A scanner's sampling rate in the vertical direction (down the page). The y-direction sampling rate is determined by the mechanical motion of the scanner's carriage as it moves down the page. Some scanners vary the y-direction sampling rate in steps of lines pairs per inch (lppi), offering more sampling rates to scale a document. Scanners with fixed, y-direction sampling rates offer fewer sampling rates or use interpolation, line dropping, or line replication to supply more sampling rates. See also carriage, x-direction sampling rate, optical sampling rate and sampling rate.

Index

W

X

Y

Z

LICENSE AGREEMENT AND LIMITED WARRANTY

READ THE FOLLOWING TERMS AND CONDITIONS CAREFULLY BEFORE OPENING THIS CD PACKAGE. THIS LEGAL DOCUMENT IS AN AGREEMENT BETWEEN YOU AND PRENTICE-HALL, INC. (THE "COMPANY"). BY OPENING THIS SEALED CD PACKAGE, YOU ARE AGREEING TO BE BOUND BY THESE TERMS AND CONDITIONS. IF YOU DO NOT AGREE WITH THESE TERMS AND CONDITIONS, DO NOT OPEN THE CD PACKAGE. PROMPTLY RETURN THE UNOPENED CD PACKAGE AND ALL ACCOMPANYING ITEMS TO THE PLACE YOU OBTAINED THEM FOR A FULL REFUND OF ANY SUMS YOU HAVE PAID.

1. **GRANT OF LICENSE:** In consideration of your purchase of this book, and your agreement to abide by the terms and conditions of this Agreement, the Company grants to you a nonexclusive right to use and display the copy of the enclosed software program (hereinafter the "SOFTWARE") on a single computer (i.e., with a single CPU) at a single location so long as you comply with the terms of this Agreement. The Company reserves all rights not expressly granted to you under this Agreement.

2. **OWNERSHIP OF SOFTWARE:** You own only the magnetic or physical media (the enclosed CD) on which the SOFTWARE is recorded or fixed, but the Company and the software developers retain all the rights, title, and ownership to the SOFTWARE recorded on the original CD copy(ies) and all subsequent copies of the SOFTWARE, regardless of the form or media on which the original or other copies may exist. This license is not a sale of the original SOFTWARE or any copy to you.

3. **COPY RESTRICTIONS:** This SOFTWARE and the accompanying printed materials and user manual (the "Documentation") are the subject of copyright. The individual programs on the CD are copyrighted by the authors of each program. You may not copy the Documentation or the SOFTWARE, except that you may make a single copy of the SOFTWARE for backup or archival purposes only. You may be held legally responsible for any copying or copyright infringement which is caused or encouraged by your failure to abide by the terms of this restriction.

4. **USE RESTRICTIONS:** You may not network the SOFTWARE or otherwise use it on more than one computer or computer terminal at the same time. You may physically transfer the SOFTWARE from one computer to another provided that the SOFTWARE is used on only one computer at a time. You may not distribute copies of the SOFTWARE or Documentation to others. You may not reverse engineer, disassemble, decompile, modify, adapt, translate, or create derivative works based on the SOFTWARE or the Documentation without the prior written consent of the Company.

5. **TRANSFER RESTRICTIONS:** The enclosed SOFTWARE is licensed only to you and may not be transferred to any one else without the prior written consent of the Company. Any unauthorized transfer of the SOFTWARE shall result in the immediate termination of this Agreement.

6. **TERMINATION:** This license is effective until terminated. This license will terminate automatically without notice from the Company and become null and void if you fail to comply with any provisions or limitations of this license. Upon termination, you shall destroy the Documentation and all copies of the SOFTWARE. All provisions of this Agreement as to warranties, limitation of liability, remedies or damages, and our ownership rights shall survive termination.

7. **MISCELLANEOUS:** This Agreement shall be construed in accordance with the laws of the United States of America and the State of New York and shall benefit the Company, its affiliates, and assignees.

8. **LIMITED WARRANTY AND DISCLAIMER OF WARRANTY:** The Company warrants that the SOFTWARE, when properly used in accordance with the Documentation, will operate in substantial conformity with the description of the SOFTWARE set forth in the Docu-

mentation. The Company does not warrant that the SOFTWARE will meet your requirements or that the operation of the SOFTWARE will be uninterrupted or error-free. The Company warrants that the media on which the SOFTWARE is delivered shall be free from defects in materials and workmanship under normal use for a period of thirty (30) days from the date of your purchase. Your only remedy and the Company's only obligation under these limited warranties is, at the Company's option, return of the warranted item for a refund of any amounts paid by you or replacement of the item. Any replacement of SOFTWARE or media under the warranties shall not extend the original warranty period. The limited warranty set forth above shall not apply to any SOFTWARE which the Company determines in good faith has been subject to misuse, neglect, improper installation, repair, alteration, or damage by you. EXCEPT FOR THE EXPRESSED WARRANTIES SET FORTH ABOVE, THE COMPANY DISCLAIMS ALL WARRANTIES, EXPRESS OR IMPLIED, INCLUDING WITHOUT LIMITATION, THE IMPLIED WARRAN-TIES OF MERCHANTABILITY AND FITNESS FOR A PARTICULAR PURPOSE. EXCEPT FOR THE EXPRESS WARRANTY SET FORTH ABOVE, THE COMPANY DOES NOT WAR-RANT, GUARANTEE, OR MAKE ANY REPRESENTATION REGARDING THE USE OR THE RESULTS OF THE USE OF THE SOFTWARE IN TERMS OF ITS CORRECTNESS, ACCURACY, RELIABILITY, CURRENTNESS, OR OTHERWISE.

IN NO EVENT, SHALL THE COMPANY OR ITS EMPLOYEES, AGENTS, SUP-PLIERS, OR CONTRACTORS BE LIABLE FOR ANY INCIDENTAL, INDIRECT, SPECIAL, OR CONSEQUENTIAL DAMAGES ARISING OUT OF OR IN CONNECTION WITH THE LICENSE GRANTED UNDER THIS AGREEMENT, OR FOR LOSS OF USE, LOSS OF DATA, LOSS OF INCOME OR PROFIT, OR OTHER LOSSES, SUSTAINED AS A RESULT OF INJURY TO ANY PERSON, OR LOSS OF OR DAMAGE TO PROPERTY, OR CLAIMS OF THIRD PARTIES, EVEN IF THE COMPANY OR AN AUTHORIZED REPRESENTATIVE OF THE COMPANY HAS BEEN ADVISED OF THE POSSIBILITY OF SUCH DAMAGES. IN NO EVENT SHALL LIABILITY OF THE COMPANY FOR DAMAGES WITH RESPECT TO THE SOFTWARE EXCEED THE AMOUNTS ACTUALLY PAID BY YOU, IF ANY, FOR THE SOFTWARE.

SOME JURISDICTIONS DO NOT ALLOW THE LIMITATION OF IMPLIED WARRANTIES OR LIABILITY FOR INCIDENTAL, INDIRECT, SPECIAL, OR CONSE-QUENTIAL DAMAGES, SO THE ABOVE LIMITATIONS MAY NOT ALWAYS APPLY. THE WARRANTIES IN THIS AGREEMENT GIVE YOU SPECIFIC LEGAL RIGHTS AND YOU MAY ALSO HAVE OTHER RIGHTS WHICH VARY IN ACCORDANCE WITH LOCAL LAW.

ACKNOWLEDGMENT

YOU ACKNOWLEDGE THAT YOU HAVE READ THIS AGREEMENT, UNDER-STAND IT, AND AGREE TO BE BOUND BY ITS TERMS AND CONDITIONS. YOU ALSO AGREE THAT THIS AGREEMENT IS THE COMPLETE AND EXCLUSIVE STATEMENT OF THE AGREEMENT BETWEEN YOU AND THE COMPANY AND SUPERSEDES ALL PRO-POSALS OR PRIOR AGREEMENTS, ORAL, OR WRITTEN, AND ANY OTHER COMMUNI-CATIONS BETWEEN YOU AND THE COMPANY OR ANY REPRESENTATIVE OF THE COMPANY RELATING TO THE SUBJECT MATTER OF THIS AGREEMENT.

Should you have any questions concerning this Agreement or if you wish to contact the Company for any reason, please contact in writing at the address below.

Robin Short
Prentice Hall PTR
One Lake Street
Upper Saddle River, New Jersey 07458

■ CD-ROM Contents

The CD-ROM provided with *Desktop Scanners: Image Quality Evaluation* provides some extra information, example images and tools for use by those people interested in testing scanners.

Installing the CD-ROM

Much of the information on the CD-ROM is stored in the form of Adobe Acrobat Portable Document Format (pdf) files. You will need Acrobat Reader version 3.0 to read these file. If you do not have Acrobat 3.0 you can install it from the CD-ROM by following these steps:

1. Insert the CD-ROM in your CD-ROM drive.

2. Double Click on "My Computer"

3. In "My Computer," right click on the CD-ROM and select "Install 32-Bit Acrobat Reader" from the menu.

If you have problems with this, look in "install.txt" on the CD-ROM. Other information on the CD-ROM is in the form of image files (tiff), spread sheets and programs.

What is on the CD-ROM

The CD-ROM is intended to provide extra reference information and tools. Except as noted, all the information on the CD-ROM is copyrighted and may not be copied off the CD-ROM (see "permission.pdf" on the CD-ROM). On the CD-ROM are:

- Example images and test results from the tests described in the book.
- Spreadsheets that can be used to convert colors from RGB to LAB and programs to calculate averages of rows and columns in tiff images.
- An on-line version of this book.
- On-line versions of various presentations about scanners and scanner image quality. Note, some of the example images in these presentations may not display as intended on computer displays.

Full content information can be found in the file "contents.pdf" on the CD-ROM.

Technical Support: Prentice Hall does not offer technical support for this software. However, if there is a problem with the media, you may obtain a free replacement copy by emailing us with your problem at: ptr_techsupport@phptr.com.